Reinventing the
Retirement Paradigm

Reinventing the Retirement Paradigm

EDITED BY

Robert L. Clark and Olivia S. Mitchell

OXFORD
UNIVERSITY PRESS

OXFORD
UNIVERSITY PRESS

Great Clarendon Street, Oxford OX2 6DP

Oxford University Press is a department of the University of Oxford.
It furthers the University's objective of excellence in research, scholarship,
and education by publishing worldwide in

Oxford New York

Auckland Cape Town Dar es Salaam Hong Kong Karachi
Kuala Lumpur Madrid Melbourne Mexico City Nairobi
New Delhi Shanghai Taipei Toronto

With offices in

Argentina Austria Brazil Chile Czech Republic France Greece
Guatemala Hungary Italy Japan Poland Portugal Singapore
South Korea Switzerland Thailand Turkey Ukraine Vietnam

Oxford is a registered trade mark of Oxford University Press
in the UK and in certain other countries

Published in the United States
by Oxford University Press Inc., New York

© Pension Research Council, The Wharton School,
University of Pennsylvania 2005

The moral rights of the author have been asserted
Database right Oxford University Press (maker)

First published 2005

Reprinted 2006

British Library Cataloguing in Publication Data
Data available

Library of Congress Cataloging in Publication Data
Data available

Typeset by SPI Publisher Services, Pondicherry, India
Printed in Great Britain
on acid-free paper by
Biddles Ltd., King's Lynn, Norfolk

ISBN 0–19–928460–1

Preface

Retirement practice and policy has become a moving target in the twenty-first century, due to volatile capital markets, rising medical-care costs, and an increased awareness of the cost of paying for old-age consumption. Indeed, over one-third of workers older than age 45 say they have altered their intended retirement age, as financial uncertainty prompts the need to work longer than initially anticipated. This book explores how rapidly changing workforce demographics combined with rising pension and medical costs—and perhaps unrealistic expectations regarding old-age benefits—have influenced retirement behavior and planning around the world.

In this book, experts explore a diverse set of issues ranging from employment trends, to pension accounting and investment management, to pension restructuring. We show how employers are proactively reformulating the definition of work and retirement, with more people working later than ever before. Not only is this a natural reaction to longer, healthier life spans, but it represents a logical response to labor shortages resulting from the slowing of labor force growth. Yet all is not rosy—trust in traditional pension offers is eroding as plans are altered and terminated, and plan sponsors are becoming increasingly aware of risks in pension investments and accounting. Experts from the UK, the USA, Japan, Sweden, and Canada share international perspectives on how the retirement institution is evolving. In the last two decades, participant-directed defined contribution (DC) plans have been an engine of growth for retirement saving around the world. In many countries, the movement to enhance participant choice has also prompted reforms of social security systems, by adding personal accounts that permit investment choice.

This book owes much to its many contributors as well as to its helpful co-editor, Robert L. Clark, professor of business management and economics at North Carolina State University. Support for the research described here was generously provided by the Wharton School and the Boettner Center for Pensions and Retirement Research at the University of Pennsylvania. In addition, we acknowledge conference support from the Employee Benefits Security Administration of the US Department of Labor. The publication also benefited from helpful editorial oversight by Virginia Jurika and Linda Brown. On behalf of the Pension Research Council and the Boettner

Center at the Wharton School, we thank each of our collaborators who helped bring this work to fruition.

Olivia S. Mitchell
Pension Research Council
Boettner Center for Pensions and Retirement Research
The Wharton School

The Pension Research Council

The Pension Research Council of the Wharton School at the University of Pennsylvania is an organization committed to generating debate on key policy issues affecting pensions and other employee benefits. The Council sponsors interdisciplinary research on the entire range of private and social retirement security and related benefit plans in the USA and around the world. It seeks to broaden understanding of these complex arrangements through basic research into their economic, social, legal, actuarial, and financial foundations. Members of the Advisory Board of the Council, appointed by the Dean of the Wharton School, are leaders in the employee benefits field who recognize the essential role of Social Security and other public sector income maintenance programs while sharing a desire to strengthen private sector approaches to economic security.

More information about the Pension Research Council is available at the website: http://prc.wharton.upenn.edu/prc/prc.html

Contents

Part I. The State of Play

Part II. Redefining Retirement

Part III. Managing the Retirement Promise

Part IV. In Search of a New Pension Paradigm: The Global Outlook

List of Figures

List of Tables

Notes on Contributors

Katharine G. Abraham is Professor of Survey Methodology and Adjunct Professor of Economics at the University of Maryland. Her research interests include the study of the labor market and economic measurement. Her labor market research has included work on firms' personnel policies, labor market dynamics and unemployment. Previously Dr Abraham served as Commissioner for the US Bureau of Labor Statistics; she also held faculty appointments in the Department of Economics at the University of Maryland and the Sloan School of Management at MIT; and she was a research associate at the Brookings Institution. She is a Research Associate of the National Bureau of Economic Research. She received the B.S. from Iowa State University and the Ph.D. from Harvard University.

Keith Ambachtsheer is President and founder of KPA Advisory Services Ltd, where he analyzes pension and investment issues and publishes the *Ambachtsheer Letter*. He is a regular contributor to numerous investment journals and textbooks. Mr Ambachtsheer advises governments, industry associations, pension plan sponsors, and money managers around the world on pension governance, finance, and investment issues.

Gary W. Anderson is the Executive Director of the Texas Municipal Retirement System where he is responsible for the overall operation and administration of the retirement system under the policy direction of the Board of Trustees. He is a member of the Government Finance Officers Association (USA and Canada), the Government Finance Officers Association of Texas, and the National Association of State Retirement Administrators. He also serves on the Pension Research Council Advisory Board at the Wharton School. Mr Anderson received the B.A. from Texas A&M University with a Major in Political Science and a minor in Economics, and the M.A. in Public Management from the University of Houston.

William J. Arnone is a Partner in the Human Capital practice of Ernst & Young LLP based in New York where he assists large organizations realign their defined benefit, defined contribution, and hybrid plans with their business imperatives and human resources objectives. He publishes on retirement issues and is co-author of a retirement planning guide. He is a Founding Member of the National Academy of Social Insurance. He received the B.A. from Fordham College and the J.D. from New York University Law School.

Keith Brainard is Research Director for the National Association of State Retirement Administrators (NASRA) where he provides services to seventy-five statewide public retirement systems. Previously he served as manager of budget and planning for the Arizona State Retirement System and performed fiscal research and analysis for the Texas and Arizona legislatures. At NASRA, he maintains the Public Fund Survey, an online compendium of public pension data, sponsored jointly by NASRA and the National Council on Teacher Retirement. Keith received the B.S. in Government and the M.S. in Public Affairs from the University of Texas at Austin.

Robert L. Clark is a Professor of Business Management and Economics at North Carolina State University. His research examines retirement decisions, the choice between defined benefit and defined contribution plans, the role of information and communications on 401(k) contributions, and international retirement systems. Dr Clark serves on the Advisory Board of the Pension Research Council, and he is also a member of the American Economic Association, the Gerontological Society of America, and the National Academy of Social Insurance. Professor Clark earned the B.A. from Millsaps College and the Ph.D. from Duke University.

Douglas Fore is a Principal Research Fellow at the TIAA-CREF Institute. His research interests include the determinants of pension type. Dr Fore earned the Ph.D. in Economics from the University of Colorado.

Susan N. Houseman is a Senior Economist at the W.E. Upjohn Institute for Employment Research. She has written widely on labor issues in the USA, Japan, and Europe. Her current research studies nonstandard employment arrangements and retirement issues. She received her Ph.D. in economics from Harvard University.

Robert Hutchens is a Professor of Labor Economics at the New York State School of Industrial and Labor Relations at Cornell University. His recent interests focus on employment prospects for older workers. He received the M.S. and Ph.D. in Economics from the University of Wisconsin at Madison.

James A. Klein is President of the American Benefits Council, a group representing major employers and those who design and provide benefits services to plan sponsors. Previously he was a legislative assistant to a member of Congress, served as associate in a law firm specializing in ERISA, and participated in the Pension Working Group of the Organization for Economic Cooperation and Development. Mr Klein received the B.A. from Tufts University and he took a law degree with honors from George Washington University Law School.

David McCarthy is a faculty member at Imperial College, London. His research focuses on pensions, finance, and actuarial studies. Previously he was a postdoctoral fellow at the University of Oxford. He received the

Ph.D. in Insurance and Risk Management from the Wharton School and he is a Fellow of the Faculty of Actuaries, Edinburgh, UK.

Olivia S. Mitchell is the International Foundation of Employee Benefit Plans Professor of Insurance and Risk Management, the Executive Director of the Pension Research Council, and the Director of the Boettner Center on Pensions and Retirement Research at the Wharton School. Concurrently Dr Mitchell is a Research Associate at the National Bureau of Economic Research and a Co-investigator for the AHEAD/Health and Retirement Studies at the University of Michigan. Dr Mitchell's main areas of research and teaching are private and public insurance, risk management, public finance and labor markets, and compensation and pensions, with a US and an international focus. She received the B.A. in Economics from Harvard University and the M.A. and Ph.D. degrees in Economics from the University of Wisconsin at Madison.

Janemarie Mulvey is Assistant Director of the Research Information Center at Watson Wyatt Worldwide, where her research focuses on employee benefits including pensions, retiree medical, and long-term care insurance. Previously she was Director of Economic Research at the American Council of Life Insurance; an economist at the Urban Institute where she forecasted the impact of Medicaid reform proposals; and Senior Analyst in the Public Policy Institute of the American Association of Retired Persons. She received the M.A. in Economics from the University of Maryland and the Ph.D. in Economics from George Mason University.

Steven Nyce is a Senior Retirement Research Associate with the Research and Information Center of Watson Wyatt Worldwide in Washington, DC. His research interests include workforce demographics, behavioral aspects of private pensions, and public and private retirement policy. He received the Ph.D. in Economics from the University of Notre Dame.

Pamela Perun is an independent consultant on retirement income policy issues. Her research examines legal issues associated with phased retirement programs, property rights in personal accounts under Social Security, proposed changes to contribution limits under pension plans, and developments in stock-based compensation and universal savings accounts. She is also the Editor of the *Pension, Compensation and Benefits Journal of the Social Science Research Network*. Previously she practiced benefits law. She received the B.A. from Wellesley College, the J.D. from the University of California at Berkeley, Boalt Hall School of Law, and the Ph.D. in Human Development (Adult Development and Aging) from the University of Chicago.

Kerry L. Papps is a doctoral candidate in labor economics at Cornell University. Previously, he was a research analyst for the New Zealand Department of Labour. He has written on the relationship between unemployment and crime, the wage curve and the effects of occupational safety and health interventions. His degrees were from the University of Canterbury and Victoria University of Wellington in New Zealand.

Silvana Pozzebon is Associate Professor in the Department of Human Resources Management at HEC Montreal (Ecole des Hautes Etudes Commerciales de Montreal), the business school affiliated with the University of Montreal. Her research interests focus on pensions and occupational health and safety management. She received the B.A. in Economics from Concordia College, and the M.S. and Ph.D. in Labor Economics from Cornell University's School of Industrial and Labor Relations.

Patrick Purcell is an economist with the US Library of Congress Congressional Research Service. He focuses on labor market and retirement saving, pensions, and Social Security. Previously, he worked at the Urban Institute, the Congressional Budget Office, and the US Department of Health and Human Services. He received the B.A. from Pennsylvania State University and the M.A. in Economics from American University.

C. Eugene Steuerle is a Senior Fellow at The Urban Institute and Co-Director of the Urban-Brookings Tax Policy Center. He currently serves on the National Committee on Vital and Health Statistics and on advisory panels or boards for the Congressional Budget Office, the General Accounting Office, the Joint Committee on Taxation, the Actuarial Foundation, and the Independent Sector. Previously he served as Economic Coordinator and original organizer of the Treasury's tax reform effort, and he undertook missions for the International Monetary Fund. Dr Steuerle received the Ph.D. from the University of Wisconsin.

Annika Sundén is a Senior Economist at the Swedish National Social Insurance Board and a Research Associate at the Center for Retirement Research at Boston College. Her research interests focus on the economics of retirement, pensions and social security, and household saving behavior. Previously, she worked as an economist at the Federal Reserve Board in Washington, DC, where she was involved in the design and implementation of the Survey of Consumer Finances. She received the B.S. from the Stockholm School of Economics and both the M.S. and Ph.D. in Labor Economics from Cornell University.

Masaharu Usuki is Senior Research Fellow at NLI Research Institute, a research affiliate of Nippon Life Insurance Company. His current research focuses on pensions and retirement benefits in public and private sectors, particularly in terms of the significance of these for Japan's economic and social policy and business management. He is also a visiting professor on the faculty of the Graduate School of Management at the International University of Japan and two other graduate schools in Tokyo.

Abbreviations

AARP	American Association of Retired Persons
ACPM	Association of Canadian Pension Management
ASB	Accounting Standards Board
BLS	Bureau of Labor Statistics
CAPSA	Canadian Association of Pension Supervisory Authorities
CATI	Computer Associated Telephone Interview system
CBO	Congressional Budget Office
CEM	Cost-Effectiveness Measurement
CPI	Consumer Price Index
CPP	Canada Pension Plan
DB	Defined Benefit
DC	Defined Contribution
DEFRA	Deficit Reduction Act
EBRI	Employment Benefit Research Institute
EGTRRA	Economic Growth and Tax Relief Reconciliation Act 2001
EPFs	Employee's Pension Funds
ERISA	Employment Retirement Income Security Act
ERSA	Employment Retirement Savings Account
FAS	Final Average Salary
FASB	Financial Accounting Standards Board
FB	Flat Benefit
FRS	Financial Reporting Standard
FTE	Full-time Equivalent
GIS	Guaranteed Income Supplement
GSP	Gross State Product
HRS	Health and Retirement Study
IASB	International Accounting Standards Board
IDA	Individual Development Accounts
IRA	Individual Retirement Accounts
IRC	Internal Revenue Code
IRS	Internal Revenue Service
JFFMR	Joint Forum of Financial Market Regulators
LFPR	Labor Force Participation Rate
LSAs	Lifetime Savings Account
MPC	Marginal Propensity to Consume
NASRA	National Association of State Retirement Administrators

NDC	Notional Defined Contribution
NIVA	Net Implementation Value Added
NSIB	National Social Insurance Board
OAS	Old Age Security
OASDI	Old Age and Survivors Insurance and Disability Insurance
OBRA	Omnibus Budget Reconciliation Act of 1993
OECD	Organization for Economic Co-operation and Development
OFE	Office of Financial Education
PBGC	Pension Benefit Guaranty Corporation
PBO	Projected Benefit Obligation
PERS	Public Employee Retirement System
PPSEA	Pension Preservation and Savings Expansion Act 2003
PUC	Project Unit Credit
QPP	Quebec Pension Plan
RHS	Retirement History Survey
RPP	Registered Pension Plan
RRSP	Registered Retired Savings Plan
RSA	Retirement Savings Account
S&P	Standard and Poor's
SARSEP	Salary Reduction Simplified Employee Pension Plan
SEC	Securities and Exchange Commission
SEPPAA	Single Employer Pension Plan Amendments Act
SIMPLE	Savings Incentive Match Plans for Employees
SSAP	Statement of Standard Accounting Practice
TEFRA	Tax Equity and Fiscal Responsibility Act
TQPPs	Tax Qualified Pension Plans
TSAs	Tax-Sheltered Annuities
USDOL	United States Department of Labor
WEFPRI	World Economic Forum Pension Readiness Initiative

Part I
The State of Play

Chapter 1

The Changing Retirement Paradigm

Robert Clark and Olivia S. Mitchell

A century ago, most workers spent 10 hours per day and six days per week on their jobs (Costa 2000). Today, the typical North American spends only five days at work per week and only 7–8 hours per day on the job; some Europeans enjoy an even shorter workweek of a mere 35 hours. This striking time-series decline in work effort has also been reflected in falling labor force attachment patterns, particularly at older ages. In 1880, for instance, 80 percent of men aged 65+ were in the labor force; only a century later, fewer than 20 percent of such older men worked or sought work (Costa 1998). These dramatic reductions in labor and effort are commonly interpreted as indicative of economic and political success. That is, as societies grew richer, and goods and services grew relatively less labor-intensive to produce, more people could afford to spend more of their lifetimes not working. This is perhaps illustrated most vividly in the dimension of leisure at older ages: people everywhere are retiring earlier, and living longer during retirement, than ever before in human history.

Yet many now believe that the race to shorten the work life is over. As the first wave of baby boomers moves into early retirement, it already is clear that some industries such as aerospace, utilities, and health care, face labor shortages. Some argue that life will change dramatically in the next two decades, particularly if employers do not find sufficient workers and if productivity fails to grow fast enough. One analyst, Steven Nyce (K@W 2004a), warns that 'companies will not be able to meet consumption needs in society, and the result will be higher inflation'.

As a result of these labor force changes, employers and employees are having to confront the need for a new retirement paradigm. The old model assumed a relatively homogeneous labor force where employee benefits, particularly pensions, were designed to reward career employees after years of loyalty, effort, and productivity. When labor force growth was the norm, many firms favored hiring plentiful younger workers over retaining more costly older employees. It was in that context that employers developed defined benefit (DB) plans that benefited mainly full-career employees, while penalizing those who remained with the firm only a few years. These traditional pension plans typically included subsidized early retirement provisions that encouraged senior employees to retire in their fifties.

As a new retirement paradigm emerges, its outlines look quite different from the old model. Several factors are key. For one, the workforce now has higher levels of labor market turnover, higher rates of female participation, and more diverse needs due to employees in increasingly complex family situations. All these changes imply a new set of expectations about the role of work and the nature of employment, including the role of company-provided benefits. Developments are occurring in the pension sector as well. Many companies must now refashion their offers so employees can accumulate retirement saving even while changing jobs, or as they move from full-time work to complete retirement. In addition, important changes in accounting standards, funding requirements, and government regulations are driving plan sponsors to revisit whether they wish to offer retirement benefits, and if so, how these benefit offers will be structured.

A key motivation for rethinking the retirement paradigm is that many people and the societies they live in cannot afford to finance twenty, thirty, or more years of inactivity. Social Security and old-age medical programs face insolvency, and many fear they will not be able to make ends meet in the very near future. A related issue is that older workers are in better health than their predecessors, and their jobs are less physically demanding than in the years gone by. These factors, combined with employees' growing attention of the many risks they face in retirement, are driving a rethinking of the types of benefits promised at the workplace.

The goal of this volume is to provide structure and new insights for the debate on the shape of the new retirement paradigm, and to help key elements of retirement policy reform. In this chapter, we review the key policy challenges, provide evidence on retirement patterns, old and new, and offer elements of the new mix. We conclude with observations drawn from the rich international experience.

Retirement Policy Challenges

Before evaluating some of the innovative practices fashioned by employers and employees confronting these new challenges, it is useful to take stock of the influential role of governmental regulation and oversight regarding the changing retirement environment. This is particularly important in the US context, since employers who offer pensions do so voluntarily. As a result, company-based pension coverage is far less than complete. Indeed, only half the civilian workforce currently has a company pension, a fraction that has remained stable for more than four decades.

Over that time, however, DB plans providing retirees with annuity payments have been supplanted by defined contribution (DC) plans such as 401(k), which offer workers incentives to save but do not require annuitization nor protection from capital market risk. Many DB plans encouraged early retirement, but today that incentive structure is often seen as a vestige of a labor surplus era. By contrast, DC plans are increasingly popular due to their portability and age-neutrality (K@W 2004*a*).

One of the major problems in the policy arena is that trust has eroded between plan sponsors and workers participating in the pension system. This is partly the result of the ongoing fallout from the Enron debacle (along with various other firms suffering earnings shocks in the last five years). The result is that regulators tend to give plan sponsors too little flexibility regarding how plans are designed and operated.

Chapters 2 and 3 discuss the current outlines of pension regulation and examine potential paths for future reforms. In Chapter 2, Klein posits that more regulatory flexibility would be desirable, in exchange for possibly harsher penalties in the event of rule violation. He also suggests the value of negotiated rulemaking. Currently, regulators ask for a wide range of views on regulations and return with a final set of regulations, where there is little room for adaptation. By contrast, a negotiated system would result in a situation where 'the parties would have greater faith in the system knowing they were more involved in the process' (K@W 2004*a*).

In Chapter 3, Perun and Steuerle point to the fact that the pension system has become inordinately complex over time. Currently, more than 110 private pension plan types are slated to come on line by 2006: a plethora of options that is simply overwhelming for most pension participants and many employers. This suggests that simplification must be high on the agenda in the near future. Two reform proposals are explored in some depth, including a more traditional 'nip and tuck' approach which tinkers with many elements of the law but does not change the fundamental framework, and a second, more fundamental approach proposed by the Bush Administration which includes Lifetime Savings Accounts (LSAs) and Retirement Savings Accounts (RSAs). The latter are simpler and tend to undermine company-based saving versus individual accounts. As Perun says, 'neither proposal is satisfactory'; indeed she states that 'we don't need more innovative savings tools; we just need one that works'. The authors' preferred middle way would boost saving incentives for a simple DC plan and would also reform the social security system to increase benefits for low-wage workers.

Looking ahead, it seems clear that policymakers must do better to clarify how pension assets are protected, prevent plan sponsor malfeasance, and provide strong incentives for the establishment and maintenance of group-based retirement plans. Yet these policies must also be assessed against the need for new retirement behaviors.

Retirement Patterns—Old and New

Important changes in the older worker labor market are evident along several dimensions. First, workers themselves are more diverse, inasmuch as they are more mobile, better educated, and healthier than ever before, even as they grow older as a group (Mitchell et al. 2003). Second, transitions in retirement patterns and expectations are beginning to emerge. For instance, in most developed nations there are rising fractions of working women spending ever greater portion of their lifetimes attached to work outside the home. At the same time, there have been dramatic increases in the number of minority workers, workers in nontraditional families, and workers with no families. These facts, combined with slower labor force growth, are altering the age structure and demands of the labor force, making it more difficult for firms to find young workers and increasing the likelihood that employers will want to retain older workers.

Research by Mulvey and Nyce (Chapter 7) reported here points out that by 2010 the US will experience a seven percentage point worker shortfall, which is forecasted to grow to 13 percent by 2020. Furthermore, all baby boomers will be older than 55 by 2020. Nevertheless, many retirement plans have encouraged workers to retire before the age 65. Partly as a consequence, the analysis by Abraham and Houseman (Chapter 5) finds that many companies today have become quite interested in employing older people. 'Employers are concerned about the ability to recruit workers,' says Abraham. Yet the data show that many employees indicate that they would like to work beyond the firm's retirement age, but few in fact do so. Indeed, only one-quarter of older workers surveyed said they planned to stop working entirely at the firm's normal retirement age; of the rest, 18 percent said they planned to work fewer hours, 5 percent said they wanted to change jobs, and the rest said they had no plans. It is of interest that, when they were interviewed two years later, most of those who planned to stop work actually did so, but most of those who planned to work fewer hours had not followed through. Abraham believes that the 'disconnect' may have to do with available jobs: most of the slots are not particularly more attractive than before.

Mulvey and Nyce go on to note that, while the US Employee Retirement Income Security Act (ERISA) of 1974 guaranteed accrued DB plan benefits, that law did not require employers to continue to provide future pension accruals. Insofar as employers offer pensions voluntarily to minimize turnover and receive certain tax benefits, at the same time they have faced soaring administrative costs over time, with costs tripling over the last two decades. As a result, almost two-thirds of companies with fewer than 1,000 workers dropped their DB plans between 1990 and 2002; among larger companies, 11 percent dropped their DB plans (K@W 2004a). Mulvey also notes that more than 20 percent of DB participants are now in hybrid plans, which combine elements of DB and DC plans which cater to a more mobile workforce. While some critique hybrid plans, suggesting that they cut employee benefits, her data indicate hybrid plans add costs to employers and protect older workers. Nevertheless some employers cannot provide any pensions because of regulatory constraints.

The question of whether employers can and do adjust their human resource policies to provide older employees more flexible work schedules is taken up again in a related study by Robert Hutchens and Kerry Papps (Chapter 8). They see phased retirement as a way to encourage older workers to extend their time in the labor force, permitting workers to transition from full-time to part-time work without changing employers. A clear advantage of such a model is that the worker would be able to curtail work hours while maintaining existing skills and job relationships. It is therefore interesting that some employers require the workers to 'officially' retire before rehiring them for shorter work hours jobs, and sometimes the time interval between official retirement and rehire is only a day.

Drawing on a special establishment survey, Hutchens and Papps find some fascinating results. First, employers favor informal arrangements regarding the rehiring of retired workers or phased employment. Second, employers who do permit some form of phased retirement do not usually restrict it to rehiring of retirees; indeed, most employers indicate they would permit informal hours reductions both before, and after, official retirement. Last, they find little support for the claim that pensions or hours constraints drive firm preferences. Instead, it appears that employers and employees find ways to reduce work hours in flexible ways, and they predict that individually negotiated arrangements will become an evermore important element of the evolving retirement paradigm.

Employers have other ways to change their incentive plans for those nearing retirement that could help extend work lives. For instance, Mulvey and Nyce suggest that employers consider offering elder care programs that assist with the care of older relatives, and phased retirement programs that allow older workers to cut back on their hours without losing benefits. In their survey, one-quarter of the women who retired early were responsible for caring for an older relative, Mulvey notes (K@W 2004b); 'These are the softer side of benefits, but they matter and they're not too costly to implement.' She also finds that men are less responsive to phased retirement programs.

Elements of the New Mix

As a result of these fundamental environmental changes, corporate as well as public sector retirement policies must also evolve. How will this new retirement paradigm be developed? Who bears the responsibility for changing the framework for retirement decisions? Answers to these questions require a new perspective regarding the role of workers, firms, financial services providers, and the government, in the provision of retirement security.

In many countries, it seems clear that pensions must be restructured to facilitate innovative retirement plans while still providing insurance and risk management features for both workers and firms. In this new environment, workers and their families will be asked to assume greater responsibility for their own retirement saving. Since retirement wealth accumulation is a lifetime responsibility, workers must be induced to start planning and saving when young, and monitor these retirement plans throughout their working careers. This is a time-intensive process, requiring frequent updating of saving targets and behavior. The retirement plans of twenty-first century workers should also embody some notion of likely changes in government benefits such as Social Security and Medicare, along with changes in company-provided pension plans and retiree health insurance.

The changing patterns of work and retirement are already creating pressures for pension reform. Innovative plan designs along with better fund management are being seen in both the public and private sectors. Ambachtsheer's study (Chapter 11) of DB pension plan investment practices suggests that pension management was guided by a set of rules that appeared to work well during the 1980s and 1990s. During this period, equity risk premiums were generally positive; equity market dips were short and soon reversed themselves, and nothing happened that a 60–40 equity-bond mix policy could not deal with. But the 'perfect pension storm' of 2000–2 developed deep cracks in the old retirement lens. DB plan surpluses turned to serious deficits, and stakeholders began to realize that the asset mixes adopted during the 1990s exposed the stakeholders of DB balance sheets to material mismatch risk. As a result, pension organizations can no longer be guided by the 'old' paradigm, but rather they require a new lens through which to see the world.

In his analysis of the pension plan type question, David McCarthy (Chapter 6) notes that recent developments in numerical analysis help researchers assess different pension plan designs using an economic framework realistic enough to assist researchers and practitioners who study and design pension plans. He develops a framework to design pension schemes to evaluate the best 'pension design'. He uses a financial economics approach to the problem of pension design, recognizing that compensation arrangements can have very distinct impacts on employees covered by these plans. In particular, pension contracts alter workers' risk exposures and the allocation of compensation over the lifecycle. As a result, having a pension changes the value that employees ascribe to different pension and compensation arrangements. His model implies that a DB plan magnifies workers' risk exposure to salary risk, while both DC and DB pension arrangements defer pay to later in the work life. As a result, younger workers therefore value DC plans because they have immediate cash needs. By comparison, DB pensions are a relatively cost-effective way to compensate older, less well-educated employees. He also concludes that underfunding the DB plan is an expensive way to pay employees, as is giving workers with 401(k) plans restricted company stock. Finally,

McCarthy suggests that a hybrid scheme might be designed to better suit both types of employees. Donald Elbaum, director of pension actuarial studies at Ford Motor Co., suggests that the idea of reducing early retirement subsidies is gaining ground in national pension plans around the world and in private schemes (K@W 2004*a*).

In their analysis of US public sector pension plans, Anderson and Brainard (Chapter 12) provide useful observations for private plans, based on their assessment of the successes of public sector pensions. They note that public sector plans in the USA cover 14 million state and local government sector participants (10 percent of the US workforce) with assets of over $2 trillion. These public sector pensions evolved before, and outside the purview of, much federal pension legislation, making their different experiences invaluable for private industry. The authors conclude that the economic boost afforded to public pension benefits will rise as Baby Boomers retire and public retirement systems distribute increasingly larger amounts. Unlike the social security system, which is mainly a pay-as-you-go program, public pension funds are almost entirely funded. The $2.3 trillion in assets have a significant, positive effect on financial markets and the economy, and the plan structures have enabled public employers to achieve important objectives related to the recruitment and retention of quality workers

As pensions plans change, financial literacy and knowledge increases in importance as workers are asked whether they will participate in a retirement saving or pension plan, as well as how much to contribute and also how to invest the funds. In this new environment, employee knowledge and financial planning become extremely important. Arnone (Chapter 9) takes up the issue of who should bear the responsibility for providing financial education, describing educational programs currently being provided. Arnone, who runs employer-investor education programs, said that companies began offering financial literacy programs in the early 1980s as they encouraged workers to take early retirement. He believes that 'the rationale was that if these older employees did the calculations, they would conclude they were better off (taking early retirement).' He adds: 'I think we're going to have a resurgence, only now they are going to conclude, "I cannot retire as soon as I thought I could"' (K@W 2004*a*). Arnone states that fewer than 20 percent of large employers initiated financial education programs. Indeed, his own firm once offered financial planning but found that other benefits, including pet insurance, were more popular.

Among investors who manage their own retirement accounts, some of the common problems include questionable asset allocation, failure to rebalance periodically, and an overconcentration in employer stock. Approximately 20 percent of DC participants have outstanding loans and many cash out at time of termination. 'The latest, biggest, hottest thing now is professionally managed 401(k) plans', says Arnone.

International Experiences

The triple challenges of an aging population, a slowly growing labor force, and increasing life expectancy confront many developed nations, and indeed most other developed countries are further along this path than is the USA. Fertility is much lower in Japan and in most of Europe and life expectancy is considerably higher in many of these countries. Many developed countries are already experimenting with reforms to their national Social Security programs and employer-based pensions. It seems likely that policymakers in all developed countries should learn from each other.

Sundén on Sweden (Chapter 14), Usuki on Japan (Chapter 15), and Pozzebon on Canada (Chapter 13) provide interesting insights into how these countries are modifying their retirement programs to address the challenges of the twenty-first century. Turning first to Sweden, Sunden notes that the Swedish Parliament passed pension legislation in 1998 transforming that country's public pension scheme from a pay-as-you-go DB plan to a notional DC. In addition, that reform introduced a second-tier DC individual account plan. This reform fundamentally changed the provision of public pension benefits and redefined the benefit promise. For instance, in the new system, government-provided benefits are closely tied to contributions, and lifetime earnings determine benefits. The reform also recognized that increased life expectancy should influence the system's financial stability, and so it built in an automatic benefit adjustment process that responds to changes in longevity. Finally, the new system also introduced a funded individual-accounts component.

In the process, Swedish policymakers recognized a fundamental and very interesting insight: namely, that pension systems are dynamic institutions which must adjust to constantly evolving demographic and economic circumstances. So as to limit political risk, the reformers proposed automatic adjustments to contribute to system stability. The downside was that the notional DC approach has all adjustments operate through changes in benefits; raising contributions is not an option since it also increases promised benefit. We also note that the Swedish system offers a minimum guaranteed benefit well above the poverty level. For such countries, pension schemes in which adjustment take place both on the benefit and the contribution side might be preferable.

In related work, Usuki points out that Japanese DB plan managers have become extraordinarily disappointed with the ineffectiveness of pension plan asset managers of late, in large part due to the narrowing risk premium in capital markets since 2000. Increasingly, they turn their eyes to the field of liability management and benefit design, seeking to control the financial risks of the pension plans offered. Recent measures taken include DB plan termination, DB benefit cuts, the put-back of the contracted-out portion, and adoption of cash balance or DC plans. As a consequence, we conclude that Japanese pension plan sponsors are using financial criteria to drive important pension outcomes. Usuki reports that determinants of DB plan termination include the volatility of return on shareholder equity, the pension plan funding ratio, and the size of pension assets and liabilities relative to the size of the plan sponsor. In addition, plan size also influenced decisions to terminate many Japanese employee pension funds (EPFs.) Turning to the decision to put back the contracted-out portion of the EPF, he again concluded that plan type choice is an important part of corporate risk management when the portfolio includes pension liabilities. Those findings imply that financial risks will remain a main concern for Japanese pension plan sponsors, with higher plan terminations and put-backs of the contracted-out portion of EPFs in the future, as well as additional conversions from traditional DB to cash balance and DC plans.

In the North American context, Pozzebon notes that the Canadian public pension system has long been seen as one of the best in the world. Indeed, to protect against the pressures of an aging population, the public system has become partially funded leading to a feeling of greater confidence among the Canadian population. Nevertheless, while some might believe that Canada's retirement system stands on reasonably solid ground, it still faces many daunting challenges. In particular, the private sector component appears to have weakened substantially during the last decade. The gradual shift from DB to DC, with a parallel move away from retirement saving arrangements covered by pension regulation, portends increasing insecurity for tomorrow's retirees. The author concludes that review of pension governance rules and analysis of the plan sponsor liability environment would strengthen the multi-pillar foundation of Canadian retirement income.

Fore (Chapter 10) illustrates how global accounting standards may influence US pensions substantially. The long phase in pension profitability came to an abrupt end in March 2000, with the bursting of the stock market bubble and the onset of the bear market. As many have noted, the fact that interest fell sharply also made matters worse, boosting the present value of DB pension liabilities. DB plan underfunding grew phenomenally: for standard and poor (S&P) 500 firms, around 70 percent of which offered DB plans, these plans were around $300 billion overfunded in 1999, but by mid 2003 were underfunded by $340 billion. Furthermore, many of those firms had an older workforce and many annuitants; most rapidly approach the day when they will begin paying out large pension cash flows on a sustained basis. Such an abrupt shift in DB plan funding status raises the question of whether pension accounting rules are consistent with the principles of pension finance.

The movement to require US pension sponsors to conform to global standards illustrates how international trends can affect retirement policies in other nations. As standard-setters move toward international convergence, it now seems clear that this trend will continue. On the whole, this new accounting paradigm appears to the author to be an improvement over the old paradigm, with its emphasis on smoothing and its decoupling of risks from returns. Opponents of fair value standards have argued that switching to these will introduce excessive volatility to financial statements for little or no benefit to users and issuers of statements. These arguments continue, yet the standards are set for adoption in Europe from 2005.

Conclusions

The new retirement paradigm must fit the realities of population aging, rising life expectancies, and the need to finance adequate retirement income. Many questions have been addressed regarding the meaning of retirement in a world with very different expectations. Slower growth in the labor force, combined with new definitions of work and retirement, clearly imply that traditional DB plans will not meet many stakeholders' needs in the labor force of the future. As a result, fewer firms will offer early retirement subsidies to encourage workers to retire in their fifties in the future; instead, company retirement policies must be amended to fit new needs. All of this is taking place against the backdrop of anticipated changes in national social security rules to improve financing, encourage continued work, and delay retirement.

A key problem noted by Rep. Earl Pomeroy (D-N Dakota) is that the US Congress tends to think in two-year bursts, which becomes a problem when it comes to legislating pension reform. 'This mismatch in long-term liabilities and short-term fiscal planning has never been starker in any period in our history,' he points out. 'Our children will pay the price'. Another is that the DB pension funding situation has become rather bleak in the US and around the world. Even with a reasonably good economy, it will take many years before these systems can be restored to solvency. And as the contributors to this volume point out, immediate application of a fair value framework would run the risk of massive DB plan terminations. On the other hand, improved disclosure rules will aid users of financial statements, and they in turn will make their voices heard concerning the quality of information disclosed.

A powerful engine driving the reform of retirement income security systems in the next decade will probably be convergence—the movement to a common approach for reporting plan assets and liabilities. This will surely change the way DB plan investments are managed and the way benefit formulas work, and it will make fixed-income investment strategies more consistent with immunization and duration than in the past. In the USA, where many DB plans have relatively old demographic structures, plan sponsors and investment managers may concentrate more on investment strategies attuned to the timing of retirement benefit cash flows.

While the old accounting conventions may have encouraged DB plan sponsors to invest too much in equity, some will claim that the new standards will encourage too much fixed income in pension fund portfolios. Ultimately, accounting rules work best when they are neutral with respect to economic decision-making, when they acknowledge that returns are coupled with risks of a long-term nature.

References

Costa, Dora. (1998). *The Evolution of Retirement: An American Economic History, 1880–1990*. Chicago: University of Chicago Press.

—— (2000). 'The Wage and the Length of the Work Day: From the 1890s to 1991', *Journal of Labor Economics*. January 18(1): 156–81.

Knowledge@Wharton (K@W 2004*a*). (2004*a*). 'How Should Retirement Policy Be Reformed? Don't Speak All Together, Please.' Viewed June 2 at *http://knowledge.wharton.upenn.edu/index.cfm?fa=viewArticle&id=986*

—— (2004*b*). 'Redefining Retirement in the 21st Century'. Viewed June 2, online at *http://knowledge.wharton.upenn.edu/article/996.cfm*

Mitchell, Olivia S., David Blitzstein, Judy Mazo, and Michael Gordon (eds.) (2003). *Benefits for the Future Workplace*. Pension Research Council. Philadelphia, PA: University of Pennsylvania Press.

Purcell, Patrick. (2004). 'Older Workers: Employment and Retirement Trends', Pension Research Council Working Paper.

Chapter 2

Looking Backward, Looking Forward: Where is Pension Policy Headed?

James A. Klein

An inescapable element of the retirement paradigm is the public policy environment within which pension laws and regulations are developed. Issues of plan design, investment choices, and financing are matters that are principally determined by plan sponsors and participants with the help of service providers and other experts. Yet all of these decisions are made against the backdrop of a retirement system that is in large part structured according to rules that were either established or reaffirmed by the key pension law, the Employee Retirement Income Security Act (ERISA) of 1974, and by amendments to that law enacted over the past thirty years.

In the future, the retirement paradigm will be reinvented because people and entities directly engaged in designing and sponsoring plans, as well as those benefiting from plans, will make countless decisions about their immediate and long-term needs. They will adjust retirement plan programs, and retirement practices themselves, to accommodate those needs. Depending on how much thought is put into the development of the new paradigm, the pension institution may be refashioned in a logical and orderly way, or reinvented piece by piece. But, either way, to effectuate many of the changes that will lead to a new retirement paradigm will inevitably require public policy changes. In the best case scenario, the public policy arena will actually facilitate the development of the new paradigm. But if we are not so fortunate, the public policy arena will be the black hole into which thoughtful ideas plunge, never to emerge again. Because the public policy dimensions will be so crucial to the reinvention of a new retirement paradigm, this chapter identifies four elements that may help in the development of a paradigm suitable for the next thirty years. These are the key role of trust in a regulatory scheme; the importance of balancing objectives in pension policy; the key importance of recognizing expectations; and the need for retirement policy champions.

The Key Role of Trust

Government officials and private sector representatives from many countries have sought to learn about the US pension system as they wrestle with the development of private sector individual and employer-sponsored retirement systems in their own countries. It seems clear that, whatever else they might accept or reject from our system as they develop their own, they should give thoughtful consideration to the concepts enshrined in Title I of ERISA dealing with fiduciary responsibilities. This is because much of the success of the US retirement system relies on the fact that workers and employers are willing to turn over large sums of money to one or more third parties, believing that this money will be responsibly managed and prudently invested, and it will be used to pay retirees benefits many decades into the future.

Commensurate with this trust is the confidence that if, by chance, the people and entities to whom these funds are entrusted should act in a negligent or dishonest fashion, then an enforcement system will hold them to account. Such faith in the system is not based on a naïve confidence in the goodness of others; rather, it is based upon a belief in the essential soundness of the structure set forth in ERISA. That this system is largely self-policing is an even more remarkable tribute to how well it works most of the time. It is not merely a linguistic coincidence that the vehicle into which pension assets are placed is called a 'trust'.

The US pension system is, of course, far from perfect. But the unfortunate instances of neglect or abuse regarding private retirement plans that are identified (and punished) are attributable more to the misfeasance of a few, rather than due to fundamental shortcomings in the legal framework of the entire pension system. What is unclear, of course, is what percentage of those who act in a negligent or abusive manner are identified under the current regulatory and enforcement regime. Thus it is with some trepidation that I call for greater *trust* between the regulators and the regulated community when redesigning the pension regulatory structure.

Pension practitioners have long decried the growing complexity of pension law in the aftermath of ERISA. Perhaps those of us with little or no experience in other policy arenas (e.g. environmental and housing) may overstate the complexity of pension policy relative to other areas of the law. Even so, in a voluntary retirement system, the concerns of those who must be relied upon to establish and maintain plans cannot be lightly dismissed. Whatever the truth might be (and 'complexity' itself is a rather subjective condition), the fact that the rules governing the pension system are often difficult to understand and expensive to implement seems to be a point conceded even by those who believe that the rules are warranted.

In some respects, the complex regulatory scheme in place today is a by-product of the breakdown in trust between the government and the plan sponsor community. This was perhaps most clearly evidenced in the reformulation of pension nondiscrimination rules in 1986, when a looser 'facts and circumstances' standard was changed to more precise mechanical rules. On one hand, the rejection of the 'facts and circumstances' approach was a response to complaints from plan sponsors themselves, who felt that the interpretation and enforcement of those standards were inconsistent and arbitrary (Gale et al. 1999). Plan sponsors had lost faith in the regulators. On the other hand, the movement toward a more rigid standard was also a manifestation of regulators unease as to whether plan sponsors were designing their plans in a way that was fair to participants at different income levels.

Yet it would be an oversimplification to attribute much of the highly regulated nature of the pension system to a breakdown in trust between the 'regulators' and the 'regulated'. The late Michael Gordon (1999), one of the fathers of ERISA, summed up the essential paradox of ERISA when he wrote about the law's 'mandatory imposition of substantial regulatory standards on a totally voluntary system'. The fact that many employers who are not required to sponsor a plan continue to do so, despite costly and complex regulatory requirements, is a testament to the underlying strength of the system and the belief of plan sponsors that retirement plans are important, despite the difficulty of maintaining them. Yet, to the extent that the regulatory burden is cited by employers as a reason not to sponsor a plan, the challenge for the future is to forge a system in which the regulatory requirements do not undermine the willingness of plan sponsors to initiate or continue a plan.

Another dimension of the regulatory scheme that governs the pension system involves the substantial notice and reporting requirements that accompany the sponsorship of a private sector retirement plan. To the extent that these responsibilities require plan sponsors to report information to participants, the enduring challenge is to make sure that the information conveyed is relevant and understandable. When reporting requirements are based on the government's need to receive information in order to ensure compliance with the law, the regulated community should accept some burden as the application of the Reagan Doctrine of nuclear disarmament ('trust but verify') to the pension system. The problem is that if the new retirement paradigm is still to be based on the premise of a *voluntary* system, Congress and government agencies responsible for developing complex rules and for requiring the reporting of voluminous information must ensure that the regulatory burden satisfies a cost-benefit analysis at least in some rough sense. Future regulators must demonstrate more clearly than in the past that the information required, and the complex testing to which plans must be subjected is, in fact, necessary to achieve some greater objective.

How might this be accomplished? At the margin, legislative and regulatory relief could be enacted to strip away some of the more obvious forms of

regulatory overkill that have developed as successive Congresses and agencies have developed new rules. Indeed in the last few years, Congressional
action has simplified the operations of the pension system. But meaningful
progress toward a new regulatory framework based on concepts of fairness
and equity will require a different mindset between the regulated community and the regulators, one where the essential ingredient is the restor-
ation of trust between plan sponsors and regulators.

From the regulators' perspective, this greater trust may need to take the
form of looser rules that afford plan sponsors more flexibility in the
operation of plans, with fewer precise hurdles that must be cleared. From
the plan sponsors' perspective, this trust might be manifested in a willingness to accept even harsher penalties for failure to meet more flexible
standards that would be established. In other words, the regulated community could be accorded more trust that they are designing and operating
plans for the benefit of participants and beneficiaries within a broader
framework of the enunciated public policy. In return, regulators would
be accorded more trust that they will enforce the law consistently and fairly
within that more flexible framework; and they would also be empowered to
impose even greater sanctions, in instances when the actions taken are
clearly inconsistent with the retirement security objectives of the underlying rule (e.g. abuse cases).

This trade-off would represent a fairly substantial gamble on the part of
both the regulated community and the regulators, yet there is reason for
optimism. In recent years, both the Internal Revenue Service (IRS) and the
US Department of Labor have initiated programs in which pension plan
sponsors are accorded more protections from sanctions for various violations if they come forward voluntarily to disclose the violation.[1]

One confidence-building measure to spur a more desirable regulatory
structure would be to engage parties with a legitimate stake in the outcome
of regulations more fully *with one another* during the development of
regulations. Since ERISA's enactment, most retirement policy rulemaking
has involved the agencies' inviting the input of parties with an interest
in the rules to provide written comments, to testify at public hearings
and to meet directly with regulators to discuss concerns. The level of
communication between the regulators and interested parties is excellent, yet the many segments of the retirement system with disparate interests rarely engage in simultaneous discussions with one another and the
regulators.[2]

The Importance of Balancing Objectives

The tax and labor aspects of pension policy have not always been in balance
over the past three decades. As a result, there is currently no consistent
legislative and regulatory regime, nor is there a coherent retirement

income policy. On the one hand, regulatory agencies with enforcement responsibilities over the pension system have well-defined roles and have avoided directly conflicting activities since the adoption of Reorganization Plan No. 4 in 1978 [543 *Fed. Reg.* 47713, Oct. 17, 1978]. On the other hand, it is probably fair to say that the Congressional committees with oversight of pension law have been less consistent than the regulatory agencies about staying within the purview of their own jurisdiction.

For instance, the numerous parallel provisions of pension law enshrined in ERISA and in the Internal Revenue Code (IRC), resulted, in part, from the lack of trust between Congressional tax and labor committee members when the pension law was crafted in 1974. Each committee wanted to protect its turf and ensure ongoing oversight authority. This dual regulatory structure may be a necessary outgrowth of the fact that pension policy is and must be an amalgam of labor and tax policy. That said, were there more collaboration between and among the Congressional committees of jurisdiction and—to a lesser extent—the executive branch agencies with jurisdiction over the nation's retirement system, the oversight of the pension system today would be a great deal simpler and more consistent.

Some observers have suggested that the dual jurisdiction of the US Department of Labor and the US Department of Treasury/Internal Revenue Service could be merged into a single federal department with retirement system oversight. In support of this idea, critics emphasize conflict between the US Treasury Department's mission of raising tax revenue, and the retirement system's goal of promoting saving (Siciliano 2004). The idea of a unified federal agency certainly bears thoughtful consideration, but it is possible to achieve greater retirement system cohesion without going that far.

The principal impetus for ERISA was the need to protect pension rights, so fiduciary concerns were a strong motivating force for its enactment. Despite its origins, however, in the intervening years, tax policy has driven the principal changes in the pension system, resulting in increasing conflict between tax and labor aspects of pension policy. From the Revenue Act of 1978 through the Economic Growth and Tax Reform and Relief Act of 2001, there were more than twenty pieces of major legislation that changed pension law, typically through changes in the tax code (even where parallel ERISA provisions were also adopted). This dominance of tax over labor aspects in pension policy is not absolute, of course. For example, attention has been devoted to participants' diversification rights and fiduciary responsibilities in the aftermath of the Enron and WorldCom problems. On the other hand, the larger conflict in pension policy over much of the past thirty years has not been the schism between 'tax' and 'labor' policy but, rather, has been the tension between tax legislation enacted primarily for revenue raising purposes, and tax legislation enacted for retirement income security purposes.

This point was made clearly during the 1980s and early 1990s, when much pension law was enacted in an effort to address substantial federal budget deficits rather than driven by the need to boost saving. Moreover, much of the legislation designed to curtail the federal tax revenue loss attributable to tax-qualified pension contributions[3] was enacted intermittently between *other* bills designed to shore up the funded status of pension plans.[4] This somewhat schizophrenic pattern exposed the absence of any coherent retirement income policy, and it also made evident the conflict between tax policy limiting lost tax revenue and tax policy protecting pension benefits. These problems were mitigated somewhat in the mid to late 1990s as the transformation of budget deficits into surpluses eased efforts to enact nearly annual tax measures curtailing tax expenditures accorded to pensions. In addition, the stronger economy until 1999 produced better funded plans and less need to legislate improvements in funding standards.

It would be unfair to attribute the revenue loss versus retirement security conflict in the pension system entirely to the regulatory environment. Some have observed that, among plan sponsors themselves, the various corporate functions which direct pension policy have not always worked in harmony. The corporate model has been compared to that of a car in which (*a*) the head of human resources is the driver, with a foot pressing the accelerator in the hope of providing progressive and generous benefits to workers and retirees; (*b*) the chief financial officer is a concerned passenger in the front seat leaning over and trying to apply the brakes and control costs; and (*c*) the company actuary is sitting in the back seat, looking out the rear window giving the other two directions. In recent years, the finance concerns of plan sponsors have often taken a 'front seat' role in the determination of companies' pension decisions, as witness some firms freezing pension accruals in light of the long-term uncertainty about the interest rate that will be required for calculating defined benefit (DB) plan liabilities.

While it would be imprudent of Congress and policymakers to dismiss the cost implications of the pension system and proposed retirement policy, many run the risk of understanding the *cost* of pensions much better than they understand their *value.* This is in part the result of extensive government focus on the tax revenue loss implications of pensions, with the annual publication of pension tax expenditure and calculations of federal revenue estimates by the Congressional Joint Committee on Taxation. Any serious effort to reinvent the pension paradigm will require much more concerted attention to questions that have been all but ignored to date. These are issues such as proper balancing of interests between the major stakeholders in the retirement system—individuals, employers, and the government; better definition of the adequacy of retirement; and benefits and drawbacks of different types of retirement vehicles.

The current economic environment and the resurgence of federal budget deficits may once again threaten the tax-favored treatment of employer-sponsored retirement plans. But if the tax expenditure accorded to pensions—the second biggest expenditure in the federal budget[5]—has been responsible for frequent Congressional efforts to reduce revenue loss through changes in retirement plans over the past thirty years, that dynamic is very likely to change over the next thirty years. For the entire period of time since ERISA's passage, the baby boomer generation has been in the workforce; the tax qualified contributions made to the retirement plans of this sizable segment of the population have dwarfed the taxable retirement benefits paid out to the smaller generation that preceded the boomers. Thus, the tax exclusion for contributions to retirement plans has exceeded the taxes collected on retirement benefits, resulting in the large expenditures. But as the boomers now begin to receive retirement benefits and pay taxes on them, these trends might reverse, and the tax structure accorded to the private retirement system may become a revenue raiser. Regardless of whether that occurs, the challenge for retirement policy in the next several years—in periods of surplus or deficit—will be largely the same: to resist formulating policy based on the revenue implications alone, but rather on the basis of what will be required to ensure retirement income security for an aging population. Clearly, the task will be made much more difficult if large deficits persist, but greater difficulty should not be permitted to interfere with the fundamental necessity of the task.

This effort will require that Congressional tax-writing committees will work in concert with the labor committees, with whom they share an interest in retirement income security. This will not be easy, as it will require collaboration over corresponding changes in both ERISA and IRC provisions. This represents a golden opportunity that public policy makers will have to address the really important questions about the future of the retirement system and retirement security.

The Relevance of Expectations

The pension system has not lacked for controversy over the course of the past several years, so it would be unrealistic to think that the future will be free of controversy or debate over the nature of the pension promise. But a new better-functioning retirement paradigm can be one in which constituencies with different perspectives and agendas make a more concerted effort to appreciate each other's expectations.

The current debate over hybrid pension plans represents a good example of where the retirement policy environment would benefit from more recognition of others' expectations. In large measure, the controversy over transitions from traditional DB to hybrid plans erupted over the issue of whether future benefit accruals could change: that is, whether the employer could modify the benefit that workers expected that they would receive if they continued to work and the plan remained unchanged. For critics of hybrid plans, the answer was an emphatic 'no', while hybrid plan advocates maintained that the law protects pension rights earned up until a certain point, but it provides no guarantee of future benefit accrual. Without delving into the details, it is plain to see that on one level, at least, the dispute is one of 'expectations'. Workers have expectations that certain conditions and events will transpire (e.g. their continued employment and the continuation of their company's pension plan). Correspondingly, plan sponsors have an expectation that they will continue to have the flexibility to change the design of their plan without being legally bound to pay benefits beyond those accrued.

It may be that these two competing expectations cannot be reconciled and will, instead, have to be resolved in the courts or in the public policy arena. Indisputably, however, the public discourse over such fundamental questions would be far more civil and productive if each side of the debate began by recognizing the other side's legitimate and competing expectations. It is possible, for example, that a hybrid plan advocate would insist that in a vibrant voluntary pension system, plan sponsors must have absolute flexibility to change their plans prospectively; while at the same time they may still acknowledge that such flexibility could be contrary to plan participants' expectations. Similarly, a hybrid plan critic would advocate that continuing certain pension plan features is more important than plan sponsor flexibility; while at the same time, they might acknowledge the harm that will be done to plan sponsors, or other participants, if employers are denied that flexibility. In practice, however, debates over the key pension questions are rarely posited to acknowledge the legitimacy of the other side's view. It is never done in a litigation context, and it seldom occurs during the course of legislative or regulatory debate.

This hybrid plan example is merely illustrative of the broader problem that plagues the retirement system debate. Of even greater concern than the resolution of any single individual policy issue is the need to make meaningful progress toward the reinvented retirement paradigm. Without a more honest recognition of others' reasonable perspectives, the nation is unlikely to make much progress on difficult retirement policy questions nor achieve the appropriate balancing of interests among participants, plan sponsors, the government, and other pension stakeholders.

To successfully implement this proposal, each of the competing interests in the retirement system debate will need to develop confidence that they can publicly acknowledge the legitimate views of others without concern that that recognition will be portrayed as a lessening in the advocacy of their position. What can be done to overcome the mistrust that often interferes with the willingness of competing interests in the retirement system to acknowledge the viewpoints and expectations of others? Initial confidence-building measures might include efforts by the media to portray in a balanced fashion competing interests involved in a variety of pension decisions. In addition, perhaps all advocacy groups could be asked, when making the case for their own agenda, to acknowledge where their own positions may be perceived as contrary to the interests of others. For example, all negotiating sessions could begin not only with a list of demands from each side, but also a rendition of each side's understanding of the other side's concerns and objectives. These measures are worth trying as a means of breaking long-standing logjams and thinking creatively about a new retirement policy paradigm.

The Need for Retirement Policy Champions

Virtually every history of ERISA portrays in glowing terms the statesmanship of a cadre of strong legislative leaders from both political parties.[6] These lawmakers possessed the vision about the need for a comprehensive law to regulate the pension system, and they also diligently immersed themselves in the minutiae of the statutory provisions needed to bring to fruition what ultimately became ERISA.

It is unfortunate that the last thirty years have produced only a handful of members of Congress who could genuinely be called legislative champions of the pension system. This is despite the prominent role that pensions play in our economy, and despite the fact that retirement security is frequently a rallying cry in congressional and presidential campaigns. Only very recently have a few members of Congress moved to lay claims to this moniker. Perhaps this change is a reflection of the aging of the workforce and the growing awareness of the need to address the demographic realities that will make retirement policy an even more prominent issue on the domestic policy agenda.

Nonetheless, the paucity of pension champions may be due to the extraordinary complexity of pension law and the difficulty of mastering what has obviously become very detailed subject matter. It may also be due to the fact that for about half of the past thirty years, Congress has struggled with substantial budget deficits. Consequently, most pension legislative activity emerged from efforts to curtail the pension tax expenditure in order to either reduce federal budget deficits or help pay for cuts in other more visible types of taxes, or both.

Whatever the reasons for the past dearth of pension legislative champions, it is difficult to imagine how positive pension policy in the future will emerge unless more members of Congress make pension issues a personal priority. There are simply too many natural obstacles to thwart forward motion on retirement policy development—tax revenue implications, jurisdictional battles between and among committees with authority over pension policy, the difficulty of mastering intricate details of pension law, and the political reality that the benefit of some pension changes are not felt, and therefore cannot be confirmed, until many years into the future. The success of prudent pension policy is often measured not in the positive conditions that it creates but, rather, in negative conditions that it prevents from occurring.

A shortage of pension legislative champions has resulted in at least two significant casualties. At the micro level, there is a lack of consistency among many of the statutes approved by Congress. At a macro level, it has resulted in the absence of a coherent national retirement income policy. The value of having retirement laws that are consistent with one another is self-evident. The arguments in favor and opposed to developing a national retirement income policy are much more complex and nuanced—and developing such a policy would be much more difficult to achieve even if there were widespread agreement that it should be done.

The challenge, therefore, is for those interested in a robust retirement system to engage in a dialogue with thoughtful members of Congress, of both parties and in both houses. Convincing lawmakers to do so should be a somewhat easier task in the years ahead than it has been in the past, because the demographic realities of an aging population and the growing emphasis on retirement policy issues in the media means that pension policy issues are much more important to the public discourse and, therefore, to elected officials.

To cultivate a larger group of retirement policy champions who will be effective, regardless of the particular agenda that they may wish to advocate, it also will be necessary to persuade more future political leaders that it is worth their while. They will have to learn the intricacies of pension policy sufficiently well that they can earn the respect of their colleagues who will *not* be retirement policy leaders, but who will rely upon the leaders' judgment in making some extraordinarily difficult decisions. It is a tall order, but it is necessary to reinvent the retirement paradigm.

Endnotes

1. Employee Plans Compliance Resolution System, Revenue Procedure 2003–44; Voluntary Fiduciary Correction Program, RIN 1210-AA76, March 28, 2002.
2. USC Sections 561–570. The Negotiated Rulemaking Act authorizes and encourages a process wherein, in real time, the disparate views of multiple interested parties and the regulators can be discussed. Apart from some Pension Benefit Guaranty Corporation rulemaking, however, the negotiated rulemaking process has been rarely employed in the development of pension regulations. It might be tried more frequently by the US Department of Labor and the Internal Revenue Service to see whether it leads to an improved pension regulatory framework. At a minimum, it might lead to a regulatory system in which interested parties more fully understand and accept the outcome of the rulemaking process. This

approach, by itself, would not represent the reinvention of a retirement regulatory paradigm. But it could offer one possible tool for building it.
3. These include the Tax Equity and Fiscal Responsibility Act of 1982 (TEFRA), Deficit Reduction Act of 1984 (DEFRA), Tax Reform Act of 1986 (TRA '86), and the Omnibus Budget Reconciliation Act of 1993 (OBRA '93).
4. These include the Single Employer Pension Plan Amendments Act of 1986 (SEPPAA), Omnibus Budget Reconciliation Act of 1987 (OBRA '87), and the Revenue Reconciliation Act of 1990.
5. Estimates of Federal Tax Expenditures for Fiscal Years 2004–2008, Joint Committee on Taxation, December 22, 2003.
6. See for instance Sass (1997).

References

Employee Plans Compliance Resolution System, Revenue Procedure (2003: 44); Voluntary Fiduciary Correction Program, RIN 1210-AA76, March 28, 2002.

Estimates of Federal Tax Expenditures for Fiscal Years (2004–2008); Joint Committee on Taxation, December 22, 2003.

Gale, William, John B. Shoven, and Mark J. Warshawsky (1999). 'ERISA After 25 Years: A Framework for Evaluating Pension Reform', *Benefits Quarterly*, 15(4): 78–81.

Gordon, Michael S. (1999). 'Twenty-Fifth Anniversary Reflections on ERISA', *Benefits Quarterly*, 15(4): 6.

Sass, Steven (1997). *The Promise of Private Pensions*. Cambridge, MA: Harvard University Press.

Siciliano, John (2004). 'Unifying the System', *Pensions & Investments*, 23: 12.

Chapter 3

Reality Testing for Pension Reform

Pamela Perun and C. Eugene Steuerle

I'm staring at documents that make no sense to me, no matter how many beers I drink.... Apparently I have until Sept. 30 (in most instances)...to comply with something (but what?) called 'GUST'... [for my Keogh plan and I]...must adopt EGTRRA prior to the end of the plan year beginning in 2002. I am, frankly, reluctant to adopt anything called 'EGTRRA,' which sounds like the name of a giant radioactive chicken that destroys Tokyo...the federal Tax Code is out of control.... It's gigantic and insanely complex, and it gets worse all the time. Nobody has ever read the whole thing. IRS workers are afraid to go into the same ROOM with it. They keep it locked in the basement, and once a day, they open the door, heave in a live taxpayer—some poor slob who failed to adopt EGTRRA in time to comply with GUST (and various other amendments)—then slam the door shut, before the screams start (Barry, 2003).

As humorist Dave Barry has pointed out, the US private pension system *is* fair game for jokes and ridicule. It is absurdly complicated and incomprehensible. Relevant tax rules and regulations include more than 3,000 pages of small, single-spaced, text and weigh more than most laptop computers. The companion labor rules under the Employee Retirement Income Security Act (ERISA) of 1974, are smaller, but not by much. There is widespread agreement that the present situation is untenable and something must be done. There is also widespread recognition that the aging of the baby boom generation will place the US private pension system under unprecedented pressure and that a comprehensive review of pension policy is long overdue (Mulvey and Nyce Chapter 7). As Klein (Chapter 2) notes, reinventing the retirement paradigm requires examining whether the current US private pension system can meet the retirement income challenges to come.

Analyses of the US private pension system typically focus on such issues as how to improve coverage or encourage saving or prevent tax abuse or generate retirement income more equitably. Those issues are important, but this chapter takes the position that reinventing the retirement paradigm will require more fundamental analysis. A critical step in the analysis is to step back and examine closely the architecture of the private pension system today. The structure and machinery of the private pension system, that is, the accumulation of plan types and rules over the past sixty years, have much to teach us about directions for reform. Accordingly we focus on the nuts-and-bolts of the private pension system, the plans that comprise it and the rules that govern them.

This is an opportune time for such an analysis. For perhaps the first time, there are two very different types of proposals for change before Congress. The first is reflected in the Pension Preservation and Savings Expansion Act (PPSEA) introduced in 2003 by Representatives Portman and Cardin (Portman and Cardin 2003*a*, 2003*b*). PPSEA is the 'traditional' type of pension reform, an omnibus bill that tinkers with almost every aspect of the private pension system to make incremental changes. The second proposal is the attempt of the Administration to effect radical change and simplification in the structure of the private pension system. The 2003 proposal, modified in budget submissions in 2004; contemplates a sweeping consolidation in the number and types of defined contribution (DC) plans (Purcell 2003; US Department of the Treasury 2004). This chapter evaluates these two approaches to change; the first one for incremental change, and the second one involving greater structural reform, and then it considers an alternative.

The Current Structure of the US Pension System

As a starting point, it is helpful to take an overview look at the current structure of the private pension system in the USA. Most people understand that the system is composed of defined benefit (DB) and DC plans, but few are aware that, legally speaking, there can be as much diversity within these types of plans as between them. Figure 3-1 illustrates the extraordinary constellation of plans that will be available when all changes brought about by Economic Growth and Tax Relief Reconciliation Act (EGTTRA) of 2001, the most recent major pension reform law, have become fully operational in 2006 (see Glossary for terminology).

The US private pension system evolved into its current complicated structure as the result of two primary factors. First, it is a tax-based system that provides tax incentives to promote saving for retirement. Second, it is a voluntary employer-based system: employers are encouraged, but not required, to provide plans for their employees. In this framework, different types of employers are subject to different tax rules. For example, for-profit and not-for-profit employers are subject to completely different sections of the federal tax code, while governmental employers are largely exempt from such rules. The theory has been that, if pension plans are to be sponsored by different types of employers, those plans should be subject to as many different rules as are necessary and appropriate for those employers. This emphasis on the tax attributes of employers largely explains the historical evolution of the private pension system. It began in the 1920s with special tax rules for plans sponsored by corporate employers.

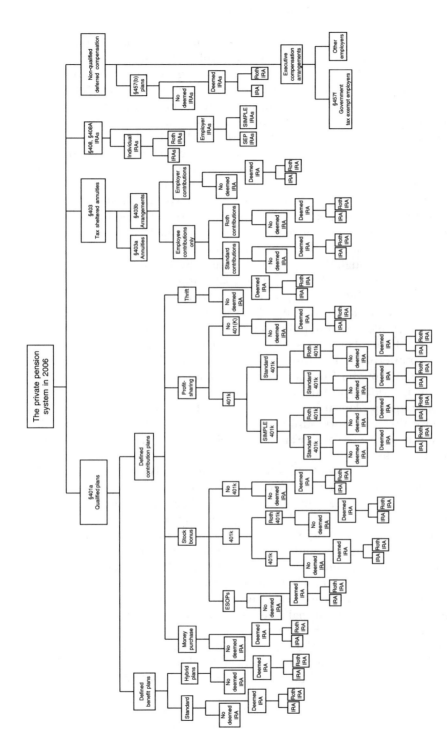

Figure 3-1. Plan types available in 2006 in the US private pension system.
Source: Perun and Steuerle (2000) (revised for EGTTRA).

Some twenty years later, new types of plans for not-for-profit employers were created. Next, special plans for self-employed individuals were developed, and then rules were imposed on plans for governmental employers. With the passage of ERISA, individual retirement accounts or IRAs were created, almost as an afterthought, to give workers without an employer-sponsored plan a limited opportunity to save for retirement. Finally, special Savings Incentive Match Plan for Employees (SIMPLE) plans have recently been created in the hope of attracting small employers to the private pension system. These are DC plans with safe harbor provisions designed to reduce the regulatory requirements of sponsoring a plan to a minimum.

The historical evolution of the private pension system is reflected in the post-EGTTRA arrangement of plan types composed of three primary families of plans. The largest group consists of qualified DB and DC plans subject to IRC § 401(a) that are subject to the full panoply of tax and ERISA rules. Although these plans were originally developed for corporate employers, now, with a few exceptions, any employer can sponsor these types of plans. The second group consists of tax sheltered annuities that must satisfy IRC § 403(b). These plans continue to be limited to nonprofit employers and public educational institutions. As might be expected, these plans are subject to much less regulation than their 401(a) counterparts. The third group consists of IRA-based plans under IRC § 408. Although IRAs were originally intended to be substitute savings plans for individuals without an employer-sponsored plan, employers can now offer group plans using these accounts. These plans are designed to minimize the regulatory burden on employers. Finally, there is a small, special category of plans available largely to governmental employers under IRC § 457(b).

Although each family of plans has its own specific rules, there has been some convergence over time. For example, most of the special rules for plans available to the self-employed have been repealed, and IRA-based plans are now available to employers as well as employees. In addition, some of the rigid barriers between plan families have been relaxed. Both nonprofit and corporate employers may sponsor 401(k) plans although governmental employers may not. This convergence, however, has not resulted in much simplification because, in most respects, the plan families retain their historical structures and traditional rules. As the pension system evolves, special rules and exceptions are created when the traditional rules do not fit a new situation. Over time, this process has produced a vast and complex array of rules that are increasingly difficult to navigate, even by the most experienced legal practitioner. These rules, which are illustrated in Table 3-1, include the EGTTRA changes that became effective in 2004.

As the US private pension system has grown more complex, both employers and workers find it more difficult and more expensive to navigate.

TABLE 3-1 Rules of the US Private Pension System in 2004

	IRC § 401(a) Plans						IRC § 403(b) Arrangements
	Defined benefit (DB)	*Money purchase*	*Profit-sharing, stock bonus, Standard 401(k)*	*Profit-sharing, stock bonus, SIMPLE 401(k)*	*Other Profit-sharing or stock bonus with no 401(k)*	*Employee stock ownership plan (ESOP)*	*IRC § 403(b)*
Eligible employer	Any employer	Any employer	Any employer except state & local governments	401(k) eligible employer with <100 employees and no other plan	Any employer	Corporate employer	Tax-exempt organizations and public schools
Overall annual limits	Annual benefit limit, per person, is the lesser of $165,000* or 100% × the highest 3 years' pay	Annual contribution limit, per person, is the lesser of $41,000 a* or 100% of pay	Per person, same as money purchase + 401(k) contributions up to a maximum of $13,000*	Annual contribution limit, per person, is a 401(k) contribution up to a maximum of $9,000* + the employer contribution		Same as money purchase	
Pay limit				$205,000*			
Required employer contribution	Amount for funding current + past service costs for each employee over future service OR the normal costs of the plan + past service liability amortized over 10 years	Amount required by plan formula	None	Employer matching contribution up to 3% of pay or fixed 2% of pay contribution		None, usually	

(*Continued*)

TABLE 3-1 Continued.

			IRC § 401(a) Plans				IRC § 403(b) Arrangements
	Defined benefit (DB)	Money purchase	Profit-sharing, stock bonus, Standard 401(k)	Profit-sharing, stock bonus, SIMPLE 401(k)	Other Profit-sharing or stock bonus with no 401(k)	Employee stock ownership plan (ESOP)	IRC § 403(b)
Employee contribution limits	Amount required by plan formula, if any	Not permitted	Maximum contribution of $13,000* + $3,000* catch-up contribution if or age 50+	Maximum contribution of $9,000* + $1,500* catch-up contribution if age 50+	Not permitted	None, usually	Same as standard 401(k)
Employer deduction limits	Lesser of 165% of current liability or accrued liability minus lesser of value of plan assets or their actuarial value	25% of aggregate employee pay	25% of aggregate employee pay (excluding 401(k) contributions)	Greater of contributions (excluding 401(k) contributions) up to 25% of aggregate employee pay or required contribution	Same as money purchase	Same as money purchase + certain dividends and interest on any loan	Not applicable
Exclusions from social security tax	Both contributions and distributions		Not for 401(k) contributions but other contributions and all distributions qualify		Yes	Yes	Not for employee contributions but employer contributions and all distributions qualify
10% Early withdrawal tax				Yes			

In-service withdrawals	Not permitted	Financial hardship[b], minimum 2 year holding period for employer contributions, loans		Minimum 2 year holding period, loans	Financial hardship, loans
Nondiscrimination rules (not governmental plans)	Top-heavy, coverage and non-discrimination rules	ADP, ACP, top-heavy, coverage and non-discrimination rules[c]	Can be exempt from top-heavy rules; no ADP, ACP or non-discrimination rules	Top-heavy, coverage and non-discrimination rules	ACP for matching contributions, availability test for deferrals and nondiscrimination rules
Integrated with social security	May be	May be (not 401(k) contributions or matching contributions)	No	No	May be
Spousal protection	Survivor annuity, consent and death benefit rights			Only death benefit usually[d]	
Vesting	Deferred	Immediate for 401(k) contributions; all others deferred	Immediate	Deferred	Immediate for deferrals; others deferred
Special requirements	PBGC guarantee and premium of $19 per participant; Minimum funding required in full each year	Special vesting rules for matching contributions	None	Forfeitures/interest payments raise annual contribution limit if 1/3 of contributions are for HCEs; 100% employer securities allowed; diversification optional at 55; put option/voting rights.	Special catch-up contributions permitted with 15+ years of service

(Continued)

TABLE 3-1 *Continued.*

	IRC §408, 408A IRAs				Non-qualified deferred compensation plans	
	Traditional IRA	RothIRA	SEP-IRA	SIMPLE IRA	Eligible 457(b) plans	Executive Arrangements
Eligibility	Anyone	Anyone with earnings less than $110,000 for individuals and $160,000 for couples[e]	Any employer	Employees of employers with no other plan and <100 employees	Employees of state and local government and tax-exempt organizations	Select group of officers or highly compensated employees
Dollar limit on contributions	$3,000* for all IRAs + $500* catch-up contributions; contributions are fully deductible if there is no employer plan or income is less than $45,000 for individuals and $65,000 for couples[f]	$3,000* for all IRAs + $500* catch-up contributions	Lesser of $41,000* or 25% of pay	Amount of employee and employer contributions	$13,000* + $3,000* catch-up contributions	None
Maximum per cent of pay limit on contributions	100%	100%	25%	Not applicable	100%	None
Employer contribution limits	Not applicable	Not applicable	Lesser of $41,000* or 25% of pay	Matching contribution of up to 3% of pay or fixed contribution of 2% of pay	None	None
Employee contribution limits	$3,000* + $500* catch-up contributions	$3,000* + $500* catch-up contributions	Not applicable	$9,000* + $1,500* catch-up contributions	Lesser of $13,000* + $3,000* catch-up contributions or 100% of pay	None
Employer deduction limits	Not applicable	Not applicable	25% of aggregate pay	Amount of contributions	Not applicable	None

Exclusion from SS tax	Yes	Not for contributions but distributions qualify	Both contributions and distributions	Not for employee contributions but employer contributions and distributions qualify	Not for employee contributions but distributions qualify	Depends on vesting
10% Early withdrawal tax		Usually not	Yes	Yes, increased to 25% in 1st 2 years	Not applicable	No (unless annuity purchased)
Early withdrawal tax exceptions	Medical, 1st home-purchase, higher education expenses, health insurance payments for unemployed	Age 59½, death, disability, 1st home purchase	Same as traditional IRA	Same as traditional IRA	Not applicable	None (unless annuity purchased)
Withdrawals permitted	Yes, may be subject to excise tax	5-year waiting period	Yes	Unforeseeable emergency only while employed	Yes	
Loans available		No			Unclear	Yes
Nondiscrimination rules		None	Uniform percent of pay contribution; top-heavy rules	Required employer contribution only	None	None
Pay limit		See above	$205,000*	$205,000* for 2% of pay contribution	$205,000*	Not applicable
Integrated with social security	No		May be	No	Not applicable	
Spousal protection			None under federal law, may be available under state law			
Vesting			Immediate			Usually deferred

TABLE 3-1 *Continued.*

	IRC §408, 408A IRAs				Non-qualified deferred compensation plans	
	Traditional IRA	Roth IRA	SEP-IRA	SIMPLE IRA	Eligible 457(b) plans	Executive Arrangements
Special restrictions and benefits	None	After-tax contributions; no tax on distributions	Employer does not have to contribute every year	Employees are generally responsible for investments	Special double catch-up contributions available during the 3 years before retirement; plans are technically unfunded but contributions to public sector plans must be held in trust	Employee taxed when benefits are paid or made available (or when vested for tax-exempts); may be a DC or DB plan

*means the amount is subject to adjustment for inflation or through a scheduled increase.

Source: IRC §§ 219, 401(a), 401(k), 401(m), 402, 403, 404, 408, 408A, 409, 410, 411, 412, 414, 415 and 416 and their regulations.

[a] The $41,000 overall limit is a cumulative limit for an employee across all defined contribution plans of the same employer.

[b] Financial hardship is an immediate and heavy financial need, even if foreseeable or voluntarily incurred, not able to be satisfied by other resources.

[c] Both the Actual Deferral Percentage (ADP) test for 401(k) contributions and the Average Contribution Percentage (ACP) test for matching and after-tax contributions are designed to limit contributions made by HCEs to a proportion based on the average contributions made by NHCEs.

[d] The surviving spouse receives the account balance as a death benefit unless he/she has consented to another beneficiary being named.

[e] The income phase-out schedule for Roth IRAs is $95,000–110,000 for individuals and $150,000–160,000 for married couples filing jointly.

[f] IRA income phase-out schedule in 2004: $45,000–55,000 for individuals and $65,000–75,000 for married couples filing together. These phase-outs are scheduled to increase to $50,000–60,000 for individuals and $80,000–100,000 for joint filers by 2007. There are also special limits for nonworking spouse.

For example, it is often not readily apparent in any given situation which plan might be the 'best' alternative among those available. Numerous consultants and other pension professionals assist in the plan selection and design process, but their services inevitably increase the cost of plan sponsorship and membership. Moreover, as rules grow more complicated, the administrative burden on plan sponsors whose plans must satisfy all relevant rules or lose their tax benefits also increases. The private pension system now includes a plan compliance industry, composed of lawyers, consultants, actuaries, accountants, and other pension professionals, dedicated to mastering and implementing plan rules. Their services are often critical to insure that plans satisfy the law, but their costs, which can be significant, must be borne by the employer as an additional business expense or charged to plan participants where they reduce the return to savings.

To be fair, it must be acknowledged that EGTTRA has resulted in some long overdue and welcome changes. For example, it rationalized the contribution limits on most employee savings plans today, 401(k), 403(b) and 457(b) plans, and the employer deduction limits on most plan types. It also eliminated some anomalies, such as the exclusion allowance for 403(b) arrangements and the coordinated contribution limit for 457(b) plans. It will result in one less plan type to worry about; by increasing the deduction limits for profit-sharing plans to those of money purchase plans; the latter (which are slightly less flexible) will become extinct. But, of course, most plan types continue to operate and the private pension system must now absorb and digest the changes EGTTRA has made in pension law.

The type of reform represented by EGTTRA and its predecessors have generally left the private pension system with more rules, not fewer; more plan types, not fewer; and more choices, even though many are not meaningful or worthwhile if and when understood. Only in a very few cases, such as the repeal of special contribution limits for 403(b) arrangements, did some rules actually disappear. In most cases, new rules are just placed on top of old rules, and new regulations must be written to harmonize and integrate them with existing law. Moreover, the private pension system has not yet felt the full brunt of EGTTRA. Rules permitting IRA contributions to employer-based plans recently became effective, and in 2006, some plans will be allowed to provide eternal tax forgiveness of future returns as long as no upfront deduction is taken, essentially by permitting the Roth-type contributions available already for Roth IRAs.

Given this background, not all of EGTTRA's changes are as benign as they might first appear. Allowing IRA contributions to be made to employer-based plans (thereby letting employees make these contributions directly to their employer's plan rather than to a separately maintained IRA) might be viewed as a good idea. Dodging the budgetary implications of backloading the cost of tax preferences to future years, allowing Roth-type contributions to employee savings plans (e.g. Roth 401(k)'s in 2006) might also be viewed as worthwhile in isolation as a pension policy. From a legal perspective, however, these additions compound the complexity now found in the private pension system. IRA contributions to qualified plans ('deemed IRAs') bring with them their special rules that will be added to plans already overwhelmed with their own rules. A plan that fails to observe the IRA rules may jeopardize the tax-qualified status of the entire plan while a plan that violates tax-qualification requirements may cost its IRAs their tax benefits too. Roth contributions too make employer-plans more complicated. Employees have traditionally made contributions on a pre-tax basis through which contributions (and their earnings) are taxed only when distributed from the plan or on an after-tax basis in which contributions are made from already-taxed income and only earnings are taxed when distributed. Roth contributions are based on a completely different tax system in which contributions are made from after-tax income but are completely exempt from taxation thereafter. Adding Roth contributions therefore means layering a third tax system on top of the traditional pre-tax and after-tax regimes. Employers will have to observe all the separate vesting rules, separate distribution rules, and separate record keeping, tax reporting and accounting requirements that apply to these different types of contributions and tax regimes in their plans. The ultimate effect of even the best-intentioned changes brought about by EGTTRA is more, not less, legal complexity in the private pension system and more, not less, of a compliance burden for employers.

Maintaining the Status Quo: The Pension Preservation and Savings Expansion Act of 2003

According to its sponsors, the PPSEA, makes 'the next generation of improvements to our nation's savings and pension systems' by providing 'a number of important new savings tools,' strengthening and expanding the employer-sponsored retirement system, offering 'new protections to participants' and 'assisting retirees in managing and preserving retirement assets and income' (Portman and Cardin 2003a). It is a massive bill, with more than 200 pages and 16 lengthy sections of highly technical changes to employee benefits law.[1]

PPSEA follows in the footsteps of EGTTRA and was crafted as a follow-on bill by EGTTRA's primary drafters, US Representatives Rob Portman of Ohio and Benjamin Cardin of Maryland. Its initial thrust was to accelerate and make permanent the changes in EGTTRA that would have expired in 2010 unless extended by Congress. Its immediate effect would be to increase the amounts individuals could contribute to 401(k)-type plans and IRAs. The bill then winds its way through almost every aspect of the private pension system, proposing changes, additions, and deletions to current rules along the way. If PPSEA were to be enacted, major legal rules throughout the pension system will be changed. These include rules on when employees are vested in plan benefits, when plans become tax-quali-fied, how DB formulas can calculate pension, and when employees must begin receiving benefits.

In addition to rule changes, there are, as always, changes to plan types. This time, the focus is on the SIMPLE plans created in 1996 that were based on plan designs intended to minimize the regulatory burden of sponsoring a plan for small employers. When SIMPLE plans were enacted, employers were no longer permitted to create new Salary Reduction Simplified Employee Pension Plans (SARSEPs), plans that could be restricted to employee, 401(k)-type contributions. SIMPLE plans required employers instead to make at least a minimal plan contribution in exchange for fewer rules and less liability. PPSEA proposes to weaken the effect of these reforms by bringing back SARSEP-type plans and permitting a smaller employer contribution. Employers would have more choices but the design of SIMPLE plans would become more complicated and, in the end, not very different from their traditional counterparts.

Not one of these changes, standing alone, is particularly problematic, and many are in fact improvements in current rules. But perhaps this is not the appropriate standard for evaluating PPSEA. The important question is not whether it does some good for some people, but rather whether it helps move the private pension system toward the systematic improvement it needs to meet the retirement income challenges to come and whether it makes the best use of the resources that are spent. A more general question is why the private pension system seems to need major reconstructive surgery every year or so. After every extensive legal revision, it usually takes about five years before the necessary regulatory guidance to imple-ment the new rules is available. Too frequent changes leave plans in legal limbo and the system in regulatory gridlock.

PPSEA tinkers with many current rules and adds new ones but does little to change the basic architecture of the private pension system. For ex-ample, there will still be eight different ways for employees to save their own money, depending on what type of employer they have and the plan it chooses to sponsor, if any: a 401(k) plan for corporate and nonprofit employers, a 403(b) arrangement for nonprofit and public employers, a 457(b) plan for nonprofit and public employers, a SIMPLE plan based on a 401(k) model, a SIMPLE plan based on an IRA, a traditional IRA, a Roth IRA, or a SARSEP. For employers, distinguishing 401(k) plans from 403(b) arrangements from 457(b) plans from SIMPLE plans will be difficult, because they will outwardly look so much alike. Employees, too, often find the intricate rules for saving perplexing. When navigating the private pension system, employers and employees are confronted with choices that appear similar but can have very different legal consequences, and this, as lawyers often say, can and will be a trap for the unwary.

EGTTRA and PPSEA exemplify the customary approach to reform in the US private pension system. For the most part, they maintain the status quo and preserve the historically distinct plan types based on employer tax attributes and their rules. At the same time, they create new plan types and tax regimes that do not fit neatly into the traditional structure. Over time, the traditional structure makes less sense and becomes less capable of supporting such changes; systemic reform is warranted but never achieved. Instead, plan types continue to be haphazardly combined, and their rules are layered on top of each other, along with the many special rules and exceptions and transition rules and historical legal quirks required to maintain the legal integrity of the system. The consequence is an all too complex and intricate private pension system.

One consequence of this approach is, frequent mutations of pension law that increase the compliance burden of employers as well as the costs of sponsoring a plan. On the positive side, it may provide employers and employees with more choices. Then again, while more choice is usually good, too many unnecessary choices may not be desirable especially if, over time, they are not sustainable. For example, adding Roth contributions will increase the complexity and cost of plan administration for employers and be a likely source of confusion for employees (Vanguard Center for Retirement Research 2001). Not only do Roth contributions require employees to project future earnings, tax rates, and statutory changes to tax law when deciding about contributing, but the tax consequences of their choice will determine pension and budget policy in part for decades to come. There is no guarantee, moreover, that Roth contributions will always have the favorable tax treatment they now enjoy. Employees, even assuming they can make a perfectly rational choice between the alternative tax regimes, may find that new tax laws (e.g. higher rates, lower rates, adoption of a consumption tax) means that the government reneged on what it once offered. It is one thing to change the law; it is another to give people choices, and then change the rules under which those past choices were made. And when eligibility for future Medicare, Medicaid, and other income-related benefits are determined, 'income' from Roth IRAs and 401(k)s probably will be counted, meaning that employees will have to maintain mini-accounting systems just for Roth contributions, even though they do not need to be reported for income tax purposes.

Ultimately, the question arises: Who really benefits from PPSEA and the type of change it represents? It certainly means more work for the lawyers, actuaries, consultants, and accountants in the plan compliance industry. New regulations must be drafted, plans must be rewritten and requalified, and administrative procedures must be reprogrammed. PPSEA also means more assets of higher-income individuals will need to flow through an extra layer of retirement plan management, thus increasing the fees paid to financial services, mutual fund, and insurance companies relative to other saving. It means that wealthier Americans can get more tax benefits from savings plans sooner because of higher contribution limits and liberalized withdrawal rules. Further, there are many special rules and provisions for almost every large group with an interest in pensions. But it is difficult to argue that it is constructive for the ordinary pension consumer—the not-so-large employer and the not-so-wealthy employee—from whom the higher costs of management attributable to the added complexity will take a much larger share of savings. For many of them, net rates of return are likely to decline. Neither have its economic benefits been demonstrated; there is no evidence (and no one has attempted to estimate) that PPSEA would result in any increase in the percent of low-and middle-income workers who reach retirement with perhaps more than $100,000 in assets.

An Alternative Direction for Private Pensions? Simplified Savings Accounts

In 2003, the Bush Administration stunned the employee benefits community by proposing a radical pruning of employer-sponsored savings plans. It advocated replacing the panoply of 401(k) plans, 457(b) plans, SIMPLE 401(k) plans, 403(b) arrangements, SEPs and SIMPLE IRAs with a new, standard plan type called Employer Retirement Savings Account or (ERSA). Although ERSAs look similar to today's 401(k) plan, contributions would not be made from pre-tax income. Instead, all contributions would be Roth contributions, made from after-tax income and exempt from taxation thereafter. Traditional and Roth IRAs would also be combined into a type of plan called a Retirement Savings Account or RSAs, modeled on today's Roth IRAs, would replace individual IRAs, and a new savings arrangement called a Lifetime Savings Account or LSAs would be created for general purpose saving.[2] LSAs are also modeled on Roth IRAs, but would have fewer rules and restrictions than either ERSAs or RSAs. In 2004, the proposal was expanded to include a fourth type of savings plan, individual development accounts (IDAs), intended for low-income workers.

The Administration's proposals were widely criticized; many felt that RSAs and LSAs were too generous to higher-income taxpayers who could arbitrage the tax system and generate tax saving with little or no increase in personal saving (Steuerle 2003). Others felt that these would destabilize the private pension system, because employers, particularly small business owners, would trade in their broad-based plans for personal RSAs and LSAs for themselves and their families. Some suggested that employees also might abandon their employer-based plans and worried that (Profit-Sharing/401(k) Council of America 2003):

Some moderate and lower income employees will make smaller, or no, contributions to LSAs and RSAs than they and their employers would have made to their qualified plans. Many employees will redirect their retirement savings to LSAs and use their accumulations for nonretirement purposes. To the extent that some employers continue to offer 401(k) plans, it may be more difficult for these plans to pass the nondiscrimination tests, even as changed in the proposal. Many employees offered a 401(k) will choose instead to save in LSAs, where they will have immediate and unrestricted access to their savings.

The plan compliance industry was distressed that it had not been consulted and the proposals were developed without their knowledge or cooperation. As a result, the proposals failed to find supporters or receive serious consideration.

Yet the following year, ERSAs, RSAs, and LSAs again returned to the policy arena, and this time, the Administration actively worked with the plan compliance industry. The most recent proposals retained some of the beneficial simplification features of the 2003 design but there were also some significant differences. Table 3-2 illustrates the major design features of each plan as currently proposed and indicates important rule changes from the 2003 proposals.

One change was that RSAs and LSAs were made modestly less attractive by reducing annual contribution limits by one-third, from $7,500 to $5,000 annually. Otherwise, the accounts were little changed: RSAs and LSAs are still essentially Roth-IRAs, funded with after-tax contributions and largely exempt from tax thereafter. In an effort to provide a balance for RSAs and LSAs that would benefit those at the high end of the income scale, the Administration added something for those at the low end—an expansion of the still-experimental IDAs. Low-income savers could contribute to an IDA and receive a 100 percent match of up to $500 annually. Matching contributions would come indirectly from the government through private financial institutions (not employers) that would receive a 100 percent tax credit in return for providing the match initially. Account assets would be available to pay for higher education, first-time home purchases, and small business capitalization.

ERSAs too were changed in the 2004 round. Figure 3-2 illustrates how ERSAs would reduce the current hodgepodge of savings plans—the 401(k) plans; the 403(b) arrangements; the 457(b) plans; the SIMPLE IRAs; the SARSEPs, and the SIMPLE 401(k)s—that now clutter the private pension system, to a single, standard plan. All 401(k) plans would become ERSAs, and all other plans could become ERSAs; those that did not would be frozen as of 2005. ERSAs could also include RSAs, subject to RSA rules.

This new direction proposed for the US private pension system, based on simplified savings accounts, has some significant merits that have largely been lost in the controversy over RSAs and LSAs. First, ERSAs would help rationalize and modernize the private pension system by eliminating some archaic, duplicate plan types. Second, they would simplify and standardize further, the rules for employee saving and thereby, reduce the burden and

TABLE 3-2 Proposed Rules for ERSAs, RSAs, LSAs and IDAs, 2003 and 2004

| | Employer plan | Employer or individual plan | Individual plan | |
	Employer retirement savings accounts (ERSAs)	Retirement savings accounts (RSAs)	Lifetime savings accounts (LSAs)	Individual development accounts (IDAs)
Sponsor/Contributor Eligibility	Any employer Not applicable	**2004:** no income limits; no age limits	Not applicable **2004:** no income limits; no age limits	Single: <$20,000* income Married: <$40,000* income
Annual funding	Optional; pre- and post-tax employee contributions; pre-tax employer contributions (broad-based and match)	Optional; post-tax only	Optional; post-tax only	Individual contributions + 100% match up to $500
Contribution limits	Employee: $30,000 + $3,000 catch-up* maximum: $41,000* or 100% pay	**2003:** $7,500* or pay **2004:** $5,000* or pay	**2003:** $7,500 or pay* **2004:** $5,000* or pay	?
Exclusion from SS tax	No, employee contribution; yes, other contributions and distributions	Not applicable		?
Early withdrawal tax	Probably, same as today	**2003:** non-qualified withdrawals subject to income+ penalty tax **2004:** non-qualified withdrawals in excess of contributions subject to income + penalty tax; 5 year holding period for conversions from ERSAs or traditional IRAs to avoid 10% penalty	No	?

(Continued)

TABLE 3-2 Continued.

	Employer plan	Employer or individual plan	Individual plan	
	Employer retirement savings accounts (ERSAs)	Retirement savings accounts (RSAs)	Lifetime savings accounts (LSAs)	Individual development accounts (IDAs)
In-service or qualified withdrawals	Probably, same as today	After age 58, death, disability	Any amount, any time	Higher education, 1st time home purchase, small business capitalization
Nondiscrimination rules	**2003**: no top-heavy rules, must have 70% coverage of NHCEs in plan, no integration or cross-testing rules. **2004**: current minimum coverage, top-heavy, integration, cross-testing rules apply; no ACP or ADP; if NHCEs' contributions (employer and employee) average <6% of pay, HCE contributions limited to 200% of NCHE contribution, otherwise no limit; design safe harbors if NHCEs get vested contributions of 3% of pay. **2004**: if 50% vested match up to 6% of pay, no testing; special rules for government and non-profit employers.		Not applicable	
Integrated with Social Security	**2003**: no **2004**: yes			
Spousal Protection	?	?	?	?

Vesting	Immediate for employee contributions; deferred for others?		Not applicable	
Special features	Consolidates 401(k), SIMPLE 401(k), 403(b), governmental 457(b)s, SARSEPs, SIMPLE IRAs. **2003**: uniform definition of HCE and compensation: HCE = pay > taxable wage base; compensation = W-2 pay + elective deferrals. **2004**: no uniform definition of HCE or compensation; Roth treatment for after-tax contributions and distributions; current rules for employee and employer contributions	Existing IRAs frozen but taxable IRAs could be converted (no income limits); Roth treatment for contributions and distributions. **2004**: no withdrawals for 1st home purchase, education, health expenses or unemployment; no minimum distribution rules; marital rollovers permitted; no income cap on Roth conversions	Roth treatment for contributions and distributions; no minimum distribution rules; can convert Coverdell accounts and 529 plans but not health savings accounts or medical savings accounts	Sponsoring financial institutions get a 100% tax credit for matching contributions plus a $50 per account credit for administrative expenses.

* indicates an amount indexed for inflation.

Source: Portman and Cardin (2003*a*, 2003*b*); U.S. Department of the Treasury (2004)

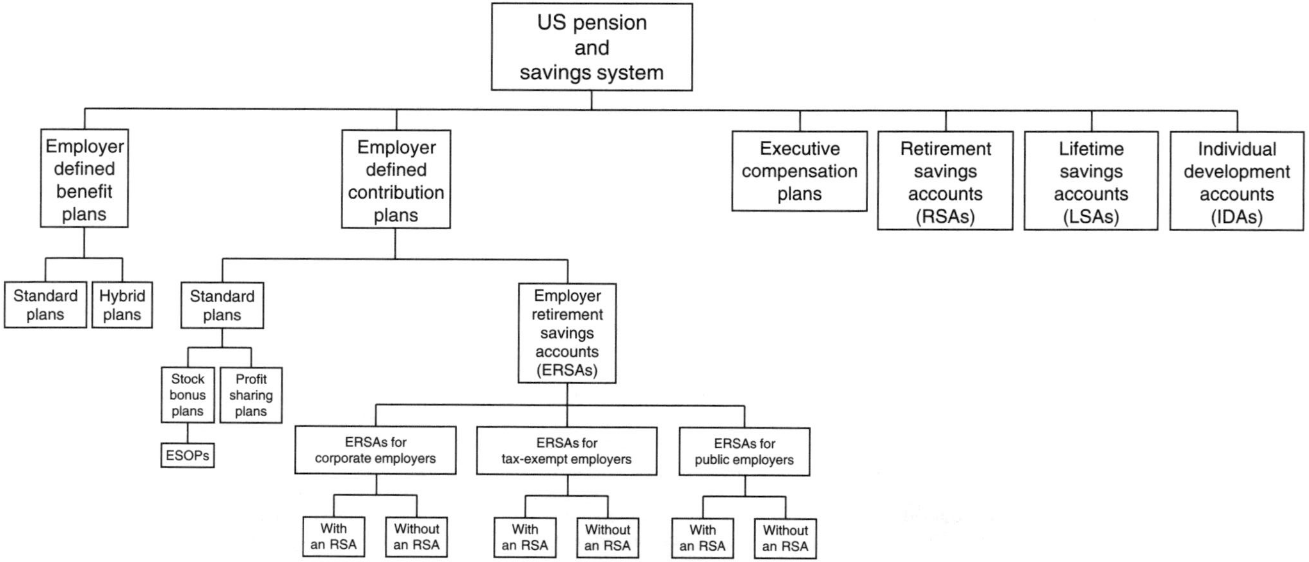

Figure 3-2. Proposed new structure for the US private pension system.
Source: US Treasury Department (2004); IRC 401(a), 4975(e)(7).

costs of plan administration. Although a single plan for employee saving makes sense, the new proposal does not go as far as it could from a design perspective. It preserves the anachronism that some separate rules are required for different type of employers, even though ERSAs are primarily designed for employee saving. There are drawbacks from a tax perspective as well, notably the Roth-type accounts. They push all costs into the future, often for decades; they add significant complication for both planning and administration when withdrawals from traditional DB plans receive more traditional tax treatment; they disfavor middle-income employees who are likely to retire and move into lower tax brackets (for whom the traditional tax treatment is better); and, as noted above, other government programs are inevitably going to require income accounting for supposedly nontax-able Roth contribution income anyway.

In addition, while the 2004 ERSAs look much like the 2003 version, they lack many of the features with the most promise for simplifying pension law. Most plans currently must perform complicated tests against the nondiscrimination rules, to prove that they are not providing high-paid employees with excessive benefits. Last year's proposal greatly simplified those rules by providing standard definitions of key concepts and less-complicated testing procedures. It minimized the special nondiscrimina-tion rules that 401(k) plans must pass every year to maintain a balance between contributions by high-paid and low-paid employees. It also dis-pensed with the top-heavy rules that come into play when plan benefits favor company owners and executives and the procedures employers can now use to shift a higher proportion of plan benefits to the high-paid such as Social Security integration and cross-testing.

The 2003 proposal promised to take the US pension system in a new direction. Through a radical pruning of plan types and their anachronistic rules, it seemed to herald a turning point in design that would reduce the administrative burden on employers and the cost of sponsoring plans. The 2004 proposal had a more limited vision. For example, the 2003 proposal retained the current nondiscrimination standard that qualified plans could not be designed or operated to favor high-paid employees but suggested simplified tests for measuring discrimination. The simplification it proposed seemed even-handed for both low- and high-paid employees. Each won and lost a little relative to the current rules but, on balance, neither seemed particularly disadvantaged by the proposed changes. By contrast, the 2004 proposal kept alive today's version of the nondiscrimina-tion rules, that massive tangle of pseudomathematical rules, regulations, testing procedures, and special exceptions, that most qualified plans must satisfy every year. By doing so, it retained such rules as Social Security integration and cross-testing that enable employers to shift more contribu-tions and benefits to high-paid employees. At the same time, ERSAs in 2004 offered nothing new for low-paid employees but were likely to enable

high-paid employees to contribute even more than they could under
current law.

Sketching a Compromise

Although it did not pass in 2003, PPSEA seems more destined for legislative
passage, since it represents a traditional approach to reform and is therefore less controversial as it makes no fundamental change to the status quo.
Moreover, almost every special interest group in the retirement benefit
field has a desired provision in it, and the muscle of employee benefits and
financial service trade associations is behind it. Budgetary constraints,
however, may prevent or slow its passage. PPSEA, like EGTTRA, was
designed in the unique 1997–2003 budget period, where almost every
major tax or expenditure bill included giveaways but little or no attention
was paid to financing the changes.

At the same time, however, the Bush Administration's ERSA/RSA/LSA
type of proposal has a support base. Although its design was initially viewed
as too radical, the 2004 changes brought the plan closer to the mainstream
and increased its appeal, though this may have eroded its potential for real
change. In reality, the Administration's proposal was never as radical as it
first appeared, but the new changes made it even less so. For example, the
design of ERSAs seemed appealing for its simplicity, but it could have been
improved without adding too much complexity. The 2004 changes not only
failed to simplify coverage and nondiscrimination standards that keep low-
paid workers from being left behind or left out, they generally were in the
opposite direction.

The 2004 proposal also retained several other design flaws. For example,
the Administration proposed to create different ERSAs for different types
of employers. Keeping special rules for tax-exempt and governmental
employers is an anachronism; the tax attributes of employers have no
relevance for plans designed for employee savings, especially now that
employee-funded plans are the primary, and often the only, source of
retirement income for millions of workers. An employee who works for a
corporation should have the same opportunity to save as an employee at a
state government. A high-paid employee of a tax-exempt hospital should
have no greater or lesser chance to save than a corporate employee with the
same income. A related issue was the failure to design ERSAs with more
incentives for savings by low-paid employees. Today's 401(k) plans, for
example, have special provisions designed to increase retirement saving
by low-paid employees that seem to have succeeded, so there is a argument
for applying them to plans of tax-exempt and state government employers
too. Another crucial reform to the ERSA proposal is to eliminate all
opportunities for Roth-type contributions. As noted, they represent substantial complexity in figuring out what type of account to open, they are all

back-loaded in costs and represent poor budget policy, and they add to complexity, with only one piece of that complexity related to the potential for conversions over time.

In Figure 3-3 we present a compromise proposal for revising ERSAs, one we first broached when ERISA turned 25. At that time it did not seem feasible in the near term, but, thanks to Economic Growth and Tax Relief Reconciliation Act of 2001 (EGTRRA) and the Administration's proposal, it no longer seems out of the realm of possibility. Like the Administration's proposal, it calls for a single, simple DC plan for employee saving, to replace the many varieties available today. It also calls for uniform contribution and deduction limits and rules on portability that have largely been achieved—thanks to EGTRRA. It provides further simplification by proposing uniform Social Security treatment for contributions, and, it ignores the tax attributes of employers when designing rules to promote employee saving.

This design also avoids the issue over which the Administration's proposal stumbled, namely overly generous individual saving vehicles which compete with employer plans, by having an individual, coordinated limit

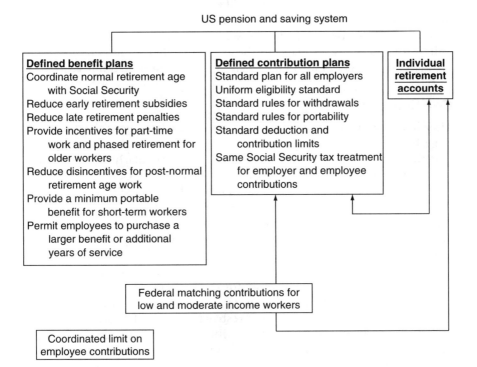

Figure 3-3. An alternative structure for the US private pension system.
Source: Perun and Steuerle (2002).

on saving between individual and employer-sponsored vehicles. This will not solve the coverage problem by itself; that is, there will still be many smaller employers who will find the current IRA limits an attractive alternative to sponsoring a plan. But, unlike the Administration's RSA proposal, the coordinated limit will keep this plan from becoming the Trojan horse of the private pension system.

Finally, this model recognizes that more needs to be done to make a tax-based system an effective saving tool for low-paid workers. It is unclear why major reform should be enacted, unless it promises to expand participation in the private pension system, so this alternative plan recommends government matching contributions for low and moderate-income workers just for that purpose. The fiscal realities facing the federal government today are very different, but three years ago EGTRRA created a tax credit for low-income savers that PPSEA now proposes to make available to higher-paid workers. It makes more sense to make EGTTRA's credits refundable, which would help the majority of low-income savers who have no tax liability and provide an incentive to save that is similar to matching contributions. This issue involves more than fairness. Those with little saving currently are the ones least likely to be able merely to transfer money out of one account into a subsidized retirement account. Thus government subsidies might be more likely to increase national saving as well, if they were less directed to those able to obtain the benefits of the private pension system without contributing any additional net saving.

Conclusions

The challenges facing the US pension system are well recognized. Despite large budgetary costs, the current structure does not provide substantial benefits for a very large portion of new retirees, particularly those who have had average or below-average earnings. Accordingly, Congress, and the country, is at a crossroads. Legislators can either decide to maintain the status quo, or they can strike out in a new direction.

Maintaining the status quo may seem the safer choice and may be the path chosen. Yet bolder action may be warranted. One approach, represented by the Administration's 2003 and 2004 proposals for ERSAs, LSAs, and RSAs, moves the private pension system toward a more efficient structure. The effectiveness of this design for increasing saving and plan participation, as well as its effect on the long-term budgetary situation, is open to question. An alternative model for restructuring the US private pension system takes some good ideas, along with the best elements of EGTRRA, PPSEA, and the Administration's proposals, and repackages them. At the same time, the appeal of a simple, standard, universal savings plan is that it avoids both the mind-numbing complexity of PPSEA and the budgetary costs and distributional effects of the Administration's proposal. In sum, the private pension system does not necessarily need *more* saving tools, but rather it needs to put them to work more effectively. This is the critical first step towards reinventing the pension component of the new retirement paradigm.

Glossary

401(a). IRC § 401(a), the federal tax statute containing the basic requirements for qualified DB and DC pension plans under US law.

401(k). IRC § 401(k), the federal tax statute containing the special requirements for a 'cash-or-deferred' savings arrangement that enables employees to save for retirement on a pre-tax basis when contributing to their employer's DC plan.

401(k) plan. A component of a qualified DC plan based on IRC § 401(k) that permits pre-tax contributions by employees. A 401(k) plan is a qualified plan.

403(b). IRC § 403(b), the federal tax statute containing the primary requirements for tax-deferred DC arrangements available to employees of educational institutions and certain non-profit organizations defined in IRC § 501(c)(3). 403(b) arrangements may also permit 401(k)-type, pre-tax contributions.

403(b) arrangements. A savings arrangement, also called a tax sheltered annuity, based on IRC § 403(b) that can permit pre-tax contributions by employees. A 403(b) arrangement is not a qualified plan.

408. IRC § 408, the federal tax statute containing the basic requirements for IRAs and SIMPLE plans based on IRAs.

408A. IRC § 408A, the federal tax statute containing the basic requirements for IRAs permitting Roth contributions.

457(b). IRC § 457(b), the federal tax statute containing the basic requirements for tax-deferred DC plans sponsored by state and local governments and tax-exempt employers that permit 401(k)-type, pre-tax contributions by employees.

457(b) plan. An employer-sponsored arrangement based on IRC § 457(b) that permits pre-tax contributions by employees. A 457(b) plan is not a qualified plan.

ACP. Average Contribution Percentage Test, one of the two primary tests for 401(k) plans that impose a ceiling on benefits for high-paid employees relative to the benefits received by low-paid employees in order to encourage their participation. The ACP test measures whether the difference between the amount of employer matching contributions and employee after-tax contributions, measured as a percentage of pay, made by NHCEs, on average, and by HCEs, on average, is within the spread permitted by IRC § 401(m).

ADP. Average Deferral Percentage Test, one of the two primary tests for 401(k) plans that imposes a ceiling on benefits for high-paid employees relative to the benefits received by low-paid employees in order to encourage their participation. The ADP test measures whether the difference between the amount of pre-tax contributions, measured as a percentage of pay, made by NHCEs, on average, and by HCEs, on average, is within the spread permitted by IRC § 401(k).

After-tax contributions. Employee contributions to an employer-based plan or IRA that are made from after-tax income so that only earnings are taxed when distributions are made from the plan.

Catch-up. Additional contributions permitted to defined contribution plans by employees who have attained the age of fifty.

Coverage. One of the two primary nondiscrimination tests for qualified plans that are intended to insure that a plan does not disproportionately favor high-paid employees. In general, this test measures whether the plan includes a sufficient number of participants who are NHCEs relative to the number of HCEs that participate and is defined IRC § 410(b).

Cross-testing. A method of testing a qualified plan for nondiscrimination under IRC § 401(a)(4) that permits a DB plan to be tested as if it were a DC plan and a DC plan as if it were a DB plan.

Deemed IRAs. An IRA that is included within a qualified plan, a 403(b) arrangement or a 457(b) plan.

Defined benefit plan. A type of plan that pays retirement benefits, usually for life. Employees earn benefits under a plan formula usually based upon their pay and years of employment.

Defined contribution plan. A type of plan that provides an account for each participant and bases benefits on contributions to that account and its earnings.

EGTTRA. The Economic Growth and Tax Relief Reconciliation Act of 2001, the most recently-enacted tax legislation to amend employee benefits law significantly.

Employee stock ownership plan. A qualified plan that is a DC plan designed to invest primarily in employer stock, defined in IRC §§ 409 and 4975(e)(7).

ERISA. The Employee Retirement Income Security Act of 1974, the primary modern law, including both labor and tax laws that governs most US employee benefit plans.

ERSA. Employer Retirement Savings Account, proposed by the Administration in 2003 and 2004 as a simplified, uniform replacement plan for 401(k), SIMPLE and 457(b) plans as well as 403(b) arrangements.

HCE. Highly compensated employee, defined in IRC § 414(q), one of the major concepts in the non-discrimination tests that qualified plans must satisfy. In 2004, an employee who earns at least $90,000 is an HCE.

IDA. Individual development account, proposed by the Administration in 2004 as a savings account for low-income individuals.

IRA. Individual retirement account governed by IRC § 408 and originally enacted as part of ERISA as a DC savings plan for individuals without an employer-based plan. IRAs now can be found in employer-based plans such as SIMPLE IRAs and SEPs, and, if the plan permits it, employees may also make contributions to an IRA through a traditional DC plan. An IRA is not a qualified plan.

IRC. Internal Revenue Code, the body of federal US tax law statutes.

LSA. Lifetime Savings Account, proposed by the Administration in 2003 and 2004 as a new DC account for general purpose saving.

Money purchase plan. A qualified plan that is a DC plan with a fixed contribution formula.

NHCE. A non-highly compensated employee, defined in IRC § 414(q), one of the major concepts in the nondiscrimination tests that qualified plans must satisfy. In 2004, an employee who earns less than $90,000 is a NHCE.

Nondiscrimination rules. The body of rules under 401(a)(4) designed to insure that qualified plans do not discriminate in favor of highly compensated employees in their plan benefits or contributions. These rules, coordinated with the coverage rules, implement the nondiscrimination standard that prohibits a qualified plan from being designed or operated in favor of HCEs.

Nonqualified deferred compensation plan. A retirement plan, usually for executives, that is not a qualified plan but is often used as a supplement to one. Plan participants are not taxed on contributions to the plan or accrued benefits until they are received or available for distribution, at which time employers receive a deduction for their contributions to the plan.

PBGC. Pension Benefit Guaranty Corporation, the federal insurer of DB plans.

PPSEA. The Pension Preservation and Savings Expansion Act of 2003, H. R. 1776, major pension reform legislation proposed in 2003 by Representatives Rob Portman and Benjamin L. Cardin, the primary sponsors of EGTTRA.

Pre-tax contributions. Employee contributions to an employer-based 401(k) plan, 403(b) arrangement, 457(b) plan or to an IRA that are made from pre-tax income and are not taxed until they (plus earnings) are subsequently distributed from the plan.

Profit-sharing plan. A qualified plan that is a DC plan with a discretionary contribution formula.

Qualified plan. A DB or DC plan that satisfies the requirements of IRC § 401(a), and other relevant legal provisions. Under the special tax treatment available to qualified plans, employers may take an immediate deduction for contributions to their plans but plan participants are not taxed until they receive benefits from the plan.

Roth 401(k). A 401(k) plan funded with Roth contributions, rather than with pre-tax contributions, enacted in EGTTRA and scheduled to begin in 2006.

Roth IRA. An IRA funded through Roth contributions.

Roth contributions. A type of contribution to an IRA, created under IRC § 408A and named for former Senator William Roth, that is made from after-tax income and is generally not subject to tax thereafter. Beginning in 2006, 401(k) and 457(b) plans and 403(b) arrangements may permit Roth contributions.

RSA. Retirement Savings Account, proposed by the Administration in 2003 and 2004 as a uniform replacement plan for IRAs and Roth IRAs.

SARSEP. A form of SEP, established before 1997, permitting employees to make 401(k)-type contributions to their employer's SEP. A SARSEP is not a qualified plan.

SEP. Simplified Employee Pension Plan, a simplified employer-sponsored plan based upon IRAs created under IRC § 408(k). A SEP is not a qualified plan.

SIMPLE. Savings Match Incentive Plans for Employees, a simplified employer-based plan created under either IRC § 401(k) or IRC § 408(k) that has individual savings accounts to which both employers and employees contribute. A SIMPLE 401(k) is a qualified plan but a SIMPLE IRA is not.

Social Security integration. A safe-harbor exception to the nondiscrimination rules that permits employers to take Social Security into account when determining benefits or contributions in a qualified plan, as described in IRC § 401(l).

Stock bonus plan. A qualified plan that is a DC plan with a discretionary contribution formula whose benefits are distributable in company stock.

Tax sheltered annuity. Another name for a 403(b) arrangement.

Thrift plan. A form of profit sharing plan that predates 401(k) plans and permits employee after-tax contributions.

Top-heavy rules. Tests found in IRC § 416 that requires qualified plans to provide minimum contributions or benefits if high-paid company officers and owners receive more than 60% of plan benefits or contributions.

Endnotes

1. The provisions of the Pension Preservation and Protection Act of 2003, H.R. 1776, can be found at: *http://thomas.loc.gov*, last accessed July 5, 2004.
2. Legislation to create Retirement Savings Accounts was introduced into the House of Representatives on June 25, 2004 as H.R. 4714, and legislation to create Lifetime Savings Accounts was introduced on March 31, 2004 into the House of Representatives as H.R. 4078 and the Senate as S. 2263.

References

Barry, David (2003). 'The Taxman Cometh, with Satan in the Van.' *The Miami Herald*, April 5.

Perun, Pamela and C. Eugene Steuerle (2000). 'ERISA at 50'. The Retirement Project, Occasional Paper No. 4. Washington, DC: The Urban Institute.

Portman, Rob and Benjamin Cardin (2003*a*). 'Portman and Cardin introduce Bipartisan Retirement Security Legislation'. Available at: *http://portman.house. gov/LegislativeAccomplishments/RetirementSavingsLegislation/PortmanCardinIntroduction/* last accessed June 23, 2004.

—— —— (2003*b*). 'Summary of the Pension Preservation and Savings Expansion Act of 2003'. Available at: *http://portman.house.gov/LegislativeAccomplishments/RetirementSavingsLegislation/SumPPSEA2003/*, last accessed June 23, 2004.

Profit-Sharing/401(k) Council of America (2003). 'President's Proposal will Reduce the Appeal of Employer Plans'. February 5. Available at *www.psca.org/press/p2003/feb5.html*

Purcell, Patrick J. (2003). 'Retirement Savings Accounts: President's Budget Proposal for FY2004.' CRS Report for Congress, RS21451. Washington, DC: The Library of Congress, Congressional Research Service.

Steuerle, C. Eugene (2003). 'Economic Perspective'. *Tax Notes Magazine*, May 5.

US Department of the Treasury (2004). 'The President's Savings Proposals: Tax-Free Savings and Retirement Security Opportunities for all Americans', February 2, JS-1131. Washington, DC: US Department of the Treasury, Office of Public Affairs.

Vanguard Center for Retirement Research (2001). 'Pension Reform in 2001: Strengthening the Private Retirement Savings System.' Valley Forge, PA: The Vanguard Group. June 16. Available at: *https://institutional2.vanguard.com/VGApp /iip/Research?Path = PUBRR&File = RetResPensionReform.jsp&FW_Event = article Detail &FW_Activity=ArticleDetailActivity&IIP_INF=ZZRetResPensionReform.jsp* last accessed July 2, 2004.

Part II
Redefining Retirement

Chapter 4

Older Workers: Employment and Retirement Trends

Patrick Purcell

The timing of retirement can change individuals' economic circumstances and also influence the entire nation's economy. The number of people retiring each year affects the size of the labor force, which has a direct impact on the economy's capacity to produce goods and services. Other things equal, fewer retirements in any given year would result in a greater supply of experienced workers available to employers and fewer people relying on savings, pensions, and Social Security as their main sources of income. Consequently, changes in the age profile of the population or the average age at which people retire have implications for both national income and the size and composition of the federal budget.

This chapter begins by describing the aging of the US population and summarizing historical data on older workers' labor force participation. Next, we turn to information on older persons' employment and receipt of pension income, which are discussed in the context information on the proportion of workers who claim retired-worker benefits before the full retirement age (65 years and 4 months for people who reach age 65 in 2004). In a final section, we discuss recent proposals to promote phased retirement through amendments to sections of the Internal Revenue Code (IRC) that govern the taxation of pension income.

Defining Retirement

To understand the factors that affect retirement behavior, it is useful to first define what it means to 'retire'. In the US context, retirement is usually defined with reference to two observable factors: nonparticipation in the paid labor force, and receipt of income from pensions, Social Security, or other retirement plans. An individual who does not work for compensation and who receives income only from retirement benefits and financial assets would meet this definition of retirement. Someone who works for compensation and receives no retirement benefits (pensions or Social Security) would not be retired according to this definition.

Between these two extremes, of course, are many who might be counted as 'retired' according to one definition but not the other. For example, someone who retired from a career in law-enforcement or the military (both of which typically provide pensions after twenty years of service) often work for many years at other jobs, while also receiving a pension from prior employment. In such cases, having retired from a particular occupation does not necessarily mean that one has retired from the workforce. Conversely, many people who retire from full-time employment continue to work part-time to supplement retirement benefits. If most of their income is provided by social security, pensions, and savings, economists typically classify them as retired even though they continue to engage in paid employment. As these examples suggest, not everyone who receives pension income is retired, and some people who work for pay actually are retired.

Labor Force Aging, 2005–35. As the generation born during 1946–64 approaches retirement age, the proportion of the US population age 65+ will rise from 12.4 percent in 2005 to 20.3 percent in 2035 (US Census 2003). The age profile of the economically active population, however, already is undergoing a substantial shift toward a greater number of older workers and a relative scarcity of new entrants to the labor force.

Evidence in Table 4-1 shows how the age profile will change between 2005 and 2035. Census Bureau estimates suggests that there will be 193 million Americans age 25+ in 2005; by 2035, this number will increase by almost 33 percent to 255 million. But the number of people age 25–54 (the ages when labor force participation rates are at their highest levels) will rise by just 11 percent. At the same time, the number of people age 55–64 is projected to increase by 9 million, or 30 percent. In other words, while the 25–64 age group will grow by about 22.8 million between 2005 and 2035, as much as 40 percent of the increase is projected to occur among people age 55–64.

TABLE 4-1 US Population, Age 25+ Projections: 2005 and 2035 (Numbers in thousands)

| Year | Age groups | | | | | |
	25–34	35–44	45–54	55–64	65+	Total
2005	39,600	43,603	42,436	30,376	36,696	192,711
2035	47,548	46,296	45,584	39,397	76,641	255,466
Change	7,948	2,693	3,148	9,021	39,945	62,755
Percentage Change	20.0	6.2	7.4	29.7	108.8	32.6

Source: US Census (2003).

Long-Term Trends in Labor Force Participation Rates. The labor force participation rate (LFPR) is the percentage of the population that is either employed or unemployed and looking for work and it varies by age and sex. Moreover, LFPRs have changed over time, as people have responded to economic developments and as social norms have changed with respect to the employment of women and the retirement of older workers. Also, as the US moved from an economy based on smokestack industries such as mining and manufacturing, to one in which producing and distributing information is paramount, demand has grown for highly educated workers, while demand has slackened for workers who perform physically demanding labor. At the same time the economy has generated jobs that can be done by workers of more varied physical abilities, the two-earner couple has become the rule rather than the exception of decades ago. Finally, with near universal coverage by Social Security and about half of all workers participating in an employer-sponsored pension or retirement saving plan, many employees now anticipate retirement as an opportunity for leisure and recreation rather than as a time of financial dependency on their children.

Men age 55+ today are less likely to participate in the labor force than were their counterparts half a century ago (Quinn 1999). The Census Bureau found in the 1950s that some 90 percent of men age 55–64 participated in the labor force (either working or actively looking for work; USBLS 1997). By 2002, only about 70 percent of men in that age group participated in the labor force (see Figure 4-1). Most of the historical

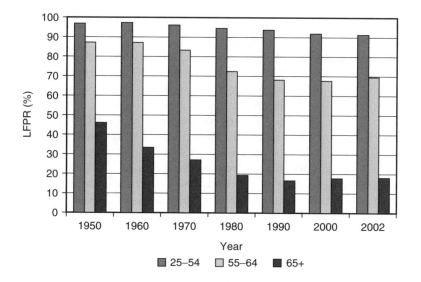

Figure 4-1. Men's labor force participation rates: 1950–2002.

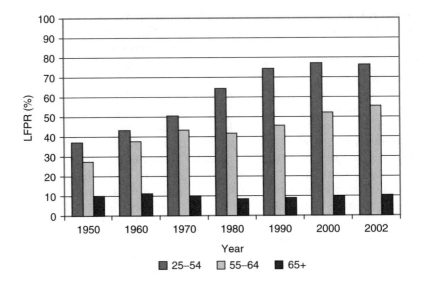

Figure 4-2. Women's labor force participation rates: 1950–2002.

decline occurred over a relatively brief period, from about 1970 to the mid-1980s. Among men age 65+, the decline in labor force participation began earlier but it also appears to have ended around 1985. Between 1950 and 1985, LFPRs of men 65+ fell from 46 percent to about 16 percent. Since the mid-1980s, the labor force participation rate among men age 55–64 has remained in the range of 66–69 percent, while for those age 65+ it has increased modestly, from 16 to 18 percent.

Women's LFPRs steadily rose from 1950 to the present (see Figure 4-2). Among women age 55–64, the rate rose from 27 percent in 1950 to 45 percent in 1990, and then to 55 percent in 2002. Among women age 65+, however, LFPRs have changed very little over the last half century, remaining between 8 percent and 10 percent over most of the 1950–2002 period.

Stability of men's LFPRs for the group age 55+ since the mid-1980s is probably attributable to several factors. First, in the USA, Social Security now covers virtually all private-sector nonfarm workers.[1] The earliest age of Social Security eligibility for retired worker benefits was set at 62, for women in 1956 and for men in 1961; this early entitlement age has not changed since. Second, in the private sector, the expansion in pension coverage that started in the 1950s had ended by 1980. About half of all workers were covered by an employer-sponsored retirement plan in 2002, virtually the same percentage as in 1980. Finally, most traditional defined benefit (DB) pension plans have minimum age and length-of-service requirements that must be met before pension benefits can be paid.

These provisions, in effect, establish a minimum age below which retirement is not a viable option for most workers. According to the US Department of Labor (USDOL 2003), 23 percent of employees in the private sector who participated in a DB pension in 2000 were covered by plans that did not allow early retirement, and 67 percent were in plans that specified a minimum age requirement for early retirement benefits. Of workers whose pensions specified a minimum age for early retirement, 79 percent were covered by plans that had a minimum retirement age of 55 or older. Labor force participation among people age 55+ might also be affected by the trend away from DB plans, which often include early-retirement subsidies and pay a guaranteed benefit for life, toward defined contribution (DC) plans which tend to be age-neutral in design and often pay out a single lump sum at retirement.

Retirement Income Among Older Workers

An important determinant of retirement behavior is whether the retiree's anticipated income will be adequate to maintain a desired standard of living. Table 4-2 shows the proportion of men and women age 55+ who reported that they received pension income of some kind in the calendar year before the survey. In Table 4-2, pension income includes employer-sponsored pensions (including military retirement), veterans' pensions, and periodic payments from annuities, insurance policies, individual

TABLE 4-2 Receipt of Income from Employer Pensions and Retirement Saving Plans

	All individuals age 55 and older	
	55–64 years (%)	*65 and older (%)*
Men		
1995	23.3	47.0
2000	19.5	45.8
2003	18.0	44.2
Women		
1995	12.1	28.8
2000	11.7	29.4
2003	11.0	27.3

Source: Author's analysis of the data in the March supplement to the Current Population Survey.

Note: Retirement plans may include a traditional pension, a retirement savings plan, or both. The income year is the year when the income was received, which is the calendar year preceding the March CPS interview.

retirement accounts, 401(k) accounts, and Keogh plans for the self-employed. Not surprisingly, the fraction of recipients increases with age. In 2002, only 18 percent of men age 55–64 received income from a pension or other retirement plan; by contrast, among persons age 65+, 44 percent had this type of income. Results for women are similar: in 2002, only 11 percent of women age 55–64 received income from pensions or retirement savings plans, while 27 percent of those age 65+ received such income.

It is interesting that the 18 percent of men age 55–64 receiving pension income reflects a decline from 23 percent in 1994. During the same period, the proportion of men age 65+ receiving pension income fell from 47 percent to 44 percent. The pattern among women was more stable: 11–12 percent of women age 55–64 had pension income throughout the 1994–2002 period. Among older women (age 65+), the pattern was again stable, with 27 percent receiving income from pensions and retirement savings plans in 2002, one percentage point less than in 1994.

The data also indicate a strong negative correlation between receipt of pension income and employment for men: during 1994–2002, the correlation was -0.75 for men age 55–64 and -0.74 for men age 65+. The statistics do not indicate why employment rose among men age 55+ while pension income receipt fell. One explanation may be that DB plan coverage is falling, and workers who have only a DC (401(k)) plan might be delaying retirement to build up larger account balances or make up for investment losses due to the market downturn. It is also interesting that employment rates and receipt of pension income are not strongly correlated for women (0.16 for those age 55–64, and 0.20 for the 65+). The lack of a relationship is partly due to the fact that women's LFPR has been steadily rising over time, perhaps masking a decline in the percentage of working women who are (or will be) eligible to receive pension distributions.

Work by Recipients of Retirement Income. Table 4-2 also indicates the number and percentage of people age 55+ who received pensions or distributions from retirement accounts. This is supplemented by evidence in Table 4-3 which show that, among men age 55–64 who received income from a pension or retirement saving plan in 2002, some 34.9 percent were employed either full or part time when they were surveyed in March 2003. Relatively few men age 65+ who received pension income also worked for pay: only 12 percent were employed, on average, over the 1995–2003 period. Women receiving pension income are also less likely than men to be employed. Among the 55–64 age group receiving income from a pension or retirement saving plan in 2002, one-third was employed in March 2003. The average rate of employment for these women from 1995 to 2003 was 30.3 percent. Among women age 65 or older who received income from a pension or retirement savings plan, only 6–8 percent, on average, were employed during the 1995–2003 period.

TABLE 4-3 Employment of Recipients of Employer Pensions and Retirement
Saving Plans, Age 55+

| | Retirement income recipients age 55 and older | |
	55–64 years (%)	65 and older (%)
Men		
1995	37.5	11.9
2000	36.7	11.6
2003	34.9	11.6
Women		
1995	31.2	6.2
2000	30.7	7.3
2003	33.7	8.0

Source: Author's analysis of data in the March income supplement to the Current Population Survey.

Note: Retirement plans may include a traditional pension, a retirement savings plan, or both. The income year is the year prior to the survey. Employment is in current year.

Age When Social Security Retirement Benefits Begin. In the USA, retired-worker benefits under Social Security are first available at age 62, but benefits taken before the normal retirement age are subject to a permanent actuarial reduction. As a result of the Social Security Amendments (SSA) of 1983, the normal retirement age will be raised to 67 incrementally over a twenty-two-year period; in 2004, the normal retirement age went up to 65 years and 4 months. Reduced benefits will continue to be available as early as age 62, but when the full retirement age reaches 67, the benefit payable at 62 will be just 70 percent of the amount that would be paid if not for the early retirement reduction.

Notwithstanding the reduction, most people elect to begin receiving social security retirement benefits before the normal retirement age. Table 4-4 shows that approximately 75 percent of men and 80 percent of women who began receiving retired worker benefits between 1990 and 2001 applied for these benefits younger than age 65. It is also interesting that in 2000, the distribution of benefits awarded to retired workers shifted substantially, with a higher-than-average percentage of new benefits awarded to persons age 65+. This was mainly attributable to the repeal of the earnings test for workers at or above the normal retirement age. Before this, benefits of recipients younger than age 70 were reduced if their earnings exceeded specific thresholds. As of 2000, the earnings test has been eliminated for people at the normal retirement age or older;[2] thereafter, the earnings test applies only to beneficiaries younger than the normal retirement age. With this change, workers who had deferred receipt of Social Security benefits now had an incentive to apply for the same

TABLE 4-4 Social Security Retired Worker Benefit Awards, by year

	Age in year when retired worker benefits began					
	62–64		*65*		*Over 65*	
	Awards	Percentage of all awards	Awards	Percentage of all awards	Awards	Percentage of all awards
Men						
1990	637,100	74.4	158,300	18.5	60,800	7.1
1995	614,700	76.1	144,400	17.9	48,700	6.0
2000	637,000	64.5	226,000	22.9	124,800	12.6
2001	650,000	75.1	179,000	20.7	36,700	4.2
Women						
1990	494,800	80.0	85,900	13.9	37,700	6.1
1995	492,900	79.9	87,800	14.2	36,300	5.9
2000	574,700	74.5	118,700	15.4	77,700	10.1
2001	556,200	78.5	102,000	14.4	50,100	7.1

Source: SSA (various years).

Note: Initial awards exclude conversions from disabled worker benefits to retired worker benefits.

benefits. Workers who delay receipt of benefits until they are beyond the normal retirement age remain eligible for a delayed retirement credit, which permanently increases their benefits, thus creating an incentive for older workers to remain in the labor force.

Older Workers and Phased Retirement

In the traditional view of retirement, a worker moves from full-time employment to complete withdrawal from the labor force in a single step. In fact, however, some workers choose to continue working after they have retired from their 'career' jobs. The process of retiring often occurs gradually over several years, with many workers retiring from year-round, full-time employment and moving to part-time or part-year work at another firm, often in a different occupation. For example, more than one-third of men and women age 55–64 who received income from private pension plans in 2002 were employed in March 2003.

As members of the baby boom generation move into retirement, millions of skilled and experienced workers will exit the labor force. As this occurs, employers may find it necessary to alter their employment practices and pension plans to induce some of those who would otherwise retire to remain on the job, perhaps on a part-time or part-year schedule. This process, sometimes referred to as phased retirement (see Chapters 5 and 8), has been described by Schopp (2000:1) as 'the situation in which an older individual is actively working for an employer part time or [on] an otherwise reduced schedule as a transition into full retirement. [It] may also include situations in which older employees receive some or all of their retirement benefits while still employed.'

Advocates of phased retirement contend that more people would choose to continue working if employers could offer them the opportunity to collect pension benefits while still on the employer's payroll. Under current law, this option can be offered only to employees who have reached a pension plan's normal retirement age. Some employers have suggested phased retirement would be embraced by more firms if this option could be offered to employees at the plan's early retirement age. Employers generally would prefer to offer the option of receiving these 'in-service' distributions only to selected categories or classifications of plan participants (CED 1999). In order for either of these actions to be taken, however, the IRC and the Employee Retirement Income Security Act (ERISA) of 1974 would need to be amended.

Current Approaches to Phased Retirement. Employer surveys often indicate that few companies have adopted formal phased retirement programs. For instance Graig and Paganelli (2000) report that 16 percent of the 586 firms participating in the survey offered some form of phased retirement to their employees. Rappaport (2001) found that of 232 employers surveyed in 2001, only 23 percent reported they had adopted formal policies to accommodate phased retirement.[3]

A number of strategies are available to retain the services of valued employees who are eligible for retirement and who might be lost to the firm if the only options provided were either full-time employment or full-time retirement. For instance, some firms allow retirement-eligible employees to work fewer days per week or fewer hours per day; others permit employees to reduce their workload through job-sharing. Occasionally companies will rehire retired employees on a part-time or temporary basis, or bring them back as contractors rather than as employees of the firm (Hutchens and Papps this volume). Two of these arrangements, hiring retired former employees on a part-time or temporary basis, and hiring retirees as contractors, require that worker separates from the firm before returning under an alternative work arrangement. This introduces considerable uncertainty into the process for both the retiree and the employer, because once the employment relationship is severed, neither party is legally bound to renew it.

Phased Retirement and Pension Distributions. Another complexity is that unless an employee has attained the pension plan's normal retirement age, that pension is not permitted to pay retirement benefits to the individual while he or she remains employed by the firm, even if only part-time. Thus to qualify for the favorable tax status granted to qualified pension plans, the plan must pay benefits only on condition of death, disability, termination of employment, plan termination, or at the normal retirement age.[4] A plan that pays benefits to an employee who has not yet reached the plan's normal retirement age could lose its tax-qualified status.[5]

An employee who has reached the pension plan's normal retirement age can begin to receive distributions from the plan, even if he or she continues to be employed by the firm.[6] Likewise, an employee who has reached the plan's early retirement age can begin to receive distributions from the plan upon separation from the firm, provided that he or she has met the required number of years of service stipulated by the plan. If a participant has separated from the employer and has begun to receive distributions from the plan at the early retirement age, he or she can continue to receive these distributions, even if at some future date the participant becomes re-employed by the plan sponsor. However, the employer may be required to demonstrate to the Internal Revenue Service (IRS) that 'both a bona fide retirement (or other termination of employment) and a legitimate rehire have occurred'.[7]

Issues Raised by Phased Retirement. Some workers would find it financially impractical to cut back to a part-time work schedule, if they were unable to supplement their earnings with pension income. Nevertheless, employers are prohibited from making in-service pension distributions to employees who have not yet reached the plan's normal retirement age. One way around this conundrum would be to lower the plan's normal retirement age. For example, if the normal retirement age under the plan were age 62 and the early retirement were age 55, the firm could reduce the normal retirement age to some age between 55 and 61. Some employers would see at least two drawbacks to such an approach. First, it could result in an unintended exodus of workers into retirement, because all eligible plan participants would be able to receive full pension benefits at an earlier age than previously. Second, it could result in an increase in the cost of funding the plan, because full benefits would be payable at a younger age.

Policy Responses to an Aging Population

The federal government influences employers' decisions about whether to offer pensions through regulation, such as the ERISA and the Age Discrimination in Employment Act; through social insurance programs such as Social Security; and through the financial incentives created for both employers and employees by the IRC. In turn, workers' decisions about where they will work and how much they will work are directly affected by employers' decisions about the amount and type of compensation that they offer to employees.

Social insurance programs and the tax code differ from direct regulation in that their primary objectives are, respectively, to provide benefits to individuals and to collect tax revenue. Nevertheless, both the Social Security system and the tax code affect the labor market behavior of employers and workers by establishing financial rewards or sanctions for certain actions. Given that the aging of the population and the impending retirement of the baby boom generation are likely to affect the supply of labor and the productive capacity of the economy, both the Social Security Act and the tax code may be amended to provide incentives for people to work longer.

As mentioned above, rules governing eligibility for Social Security benefits are believed to have a substantial influence on workers' decisions about when to retire. Some evidence indicates that more retirements occur at age 62, which is the earliest age at which reduced retired worker benefits are available, and age 65, the earliest age at which full retired-worker benefits are available, than at other ages. The earnings test and the delayed retirement credit also may influence decisions to work, and how much to work, after becoming eligible for social security benefits.

Rather than reduce the normal retirement ages in their pension plans, some employers have suggested that Congress amend the IRC to allow in-service pension distributions to employees who have reached the plan's early retirement age (or some age between the early and normal retirement ages). On the other hand, such a policy might be contrary to the main purpose of pension plans, which is to replace wage income during retirement. If employers were permitted to pay pension benefits to persons still engaged in gainful employment, the benefits would become a tax-subsidized supplement to wages, paid to individuals still able to work. Permitting in-service distributions to current employees who have not reached the plan's normal retirement age might allow employers to compensate current employees with pension funds, effectively reducing their operating expenses by shifting some costs that would otherwise be paid as wages to the pension.

An amendment to the tax code to permit in-service distributions at the early retirement age would alter incentives to work or retire, as well as how much to work and for whom to work. Consequently, it would affect both labor force participation and hours worked among older employees. The net effect of these changes in labor force participation and hours worked would be impossible to predict. Some workers who otherwise would have fully retired before the plan's normal retirement age would choose instead to continue working for their current employer on a reduced schedule, because they would be able to take partial pension distributions while still employed. Other workers who would have taken early retirement and then sought other employment might choose instead to remain with their current employer on a reduced schedule. The net effect of this change in behavior on hours worked might be close to neutral, depending on the wages available from alternative employment and the income received from pension distributions. Finally, some employees who otherwise would have chosen to continue working until reaching the plan's normal retirement age might instead reduce their work schedule and supplement their earnings with partial distributions from the retirement plan. This would tend to reduce total hours worked.

Distributions from 401(k) Plans. In the USA, in-service distributions from a DC plan that occurs before the participant reaches age $59\frac{1}{2}$ are subject to ordinary income taxes plus a 10 percent additional tax. Distributions may begin as early as age 55, however, if the employee has separated from his employer under an early retirement plan. Some advocates of phased retirement arrangements have suggested that the minimum age for in-service distributions from DC plans should be lowered from $59\frac{1}{2}$ to 55.[8] The effect on labor force participation of such a change in tax policy would likely be very similar to the effect of allowing in-service distributions from a DB plan at the plan's early retirement age. Some workers who might have fully retired from the labor force earlier than age $59\frac{1}{2}$ so that they could begin taking distributions from the plan would be induced to work longer. Others who would have taken early retirement and then sought work elsewhere would remain with their current employers, because they would be able to combine wages from part-time work with distributions from the retirement plan. Finally, some employees who otherwise would have chosen to continue working until age $59\frac{1}{2}$ or later would reduce their work schedules and supplement their earnings with distributions from the retirement plan.[9]

Flexibility versus Nondiscrimination. Section 410(b) of the IRC defines specific tests that must be applied to a pension plan to determine whether or not it discriminates in favor of highly compensated employees, in terms of either benefits or employer contributions. These tests consist of mathematical computations of the percentage of plan participants who are highly compensated employees, and the percentage of contributions to the plan or benefits paid by the plan that are made on their behalf. Pension plans that provide benefits mainly to the owners of a firm or to highly paid employees do not qualify for favorable tax treatment.[10]

It is a relatively common practice for firms to establish separate nonqualified retirement plans for company owners and senior executives. However, if a plan that was originally established as a tax-qualified plan were subsequently found to discriminate in terms of coverage or benefits in favor of highly compensated employees, it could lose its tax-qualified status. In most of these cases, the only viable options available to the plan sponsor would be to remove the discriminatory provisions or terminate the plan because covering rank-and-file employees under a nonqualified plan would result in significantly higher taxes for the participants.

In general, most employers would probably prefer the flexibility to offer phased retirement to some (but not all) pension plan participants. Yet even if Congress were to amend the IRC to allow in-service distributions from pension plans before the normal retirement age, it might do little to spur the growth of phased retirement unless employers also were permitted to limit eligibility for this benefit to employees with particular skills or abilities. But a phased retirement option that offered in-service distributions only to managerial or professional employees could result in the plan failing to meet the nondiscrimination requirements of the IRC by altering the distribution of benefits among plan participants in a way that favored the highly compensated group.[11] A phased retirement option that offered in-service distributions to all participants meeting specified age and length-of-service requirements would not conflict with the IRC antidiscrimination requirements.

Some plan sponsors would like to have the tests for nondiscrimination replaced by the more subjective method of testing that was in effect until 1994, which was based on the 'facts and circumstances' surrounding the operation of the plan. In some cases, a phased retirement option that fails the mathematical tests for nondiscrimination that are required under current law might not fail if it could be tested under the earlier, pre-1994, approach.

Conclusions

It will be necessary to help workers unlock some of their pension benefits, to permit older workers to remain with their employers on a part-time or phased basis. This is difficult under current law, since pension legislation generally requires workers to leave the firm in order to receive benefits. While proposals have circulated to permit phased retirement plans, they have not yet sparked much interest. The key question is whether tax subsidies that have been created to promote pensions should be extended to include people who have not yet retired. It may be that slowing workforce growth, along with the ongoing need for health insurance, will drive this movement in the future.

Endnotes

1. See Anderson and Brainard (Chapter 12) for a discussion of public sector employees, where about one quarter do not contribute to Social Security.

2. In 2004 a Social Security recipient under age 65 and 4 months can earn up to $11,640 without having his or her benefit reduced. Benefits are cut by $1 for each $2 earned over that amount.
3. Although the firms participating in these surveys might not be representative of all employers, their practices with respect to phased retirement offer some insights into the strategies that employers have been able to employ under current law and regulations to promote phased retirement among their employees.
4. See the Code of Federal Regulations, 1.401–1(b)(1)(i).
5. In a tax-qualified plan, employer contributions to the plan are deductible business expenses for the firm and neither the employer contributions nor investment earnings on those contributions are counted as income to the employee in the years that they occur; instead, pensions are taxed as income when the benefits are paid to plan participants in retirement.
6. If a plan participant continues to work for an employer beyond the plan's normal retirement age, the plan must meet the statutory requirements for continued benefit accruals. See 26 USC 411(b)(1)(H).
7. See Fields and Hutchens (2002).
8. It might also seem reasonable that if legislation were passed to allow in-service distributions from an employer's DB plan at the plan's early retirement age, then distributions from the employer's DC plan should be permitted at the same age (perhaps with a lower limit of 55). However, such a policy would suffer from at least two drawbacks. First, the minimum age for in-service distributions from DC plans, which is now the same for all such plans, would differ from firm to firm, thus making the retirement planning process even more confusing for workers and their families. Second, it would be administratively difficult (and in some cases, perhaps, impossible) to tie the minimum age for in-service distributions in the DC plan to the early retirement age specified in the employer's DB plan.
9. The Phased Retirement Liberalization Act, introduced in 2000 (during the 106th Congress) by Representative Earl Pomeroy of North Dakota would have amended the Internal Revenue Code to permit in-service (pre-retirement) distributions from a DB or a DC plan when the participant either reaches the plan's normal retirement age, reaches age $59\frac{1}{2}$, or completes 30 years of service, whichever comes first. The bill was not acted on and it has not been reintroduced in subsequent Congresses.
10. This section of the tax code states that a qualified pension trust is one in which 'the contributions or benefits provided under the plan do not discriminate in favor of highly compensated employees (within the meaning of section 414(q));' the term 'highly compensated employee' is defined at 26 USC 414(q) as a person who is at least a 5 percent owner of the firm or is paid compensation of at least $90,000 (indexed to inflation) 'and is among the top 20 percent of employees in the firm with respect to compensation'.
11. Employers whose approach to phased retirement does not affect eligibility for pension distributions are less likely to violate the IRC nondiscrimination provisions. Examples would be phased retirement plans that involve only reductions in hours of work, job sharing, transfers to other duties, or that are based

on rehiring retired former employees. These are conditions of employment rather than characteristics of the pension plan.

References

Committee for Economic Development (CED). (1999). *New Opportunities for Older Workers*. Washington, DC: CED.

Fields, Vivian and Robert Hutchens (2002). 'Regulatory Obstacles to Phased Retirement in the For-Profit Sector', *Benefits Quarterly*, 18(3).

Graig, Laurene A. and Valerie Paganelli (2000). 'Phased Retirement: Reshaping the End of Work', *Benefits Management* 16(2), Spring.

Quinn, Joseph F. (1999). *Retirement Patterns and Bridge Jobs in the 1990s*. Employee Benefit Research Institute Issue Brief 206, February. Washington, DC: EBRI.

Rappaport, Anna M. (2001). 'Employer Strategies for Changing Workforce: Phased Retirement and Other Options', *Benefits Quarterly*, 17(4).

Schopp, Wilma K. (2000). *Testimony on behalf of the Association of Private Pension and Welfare Plans before the U.S. Senate Special Committee on Aging*, April 3. Washington, DC: US Congress.

Social Security Administration (SSA) Various years. *Annual Statistical Supplement to the Social Security Bulletin. http://www.ssa.gov/policy/docs/statcomps/supplement/2003/*

US Bureau of the Census (US Census) (2003). 'Resident Population Projections by Sex and Age', *Statistical Abstract of the United States*. Washington, DC: USGPO.

US Bureau of Labor Statistics (USBLS) (1997). *Handbook of Methods*, Bulletin 2490. April. Washington, DC: Bureau of Labor Statistics, pp. 4–14.

US Department of Labor (USDOL) (2003). *National Compensation Survey: Employee Benefits in Private Industry in the United States, 2000*. Bulletin 2555, January. Washington, DC: USBLS.

Chapter 5

Work and Retirement Plans Among Older Americans

Katharine G. Abraham and Susan N. Houseman

As the baby boomers reach retirement age, US labor force growth is projected to slow and the share of the adult population that has withdrawn from the labor force is expected to rise (see Chapter 7; Board of Trustees of the Federal old-age and survivors insurance and disability insurance (OASDI) Trust Funds 2004). These demographic factors have raised concerns about whether the supply of labor will be sufficient to meet employer needs, and whether the Social Security and Medicare trust funds will remain solvent. Consequently, there is emerging interest in policy measures that might boost employment at older ages.

This chapter is motivated by evidence that many more people express an interest in working at older ages than actually end up doing so. For example, in the first wave of the Health and Retirement Study (HRS), 73 percent of workers aged 51–61 said that they would like to continue paid work following retirement (AARP 1998). Similarly, in responses to the 1997 Retirement Confidence Survey, more than 70 percent of baby boomers said that they expected to work at least part time following retirement (AARP 1998). Other surveys have yielded similar findings. Yet actual employment rates among older Americans are far lower than one might expect from these survey responses. Among men aged 55–64 who received pension or retirement plan income in 2002, for example, only just over a third were working in March 2003, and the corresponding share among men 65 and older was just 12 percent (see Chapter 4).

In this study, we focus on older individuals' plans for retirement and the realization of those plans. Using HRS data, we document the widespread interest among workers approaching retirement age in cutting back on their hours or changing the type of work they do, as a transition to, or in lieu of, full retirement. Next, we examine the extent to which these individuals are able to realize their plans. Whereas those who plan to stop working altogether generally do, those who plan to reduce their hours or change the type of work they do most often do not realize these plans. After documenting these facts, we consider the factors that influence whether and how older individuals realize plans to reduce their hours and remain employed.

Background

Over the next two decades, the share of the US population age 55 and older is projected to grow dramatically. This projected growth is attributable to the aging of the baby boom generation born between 1946 and 1964. In 2000, when people born in 1946 turned age 54, the group age 55+ accounted for 21.4 percent of the population. The Census Bureau projects that the population share of the 55+ will reach 25.1 percent by 2010, and 29.5 percent by 2020. Over this same period, the share of the population aged 25–54, historically the ages of maximum attachment to the labor market, is projected to fall from 43.4 percent in 2000 to 40.8 percent in 2010 to 37.7 percent in 2020 (US Census Bureau 2002). Even after 2020, increases in longevity will continue to fuel growth in the share of the population at older ages. Life expectancy at age 55 rose from 17.9 years in 1900 to 26.0 years in 2001; most observers expect life expectancy at older ages to continue to rise, at least through the end of the current century (Arias 2004; Social Security Advisory Board Technical Panel on Assumptions and Methods 2003). The Census Bureau projects that individuals 55 and older will account for one-third of the population in 2100 (US Census Bureau 2002).

Several parties have expressed an interest in boosting labor force participation at older ages. Some raise concerns about the size of the projected workforce: all else the same, slower growth in the population of prime working age will make it more difficult for employers to satisfy their growing demand for labor (see Chapter 7). Others, concerned about the solvency of the US Social Security and Medicare systems in coming decades, worry that the number of workers per beneficiary will drop from 3.3 in 2003 to 2.2 in 2030, and then continue to decline gradually thereafter. This means that there will be relatively fewer people contributing to the system to cover the costs of retiree benefits, fueling large projected system deficits (Board of Trustees of the OASDI Trust Funds 2004). It is clear that an increase in labor force participation among older Americans could be quite helpful, though it would not afford a complete solution to these problems. From workers' perspectives, if life expectancy continues to grow without a commensurate increase in saving or pension accumulations during the pre-retirement years, earnings from continued work could be a welcome supplement to old-age income. Social connections offered by work may also become increasingly attractive to individuals who, at age 55, 60 or 65, still can anticipate many more years of life.

Policy interest in facilitating employment among older workers prompted the 2000 passage of the Senior Citizens' Freedom to Work Act (PL 106–182). This Act eliminated the earnings test for Social Security beneficiaries as of the normal retirement age (age 65 for those born before 1938 and rising to age 67 for those born after 1959). This means that, in contrast to the situation for those between age 62 and the normal retirement age, there is now no ceiling on the amount those older than normal retirement age can earn while collecting their full Social Security benefits. Additional legislation introduced in the 106th Congress (the Phased Retirement Liberalization Act, HR 4837/S 2853) sought to ease restrictions that preclude workers from drawing partial retirement benefits while continuing to work for their current employers. Although that bill was not enacted into law, there is continuing discussion of methods of removing legal impediments to phased retirement, together with other reforms that might facilitate increased labor force participation at older ages (cf. Burtless and Quinn 2002; Penner et al. 2002).

What will happen to labor force participation rates at older ages remains an open question. The shares of men age 55+ employed fell steadily through the mid-1980s. Beginning in about 1985, however, labor force participation rates among older men leveled off, and since the mid-1990s, they have risen somewhat. Among women, the pre-1985 trend towards earlier retirement was offset by rising labor force participation overall, with the result that labor force participation rates among women 55+ were relatively flat through the mid-1980s. Since about 1985, labor force participation among women age 55+ has trended upwards (Quinn 1999; Burtless and Quinn 2002). Both male and female labor force participation at older ages has continued to increase over the past few years, despite relatively weak labor market conditions (see Chapter 4, this volume).

These facts are provoking considerable debate about likely future trends in labor force participation at older ages. Those who believe that labor force participation will hold constant or grow point to recent changes in Social Security rules, the shift from defined benefit (DB) to (DC) pension plans, and other changes in the workplace as factors that can be expected to make continued employment more attractive (cf. Quinn 1999). Moreover, they argue, if labor shortages due to changing demographics begin to develop, wage rates are likely to rise and employers are likely to amend their policies to encourage increased participation at older ages. Conversely, those who believe that labor force participation rates at older ages will resume their historical declines argue that, recent experience notwithstanding, retirement lifestyles have become increasingly attractive and, with the secular rise in productivity leading to continuing growth in lifetime incomes, more affordable as well (cf. Costa 1999). Even if only a fraction of the future growth in lifetime incomes is devoted to the purchase of increased leisure at the end of the work life, by this theory, longer retirement periods would be expected.

Whichever of these perspectives is correct, whether someone works at any given age depends on that person's *interest* in working and *ability* to obtain acceptable employment. This suggests the potential value of considering peoples' plans for retirement, separately from retirement outcomes. A voluminous literature on retirement and the factors that determine the age at which individuals retire already exists. Relatively little of this work, however, addresses either the formation of *ex ante* retirement plans or the extent to which actual retirement outcomes are consistent with those *ex ante* plans. Moreover, most researchers who have explored the formation and realization of plans for retirement have treated retirement as a binary outcome: a person either remains in the labor force or retires. In planning retirement, however, many people contemplate a more gradual process rather than the abrupt transition this formulation implies.

Learning about plans for retirement and the realization of those plans requires information from following individuals over time. Most research in this area has used data from either the Retirement History Survey (RHS) conducted biennially from 1969 through 1979, or the HRS initiated in 1992 and continuing. A substantial body of research shows that individuals approaching retirement age have a weak understanding of the pension and Social Security benefits for which they are eligible (Gustman and Steinmeier 1999); further there is evidence that many have done little or no financial planning for retirement (cf. Ameriks et al. 2003; Lusardi 2003).

To the extent that people's expectations about retirement do not reflect careful planning, it would not be surprising to find that their expectations are not always realized. In addition, changes in circumstances may lead to changes in plans or to discrepancies between actual as compared to planned retirement dates. Benitez-Silva and Dwyer (2003) show that developing certain health problems may lead to changes in planned date of retirement. Dwyer and Hu (2000) and Dwyer (2001) study the effects of deteriorating health status among older peoples on actual versus planned retirement outcomes. Anderson et al. (1986) evaluate whether the unexpectedly large increases in Social Security benefits paid in the early 1970s led potential recipients to retire earlier than they had planned. Coronado and Perozek (2003) examine the effect of the stock market boom of the 1990s actual as compared to planned age of retirement among older workers who began the decade with corporate equity holdings. Bernheim (1989) reports that expectations about date of retirement were relatively accurate for those within a few years of planned retirement, but less accurate for those who expected to retire further in the future. All of these studies treat retirement as a discrete event and, for those that examine actual behavior, use individuals' self-reported status to measure retirement outcomes.

Previous research also has documented the importance of 'bridge jobs,' or partial retirement, as a part of the process of withdrawal from the labor market. In these studies, the intermediate state between full labor market attachment and full retirement is defined variously in terms of the individual self-reporting his or her labor force status as 'partially retired' (Gustman and Steinmeier 1983, 1984); a fall in earnings to less than half in the worker's peak earnings year (Honig and Hanoch 1985); working on a job after leaving the firm at which the individual experienced his or her longest spell of employment (Ruhm 1990); or working fewer than 35 hours per week (Blau 1994). Gustman and Steinmeier (2000) compare a variety of different measures of both full and partial retirement. In studies that look specifically at how people leave the labor market, they find that moving from full labor market attachment directly to complete retirement is the most common path, but there are significant numbers of working individuals who pass through some intermediate state en route to complete retirement. None of these studies, however, links *plans* for bridge employment with actual transitions into this state.

Methodology

Our analysis focuses on plans that older workers may have to reduce their hours or to change the type of work they do, rather than withdrawing completely from the labor force, and on the extent to which these plans are realized. We utilize data from the HRS, which contains a representative sample of Americans born between 1931–41[1] interviewed biennially since 1992. Survey participants were asked detailed questions about many aspects of their health, work, and finances. Because we are interested in work-to-retirement transitions, we restrict our analysis to individuals who had significant labor force attachment, as reflected in their weekly and annual hours of work. We then examine the work and retirement experiences of our sample members using data from the first six waves of the survey covering the period 1992–2002.[2]

To compare work and retirement plans with actual outcomes, we draw upon questions asked in each wave of the HRS about workers' plans for retirement. That section of the survey begins with a question about the usual age of retirement at the respondent's workplace, followed by a question about the respondent's own plans. In 1992, this question read: 'Are you currently planning to stop working altogether or work fewer hours at a particular date or age, to change the kind of work you do when you reach a particular age, have you not given it much thought, or what?' In 1994 and later waves, it read: 'Now I want to ask about your retirement plans. Do you plan to stop working altogether or reduce work hours at a particular date or age, have you not given it much thought, or what?' Although individuals were allowed to give more than one response to this question, few did so. Answers to this open-ended question were coded into several categories: stop work altogether, work fewer hours, change kind of work, work for myself, never stop work, not given it much thought, don't know, and other. Beginning in the third wave of the survey, the answer 'work until my health fails' also was coded separately, although very few individuals gave this answer.[3] In the analysis that follows, we combine the categories 'not given it much thought' with 'don't know'; 'change kind of work' with 'become self-employed'; and 'work until my health fails' with 'always work'. The category that we label 'other' includes those coded as other in the HRS and those who gave more than one answer to the question.

Respondents who indicated that they planned some sort of transition, whether it was complete retirement, a reduction in hours, a change in type of work, or a move to self employment, were asked when they expected to make the change. Most respondents gave an age at which they expected to make the transition, though some provided a calendar year.

This information on timing of planned transitions was used to determine whether stated plans in one wave were consistent with actual work and retirement outcomes in the next wave, about two years later. There are at least two reasons to compare plans with outcomes over this relatively short time horizon. First, the answers to the HRS question about retirement plans may be best interpreted as providing information about the next step individuals planned to take. For instance, workers might indicate that they planned to reduce work hours in one wave, then actually reduce their hours, and in a subsequent wave indicate that they planned to stop working altogether. Because of the potentially short-term nature of the reported plans, it is appropriate to compare plans to outcomes over a short time horizon. Second, accuracy of workers' predictions about future retirement behavior can be expected to rise as the predicted retirement date draws near (Bernheim 1989). We document that many individuals do not plan for retirement much before they make the transition (cf. Ameriks et al. 2003; Lusardi 2003), so that predictions of retirement ages of any significant amount of time in advance often have little thought behind them. In addition, over a longer time period, there is more potential for life changes that affect what people end up doing (Benitez-Silva and Dwyer 2003; Dwyer and Hu 2000; Dwyer 2001; Anderson et al. 1986; Coronado and Perozak 2003). We seek to minimize this problem by comparing plans with outcomes over a two-year time horizon, and by explicitly coding as 'don't know' any responses where people say they have given little thought to future work and retirement plans.[4]

Plans for Work and Retirement

The prevalence of work and retirement plans among our sample of HRS respondents appears in Table 5-1. Here we report responses to the questions about plans asked in waves 1 through 5 (every two years from 1992–2000) provided by those working at least 20 hours per week and 1,000 hours per year at the time of the survey interview. Responses to this question have been combined across the five waves, so the figures reported in Table 5-1 contain multiple observations for given individuals.

TABLE 5-1 Plans for Retirement, by Age

Age at time of interview	Number of responses	Plans for retirement (weighted)					
		Stop work altogether (%)	Work fewer hours (%)	Change kind of work (%)	Never stop work (%)	Don't know (%)	Other (%)
50	179	22.6	12.5	7.0	5.8	46.3	5.8
51	626	17.3	14.5	10.4	5.7	47.2	4.9
52	781	18.5	16.7	7.0	5.9	46.6	5.4
53	1,104	22.9	16.9	6.9	5.7	41.6	6.0
54	1,164	23.9	14.6	5.9	6.4	43.7	5.6
55	1,398	24.4	16.0	4.3	7.2	41.1	6.9
56	1,480	25.3	17.8	5.6	7.1	38.7	5.6
57	1,630	25.5	18.1	4.7	6.9	38.1	6.7
58	1,702	25.3	19.7	4.5	7.4	34.9	8.1
59	1,732	28.0	19.2	5.3	7.7	32.1	7.7
60	1,611	26.6	19.6	4.2	8.4	33.6	7.6
61	1,330	29.8	23.0	3.1	7.2	29.5	7.4
62	814	27.3	21.7	2.2	9.8	32.7	6.3
63	616	26.2	21.7	2.5	12.0	31.4	6.1
64	419	21.5	18.9	2.0	9.4	38.1	10.1
65	298	21.0	17.2	1.6	11.8	40.1	8.4
66	186	21.2	11.9	1.4	12.8	44.9	7.8
67	106	26.1	10.3	0.0	12.4	42.2	9.0
68	77	17.6	3.2	0.6	17.8	51.3	9.6
69	23	10.3	3.3	0.0	23.8	62.6	0.0
Total	17,276	25.0	18.3	4.7	7.7	37.5	6.9

Source: Authors' calculations based on plans reported in waves 1 through 5 of the Health and Retirement Study, conducted in 1992–2000. Each interview with a person who reported working 20 or more hours/week and 1,000 or more hours/year, and was interviewed again in the subsequent wave, constitutes an observation. The tabulations thus include multiple observations for those interviewed multiple times. The 'other' category includes those who reported plans not listed or cited more than one plan for retirement. Percentages calculated using person-level analysis weights and row percentages sum to 100.

Despite the fact that all of the HRS respondents were in their fifties or sixties at the time they were asked about their retirement plans, the most common answer (38 percent of responses) was that the respondent had not given much thought to future work and retirement plans, or had no plans. A quarter of responses reflected plans to stop work altogether, while 18 percent reflected plans to reduce hours of work. Changing the type of work, always working, or other, each accounted for between 5 and 8 percent of responses. The pattern of responses was similar for men and women.

In light of the large numbers who planned to reduce their hours of work, it is interesting to consider whether these respondents viewed shorter hours as a vehicle to retire partially at an earlier age, or as a vehicle to continue working beyond an age at which they otherwise would retire. Although there is no direct evidence on this question, we can glean some insights into respondents' motivations by comparing the age at which they planned to reduce working hours, and the normal retirement age at their place of employment. A clear majority, 60 percent, reported that they planned to reduce their hours at or after the 'normal' retirement age at their workplace, suggesting that most view shorter work weeks as a substitute for full retirement.

Figure 5-1 plots the pattern of reported plans by age of respondent. The fraction indicating that they planned to stop work altogether peaks at age 61 and falls thereafter, while the fraction indicating they had no plans to retire is lowest at age 61 and rises thereafter. Even at age 61, however, only 30 percent indicated they wished to stop work altogether, while another 30

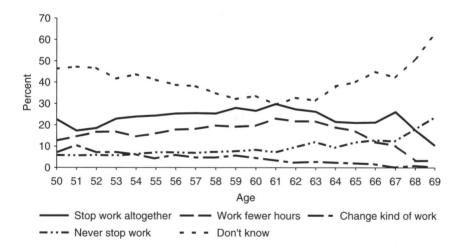

Figure 5-1. Retirement plans by age of respondent (Percent of respondents).
Source: Authors' calculations based on waves 1 through 5 of the Health and Retirement Study, conducted in 1992–2000. Percentages calculated using person-level analysis weights and row percentages sum to 100.

percent still reported having no future retirement plans. The fraction indicating they wished to cut back on their hours also peaked for workers in their early sixties. At age 61, three-quarters as many workers indicated they wished to cut back on their hours (23 percent) as reported they wished to stop work altogether (30 percent).

The fall in the fraction of workers in their mid-sixties saying they wished to make some type of transition—stop work altogether, reduce hours, or change their type of work—and the corresponding rise in the fraction indicating they never wanted to stop work or didn't know what they wanted to do, likely reflects the selected group still working at those ages. Most people who wanted to reduce their work hours or change their type of work likely already made whatever changes they were going to make at younger ages. Not surprisingly, those still working in their mid-sixties were more likely than average to want never to stop working.

We also investigated the pattern of responses by age of respondent for each wave of the survey. There is some tendency—though it is not entirely consistent for all ages—for a decline over time in the fraction of those of a given age responding 'not given it much thought' or 'don't know'. Perhaps the process of participating in a survey on retirement issues spurred respondents to think more carefully about their future. If so, the fraction of 'don't know' responses shown in the table would actually understate the fraction of the population at large that is uncertain about future work and retirement plans.

Do People Follow through on their Work and Retirement Plans?

A sizable fraction of HRS respondents reported that they planned to make a future change in their work situation. Accordingly, we next examine the extent to which people's stated work and retirement plans in one wave were consistent with their work or retirement outcomes in the subsequent wave, about two years later. Reductions in weekly hours are recorded if the sum of weekly hours worked on all jobs dropped by 8 or more hours from one survey wave to the next. We impose this threshold decline—about a day of work in the typical 5 day, 40 hour per week, full-time job—to avoid overstating minor changes in reported hours, whether due to actual variations or to misreporting of average work weeks. Of course, ascertaining whether people change the type of work they do is somewhat subjective, so we experimented with several alternative measures. Table 5-2 codes all who changed occupations as having changed the type of work they were doing.[5] Because our measure of work and retirement plans groups those who plan to change their type of work with those who plan to begin working for themselves, we also treat those who move from employee to self-employed status, or the reverse, as having changed their type of work.

Those reporting that they planned to stop work, reduce their hours, or change their type of work were asked at what age or in what year they planned to make this transition. We used this information on the timing of the planned change in conjunction with the date of the next wave interview to determine whether or not an individual would be expected to have made the transition by the time of that interview. Suppose, for example, that an individual was age 60 at the time of the initial interview, and age 62 at the time of the next interview.[6] If that individual indicated she planned to retire at age 61, then she would be expected to have retired by the time of the next interview. If, however, she indicated that she planned to retire at age 62, her expected retirement status at the next wave interview is ambiguous: she could have planned to retire by the survey date, or she could have planned to retire later in the year. Finally, if she stated that she planned to retire at age 63, she would not be expected to have retired by the next interview.

Differences in the precise timing of planned transitions are reflected in Table 5-2 which compares work and retirement plans in the initial wave with work and retirement outcomes in the subsequent wave. In general, we find that the outcomes observed in subsequent waves are consistent with the planned timing for making those transitions. That is, those planning to stop work altogether, reduce their work hours, or change the type of work they do before the next wave, were much more likely to have made that transition by the next wave. The probability of having made a specific transition is about the same for those planning that transition after the next interview, as it is for the HRS population overall.

We are particularly interested in examining whether people are more likely to succeed in making certain transitions than others. Comparisons of outcomes between those planning to stop work altogether, reduce their hours, or change their type of work, are cleanest if we restrict our attention to outcomes among those who planned to make these transitions before the next interview. These outcomes are reported in the first row of each of the first three panels of Table 5-2. Data from these three rows, along with outcomes for those who planned never to stop working, are summarized in Figure 5-2. Here, for each planned outcome—stop work altogether, reduce hours, change type of work, and always work—two columns are reported. In each case, the left-hand column represents the percent with outcomes that are consistent with initial plans, while the right-hand column represents the percent with outcomes that are inconsistent.

Differences are striking, regarding the fraction that followed through on initial plans. Nearly two-thirds of those who planned to stop working before the next wave interview did stop working by that time, and about 85 percent of those who planned never to stop working were still working, in some capacity, at the next interview. In sharp contrast, among those who planned to reduce their work hours or to change their type of work, only 35 percent

TABLE 5-2 Comparison of Plans for Retirement with Subsequent Outcomes

		Actual outcome at next interview (weighted)					
Plans for retirement	Number of responses	Working fewer hours (%)	Changed type of work (%)	Working fewer hours & changed type of work (%)	Stopped working (%)	No changes (%)	Missing (%)
Plan to stop work altogether:							
Before next interview	655	9.3	2.5	7.9	65.0	14.4	0.9
During year of next interview	529	7.0	3.0	3.0	47.8	38.5	0.8
After next interview	2,953	9.9	3.9	2.1	11.8	71.9	0.5
No date given	179	13.5	4.3	2.8	28.1	50.9	0.4
Plan to work fewer hours:							
Before next interview	474	25.7	6.7	9.6	27.8	28.8	1.4
During year of next interview	382	17.7	5.4	7.0	23.9	44.0	2.0
After next interview	2,120	13.4	8.7	4.7	7.6	65.0	0.7
No date given	160	22.3	8.5	9.4	12.2	46.3	1.2
Plan to change kind of work:							
Before next interview	118	12.2	5.4	16.7	33.1	28.1	4.4
During year of next interview	123	8.2	4.7	12.3	27.8	44.8	2.2
After next interview	529	10.4	6.8	3.9	10.6	68.1	0.3
No date given	69	14.2	13.7	5.8	10.5	54.0	1.8
Plan to always work	1,300	15.3	10.1	6.4	13.8	53.5	0.9
Don't have plans	6,544	12.7	8.0	4.5	11.6	62.4	0.8
Other plans	1,141	15.4	6.5	7.1	14.6	55.4	0.9
Total	17,276	12.9	6.9	4.9	15.8	58.8	0.8

Note: Authors' calculations. See Table 5-1. 'No changes' means that the individual did not reduce weekly hours by 8 or more and did not change occupation or move between employee and self-employed status. Missing outcomes reflect missing weekly hours data, missing occupation codes, and missing employment status information. The 'other plans' category includes those who reported plans not listed and those who cited more than one plan for retirement. Percentages calculated using person-level analysis weights and row percentages sum to 100.

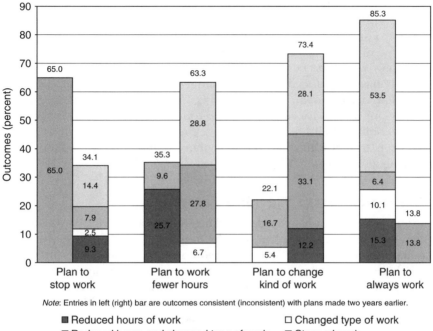

Figure 5-2. Comparison of retirement plans and outcomes.
Source: Authors' calculations based on waves 1 through 5 of the Health and Retirement Study, conducted in 1992–2000. Percentages calculated using person-level analysis weights and row percentages sum to 100.

and 22 percent, respectively, followed through on those plans. It is interesting to note that among the minority who did follow through with plans to change the type of work they were doing (measured by occupation change), more than three-quarters also significantly reduced their hours.

In sum, older workers stating they intended *to stop work* were much more likely to follow through on these plans, than individuals who planned *to reduce* their work hours or *change the type* of work they were doing. In fact, those who planned to reduce work hours before the next wave were about equally likely to reduce their hours (35 percent), to stop work altogether (28 percent), or to continue working the same or more hours (36 percent). Similarly, whereas just 22 percent of those planning a change in type of work performed before the next wave realized those plans, 28 percent continued to work the same or more hours in the same occupation, and about a third stopped working altogether; 12 percent reduced their hours of work without changing occupation. These patterns were quite similar between men and women (results available on request).

One caveat to the results thus far is that respondents might make multiple transitions in the two-year period between waves, which we do not observe. For instance, a worker who moved to a shorter work schedule or a new type of work, but then stopped work altogether before the next wave interview, would be counted as having stopped work altogether, rather than as having reduced hours or changed type of work. The HRS does not allow an assessment of more finely grained transition patterns, but we believe our qualitative conclusions are robust. In other words, people who plan to reduce their hours or to change the type of work they do are much less likely to follow through on their plans, than people who plan to stop working altogether.[7]

The Transition to Working Fewer Hours

Although nearly as many older working Americans have plans to reduce their work hours as have plans to retire fully, the former group is about half as likely as the latter to follow through on plans. We have no a priori reason to believe that people planning to reduce their hours are less committed to their plans than workers planning to stop working altogether. Why then does the transition to working fewer hours appear so difficult for older workers? While we have no definitive answer to this question, we next turn to some suggestive evidence.

Full retirement entails leaving a job completely. Unless a worker holds multiple jobs, however, reducing work hours requires either that he arrange a reduction in hours on the current job or that he find a suitable new job with shorter hours. Someone seeking to cut hours on his current job may need to obtain approval from an employer and formally renegotiate the terms of his employment, including hours, compensation, and job duties. Inasmuch as some job duties may not be easily divisible, some employers may be unwilling to reduce employee hours, even if the employee accepts a commensurate reduction in pay.

In many circumstances, therefore, the employee wishing to reduce work hours will need to find another job. Empirical support for this proposition is provided by Altonji and Paxson (1992), who show that married women who change jobs are able to adjust their hours of work more fully to changes in their circumstances, than are married women who remain on the same job. Yet, as a group, older workers find the transition to new employment particularly difficult (Chan and Stevens 2001). Many years may have passed since an older worker last sought a new job, implying a lack of good connections to other employers, or room for discouragement in the job search process. Older workers may not know how to obtain the new skills required by available positions, or they may overestimate the difficulty of skill upgrading. Some may also have unrealistic expectations about the pay and benefits they can hope for on a new job. Finally, seniors searching for work may encounter discrimination from potential employers since antidiscrimination law is difficult to enforce, particularly at the hiring stage. To the extent that older workers do not fully anticipate the obstacles to reducing work hours, those planning reductions in hours may be less likely to follow through on their plans than those planning full retirement.

Reducing hours may be easier in certain circumstances than in others. Those who hold multiple jobs can reduce their hours just by quitting one of the jobs. Self-employed individuals may have considerable flexibility to reduce their work hours if they so choose. Among those who work for someone else and hold a single job, certain tasks may be more easily divided into part-time jobs than others, and we would expect employers to be more willing to allow hours reductions among employees doing such work. Finally, employees who work very long hours, especially those working substantial amounts of overtime, may be able to cut back on work hours more easily. A sizable fraction (16 percent) of HRS older workers are employees who report working 48 or more hours per week on a single job; such individuals could substantially reduce their weekly work hours and still work what is defined as a 'full-time' schedule. And for those who are salaried rather than hourly, a reduction in work hours would not necessarily involve a formal renegotiation of employment conditions with their employer or any reduction in compensation.

We expect those holding jobs in which it is easier to transition to fewer hours to be more likely to plan to reduce hours and, to the extent that obstacles to hours reductions are not fully anticipated by those who make such plans, more likely to succeed in doing so. Table 5-3 provides some evidence on these hypotheses. The HRS includes 474 cases of workers indicating they plan to reduce hours before the next interview. We categorize these cases into five mutually exclusive categories based on the characteristics of the job held at the time that hours plans were reported: self-employed; employee with multiple jobs; employee working 48 or more hours per week; employee working less than 48 hours per week who reports that her employer would allow a reduced regular work schedule; and employee working less than 48 hours per week who reports that her employer would not allow a reduced regular work schedule.

Our tabulations are reported in Table 5-3, where the first two columns show that workers in jobs with certain characteristics are overrepresented among those planning hours reductions, whereas those in jobs with other characteristics are underrepresented. For example, whereas the self-employed account for 18 percent of the population represented by the HRS, they account for 27 percent of those planning hours reductions before the next wave interview. Not surprisingly, among employees working 48 hours or less, those who report that their employers would allow them to reduce their hours are greatly overrepresented and those who

TABLE 5-3 Subsequent Outcomes for Those Who Planned to Reduce Hours Prior to Next Interview, by Initial Employment Arrangement

Initial employment arrangement	Full sample		Sample planning to reduce hours before next interview		Actual outcome at next interview among those planning to reduce hours (weighted (%))			
	Number	Weighted percent	Number	Weighted percent	Working fewer hours	Working same or greater hours	Stopped working	Outcome missing
Self-employed	2,898	18	117	27	37	41	19	3
Multiple job holder	1,582	9	46	9	63	25	13	0
Employee with 1 job, work 48+ hours	2,758	16	53	10	48	20	29	3
Employee with 1 job, work <48 hours, believe employer would allow reduced hours on job	2,803	16	126	26	31	47	22	0
Employee with 1 job, work <48 hours, do not believe employer would allow reduced hours on job	7,235	41	132	28	27	30	43	0
Total	17,276	100	474	100	36	36	27	1

Note: Authors' calculations. See notes to Tables 5-1 and 5-2 for sample description. Individuals categorized as working fewer hours if weekly hours fell by 8 or more. Missing outcomes reflect missing weekly hours data. Because these tabulations do not require information on occupation or employment status, there are fewer observations with outcomes categorized as 'missing' than for the same group in Table 2. Percentages calculated using person-level analysis weights. Percentages in the last four columns sum to 100.

report that their employers would not allow a reduction in hours are greatly underrepresented among those planning hours reductions. These data suggest strong correlations between job characteristics and future plans, though the direction of causality is unclear. Employees whose companies would permit them to cut back on their hours face fewer obstacles in making such a transition and are more likely to find this alternative attractive. At the same time, people who think they might like to reduce hours in the future may be more likely to seek companies that will permit such hours reductions.

The four columns on the right side of Table 5-3 show that there are substantial differences in the fraction of individuals following through on plans to reduce hours, by the characteristics of their job. Although sample sizes are small, individuals with multiple jobs are the most likely to realize plans to reduce hours (63 percent), followed by employees initially working very long hours (48 percent). Among the self-employed, just 37 percent realized plans to reduce hours. Employees who work less than 48 hours and who indicated that their employers would not allow them to reduce their work schedules were the least likely to follow through on hours reductions plans. It is perhaps surprising that among employees who worked less than 48 hours per week and who reported that their employers would allow reductions in hours, the percent realizing plans to reduce work hours (31 percent) was only somewhat higher than among employees who worked less than 48 hours and who reported that their employers would not allow an hours reduction (27 percent). Interestingly, however, employees who reported that their employer ruled out hours cutbacks were much more likely to stop working (43 percent) than those who reported that their employer would allow them to reduce hours (22 percent).

Underlying the different outcomes in Table 5-3 are differences in the work hour options available, and, we argue, the difficulty people face in achieving hours reductions. For those who followed through on plans to reduce hours, Table 5-4 reports how this was accomplished. People could reduce their work hours by curtailing hours on their current jobs, changing jobs, or, in the case of multiple job holders, quitting jobs. As expected, we see that almost all multiple job holders who reduced their hours did so by leaving a second job. Almost all self-employed individuals, employees with long hours, and employees who reported that their employers were amenable to their working a reduced schedule, cut back on hours by arranging a shorter work week on their initial job. Only among employees who initially worked less than 48 hours on a single job and reported their employer would not allow hours reductions did a sizable fraction of reduced hours by changing jobs (38 percent). Nonetheless, even among this last group, almost two-thirds realized hours reduction plans by curtailing their hours on their initial job. Although the sample sizes underlying Table 5-4 are quite small, we conclude that very few

TABLE 5-4 Among Those Who Followed Through on Plans to Work Fewer
Hours, Means of Reducing Hours, by Initial Employment Arrangement
(weighted %)

Initial employment arrangement	Number of observations	Changed employer	Reduced hours with same employer	Dropped 2nd job
Self-employed	41	19	81	NA
Multiple job holder	26	0	22	78
Employee with 1 job, work <48 hours, believe employer would allow reduced hours on job	39	19	81	NA
Employee with 1 job, work <48 hours, do not believe employer would allow reduced hours on job	35	38	62	NA
Total	163	20	68	12

Note: Authors' calculations. See Tables 5-1 and 5-2 for sample description. Missing outcomes reflect missing weekly hours data. Percentages calculated using person-level analysis
weights and row percentages sum to 100.

individuals approaching retirement who realize plans to reduce hours do
so by changing jobs.

The evidence presented in Tables 5-3 and 5-4 broadly supports the argument that, if it is easier to make a transition to working fewer hours, these
people are more likely to plan such reductions and, given these plans, they
are more likely to realize them. The fraction following through on plans to
reduce hours among multiple job holders is similar to the fraction of all
those planning to stop work altogether who follow through on their plans.
In each case, realization of plans entails leaving a job, and the relative ease of
making such a transition arguably helps to account for the relatively high
fraction in these two groups who follow through on their plans. Similarly,
many who initially work long hours may be able to reduce working time
without needing to take a reduction in compensation or formally renegotiate other conditions of employment. This explains the relatively high fraction in this group that realizes plans to cut back on their hours.[8]

About a third of the self-employed and those working fewer than 48
hours per week who reported that their firms would allow them to reduce
hours followed though on plans to reduce hours. Even larger shares of
individuals in these groups continued to work the same or more hours. We
do not know the extent to which these individuals who had difficulty
arranging hours reductions, were unwilling to accept the reduction in

pay that would have accompanied a reduction in hours, or had other reasons for not following through on their plans. It should be noted that failure to follow through on plans to reduce hours may have resulted, on net, in more total work among these groups, because these individuals were more likely to continue to work the same hours rather than to fully retire. Unfortunately, the HRS data do not permit a precise comparison between planned and actual hours worked.[9]

Those working under 48 hours per week who reported that their employer would not allow hours reductions were the least likely to follow through on plans to reduce hours. These individuals presumably had planned to reduce their hours by leaving their jobs for new employment with shorter hours Instead, they proved most likely to stop working altogether; they left their jobs but failed to obtain new jobs with fewer hours. Thus, among this group, failure to follow through on plans to reduce working time appears to have resulted, on net, in less total work. In addition, among those who did reduce their hours, most managed to arrange hours reductions with their initial employer rather than moving to a new job. These preliminary findings suggest that, the need to change jobs is a major obstacle to reducing work hours and remaining employed among older Americans.

Conclusions and Implications

Our analysis of older working Americans with retirement plans indicate that about half said that they would like to cut back on work hours or change the type of work they do before, or instead of, fully retiring. But only a minority followed through on these alternative plans. Analysis of those intending to reduce their work hours—a group that represents the majority of those with alternative plans—suggests that the ease of reducing hours on a current job was strongly correlated with having plans to reduce hours and with following through on those plans. Workers whose current employment arrangements requiring changing of jobs in order to reduce work hours were the least likely to have plans to reduce hours and, conditional on having such plans, were the least likely to follow through with them. Instead, these persons were most likely to stop working entirely.

For many people, then, it appears that the only feasible way of reducing work hours is to change jobs. Nevertheless this path to a shorter workweek was taken by very few of those approaching retirement who had planned to reduce their hours. Our finding is open to several interpretations. One is that many people plan to reduce hours by changing jobs but they have unrealistic expectations about the alternative job opportunities available to them. Hence, when it is time for them to search for new employment, they find the jobs available to them unattractive and change their minds, continuing in their current jobs, or, more likely, fully retire. We note that under this scenario, there is no clear justification for policy intervention:

thus as people become better informed about their employment options, they make their choices based on this information.

A different interpretation is that many older workers face barriers to changing jobs. Despite laws prohibiting age discrimination, some firms may discriminate against older job applicants. Moreover, older workers who have not changed jobs recently may not know how to search effectively for work or how to acquire even relatively simple skills needed for a new job. Consequently, older workers in this group would likely benefit from services to facilitate job transitions, a suggestion often recommended for dislocated workers. In this scenario, policies to combat age discrimination, provide information on employment and training opportunities, and increase the efficiency of job transitions could have positive effects on employment among seniors.

Endnotes

The authors are grateful to the Boettner Center for Pensions and Retirement Security for support of the work reported in this paper; to Lillian Vesic-Petrovic and Jianzhu Li for excellent research assistance; and to Olivia Mitchell and participants in the Pension Research Council Symposium on Reinventing the Retirement Paradigm for helpful comments on an earlier draft.

1. The HRS also interviews other adults living in these households and therefore includes some individuals born before 1931 or after 1941, but we analyze only HRS participants born during this time period.
2. Wave-specific HRS person-level analysis weights are used in all calculations.
3. Except as noted, respondents' answers to the retirement plans question were coded into the same categories in all survey waves. The fraction of respondents of a given age saying that they planned to change the kind of work they did was higher in 1992, when changing type of work was mentioned explicitly as a possible response to the question about retirement plans, than in 1994 and later years, when it was not.
4. Much of the previous research comparing predicted and actual retirement outcomes from the HRS has used answers to a question included only in the first wave of the survey that asked individuals when they planned to retire fully. If individuals said they did not know, they were further prodded to give a response with the question, 'When do you *think* you will retire?' One exception is Benitez-Silva and Dwyer (2003), who draw on the same questions about retirement plans asked in successive waves of the survey that we use for our analysis. Benitez-Silva and Dwyer focus on planned age of retirement and do not consider the full range of plans that individuals report.
5. The HRS also asks individuals when they started doing their current type of work. In theory, this should measure change in the type of work individuals do, as they themselves define such change. We found, however, that measuring work change in this way was less correlated with planned work changes than measuring work change as a change in occupation.

6. Because the time elapsed between interview dates in adjacent waves could be somewhat less or somewhat greater than twenty-four months, an individual age 60 in the initial wave could also be 61 or 63 in the subsequent wave.

7. As is discussed below, workers in certain kinds of jobs—including multiple job holders, the self employed, those working more than 48 hours per week, and those who said their employers would allow a reduction in hours—are more likely to follow through on plans to reduce their hours than others. Even if we assume that all workers in these categories who planned hours reductions but instead stopped working first cut back on their hours, the fraction of people following through on plans to reduce hours would still be substantially below the fraction following through on plans to stop work altogether. People who change employers between interviews seem most likely to have changed the type of work they do. Again, however, even if all job changers are counted as having changed their type of work, plans to change type of work still are far less likely to be realized than plans to stop working altogether.

8. Unfortunately, in the HRS the time period for which data on earnings are collected does not correspond to the time period for data on hours worked. Therefore, while we suspect that many long-hours workers who reduce working time do not incur a reduction in pay, we cannot directly test this hypothesis.

9. To accurately compare the work hours planned versus those actually realized, one would need additional information on how many hours the individual planned to work, and how long the individual planned to reduce work hours before fully retiring. One would also need to examine work hours over time. It is possible that an individual who did not reduce hours as planned could work more in the short term by continuing in the same job with the same hours, but fully retire earlier than if that individual had been able to arrange a job with shorter hours, and thus work less in the long term.

References

American Association of Retired Persons (AARP) (1998). *Boomers Approaching Midlife: How Secure a Future?* AARP: Washington, DC.

Altonji, Joseph and Christina Paxson (1992). 'Labor Supply, Hours Constraints and Job Mobility', *Journal of Human Resources*, 27(2) Spring: 256–78.

Ameriks, John, Andrew Caplin and John Leahy (2003). 'Wealth Accumulation and the Propensity to Plan', *Quarterly Journal of Economics*, 118(3), August: 1007–46.

Anderson, Kathryn, Richard V. Burkhauser, and Joseph F. Quinn (1986). 'Do Retirement Dreams Come True? The Effect of Unanticipated Events on Retirement Plans', *Industrial and Labor Relations Review*, 39(4) July: 518–26.

Arias, Elizabeth (2004). 'United States Life Tables 2001', *National Vital Statistics Reports*, 52(14), February 18.

Benitez-Silva, Hugo and Debra S. Dwyer (2003). 'What to Expect When You Are Expecting Rationality: Testing Rational Expectations Using Micro Data', University of Michigan Retirement Research Center Working Paper WP 2003–37, June.

Bernheim, B. Douglas (1989). 'The Timing of Retirement: A Comparison of Expectations and Realizations', in David Wise (ed.), *The Economics of Aging*. Chicago: University of Chicago Press, pp. 335–55.

Blau, David (1994). 'Labor Force Dynamics of Older Men', *Econometrica*, 62(1), January: 117–56.

Board of Trustees of the Federal Old-Age and Survivors Insurance and Disability Insurance (OASDI) Trust Funds (2004), Annual Report. Washington, DC: Government Printing Office, March.

Burtless, Gary and Joseph F Quinn (2002). 'Is Working Longer the Answer for an Aging Workforce', Issue Brief, Center for Retirement Research at Boston College No. 11, December.

Chan, Sewin and Ann Huff Stevens (2001). 'Job Loss and Employment Patterns of Older Workers', *Journal of Labor Economics*, 19(2), April: 484–521.

Coronado, Julia Lynn and Maria Perozek (2003). 'Wealth Effects and Consumption of Leisure: Retirement Decisions During the Stock Market Boom of the 1990s', Board of Governors of the Federal Reserve System, Finance and Economics Discussion Series # 2003–20.

Costa, Dora (1999). 'Has the Trend Toward Early Retirement Reversed?' Paper prepared for the First Annual Joint Conference for the Retirement Research Consortium, May.

Dwyer, Debra S. (2001). 'Planning for Retirement: The Accuracy of Expected Retirement Dates and the Role of Health Shocks', Center for Retirement Research at Boston College Working Paper No. 2001–8, September.

—— and Jianting Hu (2000). 'Retirement Expectations and Realizations: The Role of Health Shocks and Economic Factors', in Olivia S. Mitchell, P. Brett Hammond and Anna M Rappaport (eds.), *Forecasting Retirement Needs and Retirement Wealth*. Philadelphia: University of Pennsylvania Press, pp. 274–87.

Gustman, Alan L., and Thomas L. Steinmeier (1983). 'Retirement Flows', National Bureau of Economic Research Working Paper No. 1069, January.

—— —— (1984). 'Partial Retirement and the Analysis of Retirement Behavior', *Industrial and Labor Relations Review*, 37(3), April: 403–5.

—— —— (1999). 'What People Don't Know About Their Pensions and Social Security: An Analysis Using Linked Data from the Health and Retirement Study', National Bureau of Economic Research Working Paper 7368, 2003.

—— —— (2000). 'Retirement Outcomes in the Health and Retirement Study', *Social Security Bulletin*, 63(4): 57–71.

Honig, Marjorie and Giora Hanoch (1985). 'Partial Retirement as a Separate Mode of Retirement Behavior', *Journal of Human Resources*, 20(1) Winter: 21–46.

Lusardi, Annamaria (2003). 'Planning and Saving for Retirement', Unpublished working paper. Dartmouth College, December.

Penner, Rudolph G., Pamela Perun, and Eugene Steuerle (2002). 'Legal and Institutional Impediments to Partial Retirement and Part-Time Work by Older Workers', Urban Institute Research Report, November.

Quinn, Joseph F. (1999). 'Has the Early Retirement Trend Reversed?' Paper prepared for the First Annual Conference of the Retirement Research Consortium, May.

Ruhm, Christopher (1990). 'Bridge Jobs and Partial Retirement', *Journal of Labor Economics*, 8(4) October: 482–501.

Social Security Advisory Board Technical Panel on Assumptions and Methods (2003). Report to the Social Security Advisory Board, October.

US Census Bureau. 'Projections of the Total Resident Population by 5-Year Age Groups, and Sex with Special Age Categories: Middle Series (1999–2100)', Summary Table NP-T3, National Population Projections, August 2, 2002. *http://www.census.gov/population/www/projections/natsum.html* (March 16, 2004).

Chapter 6

The Future of Pension Plan Design

David McCarthy

Three decades ago, the Employee Retirement Income Security Act (ERISA) (1974) was passed, initiating a wave of change in US private pension provision. Since that time, many traditional private-sector defined benefit (DB) pension plans were replaced or augmented with newer defined contribution (DC) arrangements, including 401(k) plans. As the system matures, it is becoming increasingly clear that the problem of optimal pension scheme design has not yet been solved. The task ahead is to ensure that pension systems of the future are adapted to meet workers' retirement needs as well as employers' objectives, a task that will require substantial effort and focus.

In the past, it has been difficult to evaluate alternative pension scheme designs from an economic point of view. This is because there was no simple theory which clearly illustrated how firms and workers actually value their pensions: that is, real-world pension contracts were far more complex than those that could be modelled with economic tools. In recent years, however, the reduced cost of computing power has changed how analysts approach the problem. It is now possible to use numerical analysis to assess different pension plan designs using a coherent economic framework which is realistic enough to assist researchers and practitioners who study and design pension plans. In this chapter we develop a framework to design pension schemes and use it to present some illustrative results.

A key part of this framework is a model of employee preferences. A realistic model of preferences must include preferences for consumption and saving, the economic environment in which workers make their decisions (for instance, by including Social Security), the major risks to which individuals are exposed, and some assessment of changes in attitudes and exposures to risk[1] as people age. In this chapter, we argue that economic life cycle models are well suited for this purpose. Previous work has applied them successfully to examine saving and consumption patterns (Carroll 1997), lifetime investment allocation (Heaton and Lucas 2003), mortgage choice (Campbell and Cocco 2003), housing purchases (Cerny et al. 2004), and the impact of state pensions (Campbell et al. 2000), and of occupational pensions (McCarthy 2003). Here we show how life cycle models can be applied fruitfully to the issue of pension design, and, further, how these models can be used to help design pension schemes which fulfil the objectives of both workers and firms.

In what follows we first identify factors that must be taken into account when designing pension schemes. Next we briefly discuss life cycle models of employee preferences and then present a specific model of this type. After sketching some results, we offer conclusions and draw implications.

Elements of Pension Plan Design

Economists recognize that pension plans are an element of employee compensation. This means that the efficiency of pension plan design can only be analyzed as a component of the efficiency of overall employee compensation. Several aspects of compensation contracts are key in this discussion, namely taxation, labor markets, employee preferences, and firm attitudes to risk. We also must acknowledge that the government is a third party to compensation contracts. That is, firms and workers can structure employment contracts so as to minimize tax revenues transferred to governments. In many countries, pensions are tax-advantaged over other forms of compensation such as cash. In the USA, for instance, pension contributions are not taxed as income in the hands of employees, and investment income on pension assets is shielded from tax. This gives employees one reason to favour pension compensation over cash compensation. Of course, tax needs to be paid on pensions when they are eventually drawn as income; Poterba (2004) examines the value of the pension tax shield from the point of view of US workers. From firms' viewpoint, pension contributions are similar to other forms of compensation such as cash, as both can be written off as an expense against taxation reducing the firm's taxation liabilities. Pensions are therefore a tax-efficient method of compensation from the point of view of employees.

We now turn to the role that pensions play in labor markets. In the simplest labor market, often called the 'spot' labor market, rational employees sell their labor services to firms each period on an open market. In this setting, there would be no involuntary unemployment and no internal labor markets in firms such as 'regular' pay scales, service-linked promotion, or retirement. Under this approach, and if employees had free access to capital markets, their firms would provide pensions in an employment arrangement only because of the tax advantage: providing for retirement via a company pension is cheaper than outside the firm. In other words, if pensions were not tax-favored, firms would not offer them to employees at all.[2]

Labor economists have developed several theories to explain why, in fact, pensions are offered as an element of labor contracts beyond the tax rationale. One prominent explanation is the deferred-wage theory, which holds that pensions can be used to induce long employee tenure at the firm.

This would be valued by firms where tenure is associated with higher worker productivity—perhaps because skills are specific to the job at hand and can only be learned on the job. Long tenure also reduces recruitment and direct training costs. Under this view, pensions are a way to pass some of the rewards of this extra productivity on to workers. The mechanism is thought to involve workers posting a 'bond' with the firm, by working for lower wages early in their employment. The deferred compensation is then returned to them in later years, in the form of a pension (or perhaps also with an upward sloping wage-tenure profile). Workers will consent to this arrangement if it pays them compensation which, in expectation, exceeds what they would earn without a pension (or with a flat wage-tenure profile). This increase compensates the fact that the worker must remain longer with the firm, and hence it has been called an 'option loss' or 'indenture premium.' DB pensions are thought to be especially useful for such backloaded employment contracts, since they explicitly defer pay until later in the contract and because they are harder for firms to renege on than unsecured promises. DC pensions with a vesting employer match may have similar effects.[3]

Another explanation offered by labor economists for pensions is that these contracts help manage the asymmetric information problem between the firm and potential workers, when firms are unable to verify the likely productivity of new hires. An employment contract which pays a pension defers payment to later in life, so jobs with pensions might be more attractive to workers who either have low discount rates, or who have greater expectations of salary increases, that is, those who expect to be more productive. Low discounters, it is believed, make better workers because they are willing to invest more in learning. As a result, offering a pension is likely to attract more productive workers, so this view is known as the 'sorting theory' of pensions.[4]

A related rationale for offering pensions is that firms which do can influence employee retirement patterns, an outcome of particular value to firms that use tilted wage profiles to control turnover (Fields and Mitchell 1982). This is because with tilted wage profiles, employees will earn more than their alternative opportunities before they retire, which is a disincentive to retire. Consequently, a firm can design its pension to induce workers to retire as part of the retirement contract. There are also sociological reasons why firms might wish workers to retire, including the transactions costs associated with forcing older employees with long service to retire if they are unable to fulfil their job responsibilities. Some types of pension are better at achieving these different goals than others: for instance, some pensions may have only a small effect on job turnover or sorting depending on how they are designed. The literature shows that DB pensions are especially effective at influencing retirement by means of nonactuarially neutral benefit formulas; by contrast, DC plans tend to be less influential of retirement outcomes, depending on the workers' accumulated values as they near retirement.

All of the labor market explanations of pensions have one factor in common: they downplay the fact that employees are more risk-averse than firms, yet they can access the same capital markets as can firms. Workers are believed to be more risk-averse because investors who own the firms can diversify their exposure by trading in securities, while employees are unable to do the same with their wage income.[5] Thus a financial economics approach to pensions would include the fact that different compensation arrangements can have very different implications for employees' portfolio costs in these plans. A further aspect of pensions to be considered in the financial economics context is the corporate finance aspect of pensions. That is, different pension strategies impose different risks on employers, which should be acknowledged in the modeling approach. For instance, DB pensions expose employers to investment risk and mortality risk. Also firms may have different risk preferences than their workers: for instance, a small family-owned business might react differently to risk than a public-sector employer. Some firms may also be able to hedge risks more easily: for instance, wage fluctuations might be reasonably well hedged by firm income in larger companies, while mortality risk would be very difficult for any firm but the government or a large life insurance company, to hedge effectively.

Another aspect of pension compensation which needs to be considered is the role that pensions play in workers' overall portfolios. Pension contracts change workers' risk exposures, and they also alter the allocation of compensation over the life cycle. For instance, DB pension arrangements magnify the risk exposure of an individual to salary risk, and both DC and DB pension arrangements defer the pay of younger workers to later in their lives. Younger workers might therefore value cash in hand highly, because they have immediate cash needs, while older workers might be more willing to defer compensation to later in life as they are saving anyway.

Both of these effects are portfolio costs that depend on how effectively employees can access capital markets on their own. To the extent that employees and employers can trade freely in capital markets, the portfolio efficiency of pension compensation is irrelevant, because well-informed employees will simply adjust their portfolios to achieve any desired risk exposure. By contrast, if employees cannot trade freely on capital markets—for instance because of portfolio restrictions, liquidity constraints, moral hazard or incomplete markets—then the portfolio efficiency of pensions becomes important. An example might make this clearer. For instance, imagine that employees were offered movie tickets as part of their compensation package. Two movie tickets per month might be an effective way of compensating employees who like to go to the movies. But if employees were paid a large fraction of their wages in movie tickets, the value they place on this compensation would decline dramatically because they cannot cheaply sell large numbers of movie tickets for cash. By choosing to pay employees in movie tickets, the firm imposes on workers a portfolio cost. We might therefore call this form of compensation portfolio inefficient, in this case entirely because of the transactions costs involved in regularly selling large quantities of movie tickets.

In some respects, paying individuals pensions is akin to paying them movie tickets: pensions cannot be traded or borrowed against, and they impose liquidity constraints on workers. Pensions also increase worker exposure to risks which cannot be traded, such as wage risks. Unlike movie tickets, of course, pensions produce income in retirement and may also protect workers from some risks.

A general framework for deciding optimal pension design should take account of all four of these aspects: tax efficiency, incentive compatibility, portfolio efficiency, and corporate finance. Yet only a partial list has been considered in previous studies. For instance, Ippolito (1994) assessed compensation strategies which account for some labor incentive aspects, but he ignores worker portfolios. Bodie et al. (1988) examine pensions from the point of view of portfolio efficiency, but they ignore labor market aspects, taxation, and corporate finance issues. McCarthy (2003) has a more complete model of portfolio efficiency and mentions firm risk, but he assumes that firms can hedge all their pension risks away.

A Model of Pension System Design

We have argued that a comprehensive framework for a theoretically optimal pension compensation strategy would recognize the key role of the following elements:

1. A *firm* which chooses a compensation strategy (i.e. designs a pension plan) based on some criterion, for instance, maximizing expected profits. Risk-averse smaller firms might take some of the risk they are exposed to by pension arrangements into account, too, in determining the optimal pension.
2. Workers who respond to the *incentives* provided by compensation strategies. Pension design affects firm profits via the direct cost of the compensation, and also via the effect that compensation has on worker recruitment and behaviour. This would include labor market aspects such as sorting, tenure and retirement.
3. An *incentive compatibility constraint* to ensure that the pension does not cause worker and firm incentives to be misaligned; and
4. A worker *participation constraint*, which ensures that the firm is able to recruit the quality and quantity of workers it needs to produce its output. To take into account worker preferences, this would need to be expressed not in terms of the wages that the worker is offered, but in terms of the lifetime utility that the worker expects to achieve. This

measure takes into account the portfolio efficiency of the pension scheme within the context of the worker's entire portfolio. This portfolio includes worker's future wages, the major risks to which the workers are exposed (investment risks, mortality risk, income risk), the preferences of the worker, any portfolio restrictions on the worker, and how all of these factors change over working life and retirement.

These ideas may be illustrated using a simple three-period model of employment and pensions, building on Ippolito (1994) who examined indenture premia, and Bodie et al. (1988) who assessed the portfolio effects of different pension arrangements. Here we posit two work periods and one retirement period. Employers may pay remuneration during the retirement period which is the pension. Workers have access to capital markets but they can only save, not borrow against future wages. There is only one asset and it is not risky. Workers have no assets except what they have saved and their future wages, called here their human capital. Workers must save to smooth out consumption over their lifetimes. In this simple formulation, there is no Social Security system and compensation including only wages and (possibly) pensions. We further abstract from taxes and uncertain mortality. For simplicity, the interest rate on the risk free asset and workers' discount rates are assumed to equal zero. The model also assumes that per period hours of work are fixed and that the firm faces an infinite demand for goods at the current price.

The firm can choose a wage profile w_1 and $\tilde{w}_2$, and a pension $\tilde{p}$. At the beginning of period 1, the employee knows w_1 but not $\tilde{w}_2$ or $\tilde{p}$. The values of these are revealed at the beginning of period 2 and may be random. However, the worker knows the statistical distribution of likely second-period wages and pension payments. Then, given a compensation structure, the employee chooses his consumption in periods 1 and 2 to maximize:

$$U(w_1, w_2, p) = \max_{c_1, c_2} u(c_1) + E[u(c_2) + u(c_3)]$$

s.t. $0 < c_1 \leq w_1$, $0 < c_2 \leq w_1 - c_1 + \tilde{w}_2$ and $0 < c_3$
    $= w_1 - c_1 + \tilde{w}_2 - c_2 + \tilde{p}$.

The constraints come from the fact that the employee is assumed to start off with no assets and cannot borrow against future income. In the final period, the worker consumes all his assets. This is a particularly simple model of preferences: in principle, it could be made as complex as desired.

Let the pension $\tilde{p}$ be a final salary DB pension with accrual rate α. Contributions to the pension are deducted from cash wages, and because the interest rate is zero, expected contributions must sum to the expected pension. If we assume that $E[w_2] = w_1$ and that $p = 2\alpha w_2$, for $\alpha \geq 0$, and that the employer is risk-neutral, then the employer's optimization problem is:

$$(w_1, w_2, \alpha) = \arg \max_{w_1, w_2, \alpha} R(w_1, w_2, \alpha) - w_1 - w_2 E[\tilde{Z} + 2\alpha\tilde{Z}]$$

$$\text{s.t.} \quad U(w_1, w_2, \alpha) \geq \overline{U} \text{ and } \alpha, w_1, w_2 \geq 0$$

Here the term $R(w_1, w_2, \alpha)$ represents the revenue the firm earns from selling its products, net of training and recruitment costs. If the compensation structure makes workers work harder, then net revenue will be higher, which is why revenue is a function of the compensation structure.

The participation constraint $U(w_1, w_2, \alpha) \geq \overline{U}$ shows that employers design a compensation contract which attracts workers. In this model there is no incentive compatability constraint: this could be introduced by stipulating that in all periods, workers may not sell future labor for current wages.

The implications of this simple model are interesting. First, firms have an incentive to pay workers in ways which are beneficial for the worker. It is not necessary for firms to 'care' about workers for this to be so: by paying employees in a form the employees value, employers reduce their total compensation bills and potentially increase profits. Alternatively, by paying workers in a form they do not value, firms increase their total compensation bill and therefore earn fewer profits. A familiar example of this phenomenon involves taxation. Arguably, in the USA, firms are fairly indifferent between 401(k) pension and cash compensation from a tax point of view: both can be written off against income to reduce the firm's tax liability.[6] However, because workers face a lower tax bill on pension compensation, firms can give workers a higher post-tax wage by paying part of the wage as a pension. A less familiar example might be the form of the benefit itself: if workers are paid a risky pension which they cannot hedge, as in the above example, firms must boost wages to compensate employees for taking on this risk.

If we introduce into the above analysis risks that workers and firms can hedge by trading on capital markets, some perhaps surprising results obtain. For instance, firms derive no value from protecting workers from risks that workers can hedge, such as investment risk, and they will get no benefit from exposing workers to these risks. The reason for this is that workers could choose to buy this protection on the markets themselves, and they would pay the same price as the firm. In this setting, employees are indifferent between receiving protection from traded risks as part of their compensation (which they could then sell for cash if they wished), or receiving cash and buying the protection themselves. Of course, in the real world, workers cannot trade freely on capital markets for many reasons, one of which is the cost of learning how to manage assets. Yet this model suggests that the cost of prescribing an investment strategy for workers in their pension plans is relatively low, if workers are able to trade competently themselves. If workers are unable to trade competently, the benefits of prescribing an investment strategy may be quite high.

Two other implications of this analysis need to be mentioned. The first is the issue of underfunded DB pension plans. If promising workers a stake in an underfunded pension plan has no effect on effort, then this is an expensive way to pay workers. This is because workers already have substantial undiversifiable exposure to the firm: if the firm goes bankrupt, they stand to lose their jobs. Giving workers a claim on an underfunded pension is paying them partly with long-term credit notes on the company, which boosts their exposure to the firm's credit risk. If the firm is a publicly traded corporation, workers could hedge this risk by selling the company stock short, or by buying credit default swaps on the firm's debt instruments (assuming these can be purchased). Of course there may be incentive problems caused by the workers effectively holding a short position in the company stock, and workers will suffer transactions costs and will need to be reimbursed for these in the form of higher total compensation. The firm could thus reduce compensation costs by paying workers with a fully funded pension. If the firm is not publicly traded, then workers have no way of diversifying this risk away and will have to be compensated for the credit risk of the firm in the form of higher total wages. Paying workers in the form of insecure, underfunded pensions is therefore an expensive way to compensate them.

A second issue is compensating workers with 401(k) plans that contain restricted company stock. Exactly the same theoretical analysis as performed above applies: in the absence of incentive effects, this is an expensive way for firms to remunerate employees because they are already heavily exposed to company risk. Watson Wyatt (2004) reports the results of a US survey showing that workers routinely value options and restricted stock at a discount to their true cost. It is interesting that some employers say they pay employees in this form because they believe that it will help to align the incentives of workers and owners, partly to induce workers to sort themselves, and partly to retain workers.[7]

More Realistic Pension Designs

Next we turn to a life cycle model which extends the framework above, by using a computational approach that permits an evaluation of how workers might value pensions of different types, and how one might develop optimal pension compensation strategies for employers, under a range of economic and demographic assumptions. We build on McCarthy's (2003) life cycle model to characterize the major risks to which workers are exposed (investment risks, wage risks, and mortality risk), and how the workers exposure to these, changes as they age, retire, and finally die. In this approach, the worker is assumed to maximize utility and work until age 65 when he retires; death happens with certainty before age 100 but he might also die before retirement. (In practice, we use mortality patterns of

US females born in 1980.) Each period he works, he receives a risky wage which may be consumed or invested in stocks or bonds, with the asset allocation redetermined each year. The bond pays a constant real rate of return, while stocks pay a risky rate of return. The worker cannot borrow against future wages or stock holdings, and he cannot sell stocks short in order to buy bonds. To keep the analysis tractable, we abstract from a Social Security system and housing assets in this model. The structure of the model is outlined in Table 6-1.

To represent real-world earnings data, we assume that wages are subject to transitory and persistent shocks. The transitory shocks affect only current earnings and have no effect on future pay (e.g. a sales agent might have a bad week because she had a cold), while persistent shocks are

TABLE 6-1 Structure of the Life Cycle Model

	Working period				Retirement period		
Time	1	2	...	T	$t+1$	...	$t+s$
Income	W_1	W_2	...	W_t	0	...	0
Wealth	A_1	A_2	...	A_t	A_{t+1}	...	A_{t+s}
Pension	P_1	P_2	...	P_t	P_{t+1}	...	P_{t+s}
Consumption	C_1	C_2	...	C_t	C_{t+1}	...	C_{t+s}
Risky asset return		R_2	...	R_t	R_{t+1}	...	R_{t+s}

Notes: At each time period the individual chooses how much to consume and how much to save from current income. The asset mix of savings (between bonds and equities) can be adjusted each period. Income is stochastic with permanent and temporary errors. Risky asset returns are assumed to be log normally distributed with a constant mean and variance. Retirement is assumed to be at age 65. The individual is assumed to face mortality while working and retired. The maximum possible length of the retirement period is 35 years. At time 0, the individual is offered a pension contract, which may be a defined benefit (DB) or a defined contribution (DC) pension. At retirement, the individual can choose to purchase an annuity from private savings on the private market. To model the costs of adverse selection, the annuity is not priced fairly but has a multiplicative loading factor incorporated into the price. This annuity pays a level annual pension for life. The individual can purchase an annuity regardless of the pension plan arrangement. Annuities that are mandatory do not attract an adverse selection charge; voluntarily-purchased annuities attract a charge for adverse selection. There is no bequest motive, labor supply is assumed to be exogenous and the individual is not permitted to borrow either stocks or bonds. The individual maximizes:

$$\max_{\{Y,\,C_i,\,\alpha_i\}} E_0 \sum_{i=1}^{t+s} \beta^i \pi_i u(C_i)$$

where

$$u(C) = \frac{C^{1-\gamma}}{1-\gamma}, \ \gamma \geq 1,$$

and π_i is the assumed probability the individual is alive at time i conditional on being alive at time 0. The individual is offered one of several pension arrangements as described in the text.

assumed to influence future wages (e.g. a professional skier might have a serious accident). Such shocks cause wages to fluctuate around age and education-dependent wage profiles derived from US data (see the notes to Table 6-1). Workers with different educational backgrounds are permitted to have different mean earnings as well as different earnings shocks. The data also show that more educated workers tend to have more permanent wage shocks, a fact with important implications for pension design.

Just after retirement, at age 65, we assume that the retiree can buy an annuity in the private annuity market at an actuarially unfair price—which means that the expected present value of the lifetime benefit is below the annuity premium. The price is set to be unfair to reflect the possibility of adverse selection in the annuity market. During the retirement period, the retiree then receives income equal to any pension plan income, plus his private annuity income. The individual is assumed to choose his consumption, investment strategy, and annuitization to maximize his expected discounted lifetime utility. Using numerical techniques discussed in McCarthy (2003), we calculate the total expected discounted lifetime utility workers of different ages and types. By calibrating the parameters of the model to actual US data, we can use the model to approximate preference structure of US workers. This allows us to examine how these workers might value pensions of different types.

To implement the model, we must further specify tastes for consumption in each period, the worker's degree of risk aversion (which affects how much he would willingly pay for insurance against risk), and his personal discount factor (the higher the discount factor, the more valuable is consumption today versus tomorrow). We denote the expected discounted lifetime utility of the worker with no pension benefit as $U_0(1)$; the lifetime utility of a worker with no pension benefit but having an initial endowment and lifetime income is higher by a factor of m, so his utility may be written $U_0(m)$. To introduce different pension arrangements into the model, we let the lifetime utility of a worker with a pension of type i be denoted by $U_i(1)$. More details appear in Table 6-2.

The specific pension arrangements to be examined here include the following:[8]

1. *A noncontributory DB pension with varying replacement rates.* This pension pays a benefit from retirement (age 65) until the individual dies, with the benefit set to equal a fraction α of the individual's final salary (hence α is the pension replacement rate). We define the worker's expected discounted lifetime utility with this pension benefit as $U_1(1)$, and the expected discounted cost of this benefit to the employer is C_1.
2. *A DC pension with contributions over and above cash wages of 10 percent of pay; here there is no investment choice and no mandatory annuitization.*

TABLE 6-2 Model Parameterization

	Assumption[a]		
Risk aversion	5		
Time preference	4%		
Risk-free interest rate	2%		
Equity risk premium	4%		
Equity uncertainty	$\sigma_\eta = 0.157$		
Permanent income profile	Polynomial profile[b]		
Income uncertainty	$\theta = 1$	$\theta = 1$	$\theta = 1$
	$\sigma_\xi = 0.130$	$\sigma_\xi = 0.136$	$\sigma_\xi = 0.162$
	$\sigma_\varepsilon = 0.121^c$	$\sigma_\varepsilon = 0.103^c$	$\sigma_\varepsilon = 0.102^c$
	(College)	(High School)	(No High School)
Mortality		US Females[d]	
Equity/permanent wage error correlation	$\rho_{\eta\xi} = 0.15$	$\rho_{\eta\xi} = 0.10$	$\rho_{\eta\xi} = 0.10$
Liquidity constraints		Imposed	
Private annuity market		$\lambda = 10\%^e$	

Notes
[a] No bequest motive is assumed and labor supply is assumed exogenous.
[b] This profile, from Campbell et al. (2000), was estimated from the Panel Study on Income Dynamics (PSIS) separately for college-educated individuals.
[c] These estimates are from Campbell et al. (1999) PSID analysis; his temporary standard deviations for college-educated individuals were halved to allow for measurement error. These values are slightly higher than those found in Hubbard et al. (1995), Heaton and Lucas (2000), and Carroll (1996).
[d] We use projected mortality for the 1980 cohort of US females calculated by the Berkeley mortality database with data from the Social Security Administration; see *demog.berkeley.edu/ wilmoth/mortality*
[e] Mitchell et al. (1999) estimate adverse selection and loading costs to be around 10 percent of the cost of annuities.

Under this plan, contributions accumulate in a separate account which the worker will not be permitted to access before retirement. At retirement, the DC assets are added to the retiree's other assets and these may be used in whole or in part to buy a private annuity, or they could be consumed freely. We denote the expected discounted lifetime utility of the worker with this pension benefit as $U_2(1)$, and the employer's expected discounted cost of this benefit as C_2.

3. *A DC pension with contributions over and above cash wages of 10 percent of pay; here there is no investment choice but annuitization is mandatory.* In this case, the contributions accumulate in a separate account as before, but after retirement the worker receives a lifelong annual pension payment equal to the accumulated DC balance at retirement, divided by the price of a fair annuity. We denote the expected discounted

lifetime utility of the worker with this pension benefit $U_3(1)$, and the employer's expected discounted cost of this benefit as C_3.

To calculate the value of the different pension arrangements to the individual we solve for m_i in the following equation: $U_0(m_i) = U_i(1)$. In economic terms, m_i is the 'compensating variation' if pension arrangements change. It is the factor by which a worker's initial endowment and lifetime income would have to be changed, in order to exactly compensate him for the change in that pension. If m_i is high, we can conclude that this particular pension is more highly valued than when m_i is low. We solve this equation by noting that, from the preference function assumed, a change in m is nothing more than a change of currency or numeraire, and therefore that:[9]

$$m_i = \left[\frac{U_i(1)}{U_0(1)}\right]^{\frac{1}{1-\gamma}}.$$

It should be noted here that this specification only focuses on employee preferences: there is no explicit employer in this model so it includes only part of the more complete framework discussed previously.

Results

To make the different pension arrangements comparable, the results in Table 6-3 constrain the costs of each pension offer to the same proportion of workers' lifetime cash wages (this version of the model abstracts from taxes). These results have implications of offering an employee different pension schemes, each of which has the same cost. The cost for each DC arrangement is therefore set at 10 percent of lifetime income from the point that the worker joins the plan onward. The DB plan generosity is adjusted at each age to ensure that its cost is equal to that of the DC arrangement. For instance, for a worker with no high school education who joined the DB plan at age 30, a contribution of 10 percent of cash wages until retirement was sufficient to purchase a DB pension with a replacement rate of 40 percent; by contrast, for a worker with no high school education joining the plan at age 50, this contribution would only be sufficient to purchase a pension with a replacement rate of 12 percent. The generosity of the DB pension declines in a nonlinear way with the age at joining, because of the effect of earnings, mortality, and interest rates over the life cycle. Workers with different educational backgrounds who pay contributions worth 10 percent of wages into a DB pension plan will end up with pensions of slightly different generosity, because of different expected wage profiles.

A key variable of interest in the pension design arena is the difference between the cost of the pension, paid by the firm in this model, and the

TABLE 6-3 Pension Value Minus Pension Cost (Welfare Loss) Under Various Plans, as a Percentage of Pension Cost

	Age 30			Age 40			Age 50		
	College	High School	No High School	College	High School	No High School	College	High School	No High School
Model 1: DB plan	39	27	26	22	14	12	8.7	1.3	2
	(38)	(37)	(40)	(25)	(24)	(25)	(13)	(12)	(12)
Model 2: DC plan									
30% equities	5	8	15	10	7	8	7	12	14
70% equities	10	12	18	12	7	10	7	12	14
100% equities	15	16	22	14	9	12	8	12	15
Model 3: DC plan									
30% equities	12	17	21	19	15	7	6	11	14
70% equities	16	18	24	19	15	8	6	10	13
100% equities	22	24	28	22	16	9	6	10	13

Notes: The table shows the value of $(10\% - m_i)/10\%$, where m_i is the increase in lifetime cash wages required to compensate the worker for the loss of the pension arrangement described. The value m_i solves the equation:

$$m_i = \left[\frac{U_i(1)}{U_0(1)}\right]^{\frac{1}{1-\gamma}}$$

where $U_0(m_i)$ is the expected discounted lifetime utility of an individual with no pension (see Table 1), and $U_i(m_i)$ is the expected discounted lifetime utility of the same individual but with the pension arrangement described in the first column of Table 3. Model 1 is a DB final salary pension that pays a life annuity with a replacement rate shown in brackets, multiplied by the worker's final annual salary. The cost of each DB pension is 10 percent of lifetime income from that age until retirement. Model 2 is a mandatory DC scheme with contributions equal to 10 percent of earnings and with an investment mix as shown (the first number refers to equities), but with no mandatory annuitization. Model 3 has the same DC scheme but requires mandatory annuitization. The DC figures are evaluated with temporary wage fluctuations turned off. All figures assume non-pension wealth in the first year (e.g. age 30, 40 or 50) equal to expected wages in that year.

cash-equivalent value of the pension, which is the compensating variation to the worker. If a worker felt that the cash equivalent of a pension was worth less than the cost of the pension to the firm, then that pension would be an inefficient way to pay people (or the difference would have to be due to some other aspect not in the model, such as tax efficiencies or labor market effects of the pension on sorting and turnover). Table 6-3 shows the difference between the cost of the pension (assumed at 10 percent of cash wages for all pension types), and the compensating variation of the pension; the gap is then expressed as a percentage of the cost of the pension.[10]

One striking result in Table 6-3 is that all the values are positive: that is, the compensating variation of pensions is always less than the cost of the pension. This is because, in the absence of tax effects, workers are always better off with cash than with pensions because of the undiversifiable risks to which pensions expose them, and because of the forced savings aspects and illiquidity of pensions. Consider a worker age 30: in the DB plan, the figures in parentheses show the pension replacement rates that could be purchased by contributions worth 10 percent of cash wages. For a college-educated 30 year old, 10 percent of lifetime cash wages will purchase a DB pension with a replacement rate of 38 percent. But the table shows that this worker would receive equal lifetime utility from a boost in cash compensation worth 39 percent *less* than the pension plan's cost. In other words, unless the labor market and taxation effects of paying a DB pension are worth 39 percent of the pension cost, it is an expensive proposition to pay the worker such a DB pension. Workers of the same age but with less education value a DB plan only slightly more: the welfare loss is 27 percent of the cost of the pension for those with a high school education, and 26 percent for those with no high school education.

It is of interest that, under Model 2, the loss from a DC plan is lower than for a DB plan for some individuals but not others, such that college-educated individuals have a lower loss (15 percent for a plan invested all in equities) than the less educated (22 percent for the same portfolio). It is also worth noting that the value of a DB plan is relatively higher for low-educated workers than for highly educated, particularly for those entering the firm at older ages. We also find that mandatory annuitization under the DC plan reduces the welfare loss of DC pension arrangements by roughly 7 percent, comparing Model 2 with the voluntary annuitization results for Model 3. This result may overstate the appeal of annuitization to the extent that other alternatives are available (cf. Yaari 1965).

The impact of mandatory investment policy in the DC plan on welfare losses is much smaller than some may have anticipated: for instance, the welfare loss grows by only about 10 percent of the pension cost, when the investment strategy changes from 30 percent to 100 percent equities. The reason is that the investment strategy is only important while workers are liquidity-constrained. Once they have amassed sufficient assets outside the pension plan, they can alter the investment mix of those other assets to achieve any desired overall asset allocation.

We now examine the results for a worker aged 40, with 25 years until retirement. Here the DB pension plan imparts a lower welfare loss than before, because wage uncertainty for older workers is lower due to the fact that fewer years remain until retirement. In addition, because they are nearer to retirement, the liquidity constraint associated with forced saving in pensions is not as binding because these workers are starting to antici-pate retirement and increase their savings. The DB plan is still less favor-able for college-educated workers than for other types of workers, for the reasons discussed. For DC pensions, the welfare loss is smaller for older workers because the natural propensity to save of workers increases with age. Therefore the forced savings aspect of DC pensions is smaller, and the illiquidity of the DC pension wealth is less of a factor. In addition, the DC investment strategy has a much smaller effect on wellbeing, because of the fact that with higher savings, the range of achievable overall investment strategies is greater despite the pension investment restrictions. Differ-ences between subjective valuations of the DC pension by different classes of worker are surprisingly large. This may be due to the different age-wage profiles of the different classes of worker or the different pattern for wage shock variance and persistence.

By age 50, the welfare loss associated with the DB plan is less than that associated with the DC plan, for low-educated workers. This is due to the effect of declining human capital and increasing financial capital on the valuation of DB pension plans, as discussed above. The welfare loss of DC pension falls due to the fact that most workers at age 50 are saving for their retirement which looms near, at age 65. There is now almost no difference between the welfare losses of DC pensions with very different investment strategies, as most individuals are saving enough to ensure that they are able to achieve their optimal desired overall asset allocation. Once again, there are surprisingly large differences between workers of different types.

Implications and Conclusions

Though many forms of pensions have been tried in the marketplace to date, it is fair to say that the pension environment is in flux around the world. Much work remains to design pension systems that best meet em-ployee needs as well as employer objectives. This chapter draws together the literature on pension compensation and optimal portfolio choice to seek solutions to the 'pension design' problem.

Inasmuch as pension schemes are an element of employee compensa-tion, we propose that pension design must be evaluated in terms of how well any given plan format fits into the objectives set for employee com-pensation more generally. Our financial economics approach to pension

design recognizes the fact that compensation arrangements can have very distinct impacts on employees covered by these plans. In particular, pension contracts alter workers' risk exposures and the allocation of compensation over the life cycle. As a result, having a pension, changes the value that an employee would ascribe to different pension and compensation arrangements.

Our results suggest that DB pension arrangements magnify the risk exposure of an individual to salary risk, and both DC and DB pension arrangement defer the pay of younger workers to later in their lives. Younger workers therefore value cash more highly, and DC plans in particular, because they have immediate cash needs. In contrast, DB pensions may be a cost-effective method of compensation for older, less well-educated employees. We also conclude that promising workers a stake in an underfunded pension plan is an expensive way to pay employees, particularly if the underfunding has no positive impact on effort. Of course, giving workers 401(k) plans holding restricted company stock is also an expensive way to remunerate employees, because they are already heavily exposed to company risk.

Our results also imply that a hybrid scheme might be designed to better suit both types of employees. Such a plan would have workers beginning their careers with a DC pension heavily invested in bonds, and then later they would switch to a fully-funded DB scheme; this would likely be a cost-effective way of remunerating employees. Several factors which have not yet been incorporated in our model strengthen this conclusion. The first has to do with job turnover, which makes DB plans riskier for younger employees because of the fact that most vested DB pensions in the US are not indexed to inflation after workers terminate. This exposes individuals to inflation risk in their DB pensions and imposes a pension capital loss on these workers. Awareness of such risk would further reduce the attractiveness of DB plans for younger employees.[10] Also if employees find it is costly to make pension investment decisions, having the employer select a DC investment strategy would benefit the employees while imposing few costs on those workers able to adjust their own portfolios to compensate for the imposed pension investment mix. An alternative design might be a form of fully matched cash balance plan for younger workers, which changes to an explicit salary link for older workers.

We must note that our model here does not include taxes, which prevents us from inferring the overall level of pension generosity relative to cash wages. Poterba (2004) computes the value of the current tax shield accorded to US retirement accounts, and he finds that in the case of fixed-income assets, the tax shield is not very large unless very long time horizons are used (and even then only for workers with high marginal tax rates and high interest rates). For equity investments, the tax protection of pensions is significantly lower in all cases. While the tax effects might have been

larger in the past, currently the tax effects appear small, implying that the labor market effects of pensions—and especially DB pensions—would have to be substantial, to justify their use as a compensation tool for younger workers.

Future work will extend our analysis of optimal pension design. We anticipate including worker preferences more explicitly within this framework to derive optimal pension compensation strategies for workers of different types, who are engaged at firms having varying attitudes toward risk. A further area needing more work in the financial economics context is the corporate finance aspect of pensions. That is, different pension strategies impose different risks on employers, which should be acknowledged in the modeling approach. We also expect to evaluate the sensitivity of results to assumptions regarding worker responses to pension incentives, and we hope to test model predictions using firm-level pension data.

Endnotes

1. This is a simple model of the labor market which ignores issues such as transactions costs, skills specificity, on-the-job training, customs, indenture premia, differences in risk aversion between firms and employees, asymmetric information and incentives, all of which may have implications for pensions. Bulow (1982) presents an early discussion of labor markets and pensions from a financial point of view.
2. Lazear (1979) discussion of wage-tilt and tenure, and Ippolito (1997) covers the compensation aspects of DC pensions.
3. Allen et al. (1993) and Ippolito (1997) discuss pensions and sorting.
4. Of course, some firms may be more risk averse than others: for instance, the attitude to risk of a small family-owned business is likely to be very different to that of a publicly traded multinational company.
5. This abstracts from the fact that 401(k) contributions are subject to social security payroll tax.
6. See Oyer and Schaefer (2004) for an empirical investigation of why employers pay employees with stock options.
7. Euler equations are derived in McCarthy (2003).
8. The model was checked by solving the same equation numerically, and the results were found to agree with the analytical results to the degree of precision reported in the tables.
9. It should be noted that further assumptions are required to interpret the results as speaking to the efficiency of different pension formats. If pensions have no labor market effects, and the firm is risk neutral or can hedge all pension-related risks (such as wage changes and mortality changes) perfectly, then the results may be interpreted as informative about the efficiency of pension compensation from the firm's point of view. The results can also be used to assess how large the labor market effects of pensions need to be, to make them an efficient compensation strategy.

10. Of course, if the presence of a DB pension plan had significant effects on the turnover of younger employees, this higher cost might be offset by lower recruitment and training costs.

References

Allen, Steven G., Robert L. Clark, and Ann A. McDermed (1993). 'Pensions, Bonding, and Lifetime Jobs', *Journal of Human Resources*, 28: 463–81.

Bodie, Zvi, Alan J. Marcus, and Robert C. Merton (1988). 'Defined Benefit versus Defined Contribution Pension Plans: What are the Real Tradeoffs?', in Z. Bodie, J. Shoven and D. Wise (eds.), *Pensions in the US Economy*. Chicago: University of Chicago Press.

Bulow, Jeremy I. (1982). 'What Are Corporate Pension Liabilities?', *The Quarterly Journal of Economics*, 97(3): 435–52.

Campbell, John Y. and Joao Cocco (2003). 'Household Risk Management and Optimal Mortgage Choice', Working Paper, London Business School.

—— —— Francisco J. Gomes and Pascal J. Maenhout (2000). 'Investing Retirement Wealth: A Life Cycle Model', in Martin Feldstein and John Y. Campbell, (eds.), *Risk Aspects of Investment-Based Social Security Reform*. NBER, Chicago: University of Chicago Press.

Carroll, Christopher (1996). 'Buffer Stock Saving and the Life Cycle/Permanent Income Hypothesis', *Quarterly Journal of Economics*, CXII(1): 1–56.

Cerny, Ales, David K. Miles, and Lubomir Schmidt (2004). 'A Calibrated Model of Saving, Portfolio Allocation and Housing Choices', Working Paper, Imperial College.

Fields, Gary and Olivia S. Mitchell (1982). *Retirement, Pensions and Social Security*. Cambridge, MA: MIT Press.

Heaton, John and Deborah Lucas (2000). 'Portfolio Choice in the Presence of Background Risk', *The Economic Journal*, 110 (January): 1–26.

Hubbard, R. Glenn, Jonathan Skinner, and Stephen P. Zeldes (1995). 'Precautionary Saving and Social Insurance', *Journal of Political Economy*, 103(2): 360–99.

Ippolito, Richard A. (1994). 'Pensions and Indenture Premia', *Journal of Human Resources*, 29(3): 795–812.

—— (1997). *Pension Plans and Employee Performance: Evidence, Analysis, and Policy*. Chicago: University of Chicago Press.

Lazear, Edward P. (1979). 'Why Is There Mandatory Retirement?', *Journal of Political Economy* 87: 1261–84.

McCarthy, David G. (2003). 'A Life-cycle Analysis of Defined Benefit Pension Plans', *Journal of Pension Economics and Finance*, 2(2): 99–126.

Mitchell, Olivia S., James M. Poterba, Jeffrey R. Brown, and Mark Warshawsky (MPBW) (1999). 'New Evidence on the Money's Worth of Individual Annuities', *American Economic Review*, 89: 1299–1318.

Oyer, Paul and Scott Schaefer (2004). 'Why Do Some Firms Give Stock Options to All Employees? An Empirical Examination of Alternative Theories', NBER Working Paper, 10222.

Poterba, James M (2004). 'Valuing Assets in Retirement Savings Accounts', Boston College Working Paper, 2004–11.

Watson Wyatt (2004). 'Employees Undervalue Stock Option Grants', News Report, <*www.watsonwyatt.com/news/press.asp?ID=13001*>

Yaari, Menahem. (1965). 'Uncertain Lifetime, Life Insurance and the Theory of the Consumer', *Review of Economic Studies*, 32: 137–50.

Chapter 7

Strategies to Retain Older Workers

Janemarie Mulvey and Steven Nyce

As the baby boomers begin to retire over the next two decades, their exodus from the labor force will adversely affect the supply of labor available to employers. These retirement decisions will be affected by both economic and noneconomic factors. For instance, generous early retirement subsidies in defined benefit (DB) plans, along with retiree medical coverage, provide strong incentives for workers having these plans to retire before age 65. In addition, factors influencing retirement go beyond the economic issues: for example, many older workers must care for aging parents, time demands that make full-time work challenging.

Looking ahead, then, many boomers will be searching for ways to *transition* into retirement rather than abruptly ending their working careers, which will change the nature of retirement in coming decades. Some employers will respond with strategies that encourage older workers to defer retirement, while still preserving the 'retirement promise'. Such strategies could include work/life benefits including phased retirement programs, which would permit phasing out of work slowly; they also might involve employer-sponsored eldercare programs which help workers identify and evaluate caregiving alternatives for aging relatives or spouses.

This chapter begins by outlining the economic and demographic realities facing employers and spells out how these change the 'retirement promise'. To understand the process, we quantify the effect of several factors on older workers' retirement patterns, including early retirement incentives in DB plans, retiree medical coverage, and various work/life benefits including phased retirement and eldercare programs. Next we estimate the potential increase in older workers' labor force participation from changing these benefit offerings, and we conclude that these will only marginally offset expected gaps between labor supply and demand in the coming decade.

The Nature of the Pension Promise

In the mid-1960s, when the baby boom generation began moving into the workforce, the private pension system was largely unregulated. The seeds of reform were sown during the Kennedy administration, prompted by funding, fiduciary, and vesting lapses that drew concern from many quarters (Sass 1997). These reform efforts faced immense political resistance by both labor and business, but eventually they culminated in the Employment Retirement Income Security Act (ERISA) of 1974. One key element of ERISA was the protection of employee benefits (Title 1): the law held that private sector employers had an obligation to provide promised benefits and satisfy a set of requirements for managing and administering private pensions and welfare plans. The law also granted workers a legal 'vested' right to their accrued pensions based on past service. Previously, employees often lost their accrued pension when they left jobs before retirement (Sass 1997).

Before the enactment of ERISA, many employees trusted that their companies would stand by their benefit promises. However, some employers drafted their plans with protective language to avoid paying benefits at all, raising questions about the soundness of the implied contract (Schieber 2003). Accordingly, the main thrust of ERISA was to protect accrued benefits and to ensure that if a company went bankrupt, there would be a federal insurance fund to cover those DB liabilities. It is worth noting that ERISA did not require firms offering pensions to insure benefits that might be accrued in the future; thus, the pension promise related mainly to benefits accrued to date.

Since company pensions in the USA are voluntarily provided, sponsors continually weigh the costs and benefits of providing this benefit to the workforce. In addition to the tax benefits pensions offer, DB pensions have also helped employers to shape their workforces in key ways. An initial reason companies adopted DB plans was to promote an orderly retirement process (Ghilarducci 1992), and many of these plans were coupled with retiree health insurance as well. At that time, labor was plentiful due to the wave of boomer workers. Of course, over time, employers discovered additional benefits of traditional DB plans, most important among them the finding that they provided an important retention mechanism. Turnover rates were lower in firms with pensions (Mitchell 1982) and tenure proved to be higher (Turner 1993).

Notwithstanding the positives of DB plans, the costs of offering them have risen substantially over time. For one, administrative costs of complying and funding these plans grew markedly following the implementation of ERISA. One analyst found that administrative costs rose nearly three times between 1981 and 1996 (Hustead 1998). For another, regulatory actions during the 1980s also curtailed employers' ability to fund their future pension obligations. First Congress restricted the level of pension funding allowable under the federal tax code with the Tax Equity and Fiscal Responsibility Act (TEFRA) of 1982. Next, it changed full funding limits on pensions, tying these caps to current liabilities instead of projected benefit obligations, with the Ominous Budget Reconciliation Act of 1987

(Schieber 2003). These policies prevented employers from pre-funding their future obligations, so the size of unfunded DB liabilities began to rise and threaten to grow further as the workforce ages.

Higher administrative costs and funding restrictions altered the fundamental economic value of employer-sponsored retirement plans particularly for smaller firms and those with lower wage workers (Clark et al. 2004). For these organizations, it became more cost-effective to instead adopt a 401(k) plan, which partly explains why DB plans have declined in number (Papke 1999). The Pension Benefit Guaranty Corporation (PBGC) in 1990 insured 87,564 small DB plans, with fewer than 1,000 employees; by 2003, that number fell by 70 percent to only 25,812 plans (PBGC 2004). Larger employers often maintain their DB plans because they are able to spread the large administrative costs over a larger number of workers, yet even so, funding restrictions and falling equity markets have accelerated the rate of decline in that sector as well. Between 1990 and 2003, the number of PBGC-insured DB plans among firms with more than 1,000 employees fell 15 percent, from 4,335 to 3,700 plans (PBGC 2004).

Employers who have retained a traditional DB plan seek to adapt them to the changing workforce and marketplace. One approach has been to convert them to hybrid plans: for instance, in 2000, one in five DB participants worked for companies with hybrid pension plans (PBGC 2004). As their name suggests, these hybrids combine features of both DB and defined contribution (DC) pensions. Similar to a DC, a hybrid plan accumulates benefits in the form of a hypothetical account balance which is paid out in a lump sum. Also like a DC, the benefits are portable; if the worker leaves an employer before normal retirement age, the assets can be rolled over and re-invested. Yet a hybrid plan retains many of the advantages of a traditional DB plan, in that the plan sponsor bearing investment risk and it is federally insured by the PBGC.

Despite their advantages, growth in hybrid conversions has slowed substantially in recent years due to increased regulatory and legal uncertainty. Some critics have argued that employers converting from a traditional DB plan to a hybrid plan do so to cut costs at the expense of long-service workers. Nevertheless, the data show that hybrid conversions since 1999 have actually increased plan sponsor pension costs by an average of 2.2 percent, and employers who converted their DB to hybrid plans also protected older workers nearing retirement (Goodfellow et al. 2004). That is, some 89 percent of plan sponsors implemented specific protections for older workers, including 'grandfathering' benefits, offering workers a choice between plans, and offering transitional credits. This suggests that a better explanation for why firms have converted to hybrid plans is that they are doing so to adapt to the changing workforce. Not only are workers older, but they are more likely to change jobs, meaning that the traditional backloaded DB plan is less attractive. For instance, research has found that industries with younger, more mobile workers and tighter labor markets were most likely to undertake hybrid conversions (Coronado and Copeland 2003). Clearly, as long as employer-provided pensions are a voluntary benefit, it stands to reason that restricting hybrid conversions may detract from both employer and employee well-being.

The Changing Demographic Landscape and Potential Labor Shortages

As the leading edge of the baby boom generation approaches retirement, labor markets face a massive exodus of talent over the next several decades. How employers will adjust to these demographic changes will be very important for the economy. Figure 7-1 illustrates the trend: growth rates in the civilian US labor force from the 1950s through the 1990s, versus

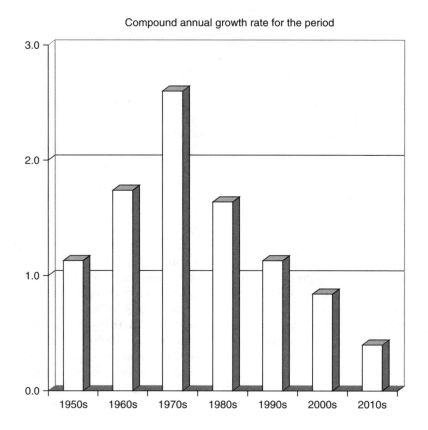

Figure 7-1. US civilian labor force growth rates for selected decades.
Source: Council of Economic Advisors (2004); Social Security Administration (2000).

projections of slowdown thereafter. Indeed, Social Security Administration actuaries estimate that labor force growth to 2010 will be only about 75 percent of that seen during the 1990s, and after that it will be only about one-third as high. Consequently, a key question arises as to whether growing demand for goods and services might outpace a slow-growing workforce.

The demand for labor ultimately depends on the efficiency with which workers are employed in producing output, and the level of output that firms produce. In turn, output is driven by the demand for goods and services and the role of international markets. The USA has historically demonstrated a strong appetite for higher living standards, measured here by gross domestic product (GDP) per capita.[1] Table 7-1 illustrates per capita GDP over the last half of the twentieth century, along with US population estimates, and GDP levels in 1996 dollars. It is interesting that per capita GDP growth over the last half century was fairly stable, notwithstanding year-to-year fluctuations.

There are several ways of estimating future national output levels.[2] Here we rely on ten-year macroeconomic projections developed by the US Congressional Budget Office (CBO), similar to private sector estimates of economic growth projections (Lofgren et al. 2003). The last column of Table 7-1 also provides our projections for growth in standards of living to 2020.[3] Here we assume an annual real per capita GDP growth rate of 2 percent to 2010, an estimate consistent with the pattern of historical improvement in standards of living. In the following period to 2020, the growth in output per person is anticipated to slow to roughly 1.66 percent

TABLE 7-1 Population and Output Measures in the USA for Selected Periods and Expectations for the Future

	Resident population (in millions)	GDP in 2000 chain weighted dollars (in billions)	Annualized GDP growth rate from prior date (%)	GDP per capita in 2000 (dollars)	Annualized growth rate in per capita GDP from prior date (%)
1950	152.3	1,777.30		11,669.73	
1960	180.7	2,501.80	3.48	13,845.05	1.72
1970	205.1	3,771.90	4.19	18,390.54	2.88
1980	227.8	5,161.70	3.19	22,658.91	2.11
1990	249.5	7,112.50	3.26	28,507.01	2.32
2000	275.3	9,817.00	3.28	35,659.28	2.26
2010	299.9	13,030.50	2.87	43,449.48	2.00
2020	324.9	16,646.90	2.48	51,237.00	1.66

Sources: CBO, Census Bureau and US Department of Commerce, Bureau of Economic Analysis.

per year, a rate of improvement roughly in line with previous periods. A key determinant of strong economic growth, despite slower labor supply expansion, is workforce productivity. Examining historical productivity growth (average GDP per hour) may offer insights for the future. During the 1950s and 1960s, average GDP per hour of labor grew at a rate of 2.66 percent per year, but over the last three decades, average annual growth in productivity has been a modest 1.5 percent. Just recently productivity has seen a resurgence, with the last half of the 1990s reporting a 2.1 percent per year, and an average of around 2.3 percent in 2002 and 2003.[4]

These growth projections have important labor force implications. To describe the challenges, we examine the relationship between the potential labor supply and the demand for labor under a range of alternative productivity scenarios. The analysis begins by projecting labor supplies on the basis of the existing workforce and expected changes in the population over the coming decade.[5] The most conservative projection scenario assumed that output per worker hour would rise at 1.5 percent per year, the average rate of increase in output per hour over the past three decades. In the second and third scenarios, we assumed that output per hour would increase at a rate of 1.75 percent and 2.0 percent per year, respectively, reflecting the ranges experienced in worker productivity growth during the past decade. Two last scenarios assumed that output per hour increases at 2.44 percent and 2.23 percent per year, roughly in line with those of the 1950s and 1960s (but unmatched for any extended period since then).

Table 7-2 presents the results of these projections in terms of full-time equivalent (FTE) workers.[6] Our approach poses the problem as measuring how much labor force participation rates of workers over age 55 would have to change to meet the gap. Of course, boosting employment could also happen at other age groups, drawing in more women and younger cohorts.[7] Yet we focus on the age 55+ bracket, inasmuch as these workers are

TABLE 7-2 Labor Supply Gap under Alternative Productivity Growth Scenarios
(Millions)

	2010	2020	Gap 2010	Gap 2020
Labor Supply FTE	134.6	139.9	—	—
Labor Demand FTE				
at 1.5% Productivity	143.6	158.0	8.9	18.1
at 1.75% Productivity	141.1	151.5	6.5	11.7
at 2.0% Productivity	138.7	145.4	4.1	5.5
at 2.23% Productivity	136.5	139.9	1.9	0.0
at 2.44% Productivity	134.6	135.1	0.0	−4.8

Source: Authors' calculations from unpublished projections provided by the SSA (2001); the US Department of Commerce (2004: D-3); Unicon (2003); the US Census Bureau (2000: NP-D1-A); and the CBO (2004: Table E-1).

those most affected by pension and other retirement programs over the next two decades.

Under the most conservative productivity improvement scenario, there will be a labor shortfall estimated at 6.6 percent in 2010, representing roughly 8.9 million FTE workers. As seen in Table 7-3 the shortfall is reduced when productivity rises. Labor supply will be sufficient to meet labor demand only if productivity improvements meet or exceed 2.44 percent per year. Projecting further, to the year 2020, the gap between labor supply and demand widens to 18.1 million FTE workers under the most conservative scenario (a 13 percent shortfall). In order to close the gap under the 2020 projection, labor productivity would need to sustain an annual rate of 2.23 percent, if current workforce patterns persist. The fact that the required productivity rate is lower for the 2020 scenario compared to the 2010 scenario reflects the slowdown in output growth anticipated by the CBO over the 2010s.

If the required boost in labor productivity is not achievable in the coming decades, higher rates of workforce participation will be needed to avoid disappointing future standards of living. Employers will either have to entice some people into the workforce who are outside it today, or convince their current workers to work longer hours. Since here

TABLE 7-3 Required Changes in Labor Force Participation Necessary to Meet Future Growth Prospects under Alternative Productivity Growth Scenarios

		1.5% Productivity		1.75% Productivity		2.0% Productivity	
	2003	2010	2020	2010	2020	2010	2020
Males							
55 to 59	77.6	105.6	124.1	97.9	107.5	90.4	91.6
60 to 64	57.2	77.8	91.5	72.2	79.3	66.6	67.5
65 to 69	32.8	44.6	52.5	41.4	45.4	38.2	38.7
70 to 74	18.8	25.6	30.1	23.7	26.0	21.9	22.2
75+	8.3	11.3	13.3	10.5	11.5	9.7	9.8
Females							
55 to 59	65.5	89.1	104.8	82.7	90.8	76.3	77.3
60 to 64	45.3	61.7	72.5	57.2	62.8	52.8	53.5
65 to 69	22.7	30.9	36.3	28.6	31.5	26.4	26.8
70 to 74	11.2	15.2	17.9	14.1	15.5	13.0	13.2
75+	4.1	5.6	6.6	5.2	5.7	4.8	4.8

Source: Authors' calculations unpublished projections provided by the SSA (2001); the US Department of Commerce (2004: D-3); Unicon (2003); US Census Bureau (2000: NP-D1-A); Congressional Budget Office (2004: Table E-1).

we focus on the labor supply of older workers, Table 7-3 illustrates how much rates would have to rise for males and females aged 55+ to eliminate the labor supply shortage. As noted above, under our most conservative productivity scenario, we estimate a 6.6 percent shortfall for 2010, which rises to 13 percent by 2020. Under the 1.5 percent productivity improvement scenario, participation rates would need to rise by more than one-third compared to current levels. For men aged 55–59, participation rates would have to increase from 77.6 percent in 2003 to 105.6 percent by 2010. Likewise, female participation rates in the same age cohort would have to climb from 65.5 to 89.1 percent over the decade. These increases are implausible since then participation would be above the natural limit of 100 percent for men, though people would need to work increasingly longer days or hold multiple jobs. Looking at the 1.75 percent and 2.0 percent productivity growth scenarios, participation rates would need to rise by 26.2 percent and 16.5 percent, respectively, by 2010.[8]

If we extend the period out to 2020 under the 1.5 percent productivity scenario, activity rates would need to rise by nearly 60 percent among older workers over the next two decades to close the gap between labor supply and labor demand. Participation rates for both males and females aged 55–59 would need to rise above 100 percent, of course an improbable outcome. Under the 1.75 percent productivity scenario, participation rates would need to rise by 38.5 percent, and for the 2.0 percent scenario rates would have to increase by over 18 percent.

Next we turn to a discussion of how pensions and retiree medical plans influence early retirement, and finally we evaluate several strategies that employers can use to induce workers to retire later.

The Importance of Pensions and Retiree Medical Plans to the Retirement Decision

These economic and demographic realities suggests that employers will likely launch a search for strategies to retain their older workers. Because DB pensions have the strongest early retirement incentives, these will naturally be a prime target for change. Evidence suggests that early retirement subsidies in DB pensions and Social Security strongly influence the decision to retire before normal retirement age (Coile and Gruber 2000; Gustman et al. 1994). Traditional DB plans generally encourage early retirement by offering early retirement subsidies and delayed retirement penalties (Luzadis and Mitchell 1991). While most early retirement benefits are actuarially reduced to reflect a longer payout period, these reductions generally are small and tend to provide a more than actuarially fair early retirement benefit. For instance, two-thirds of DB plans had an early retirement subsidy in 1994 (Foster 1996).

TABLE 7-4 Pension Coverage of Baby Boomers (1998)

	Percent with Defined benefit plans				
	Overall	*Men*	*Women*	*⇐ $30K*	*>$30K*
Boomers	32.4	33.6	31.1	23.6	43.7
(Age 33–52)					
Younger boomers	28.9	29.7	28	21.5	39.4
(Age 33–42)					
Older boomers	36.7	38.5	34.6	26.4	48.3
(Age 43–52)					

Source: Verma and Lichtenstein (2003).

Though pension coverage has declined for the workforce as a whole over the past decade, it is still prevalent among baby boomers, particularly the older segment (see Table 7-4). Overall, 37 percent of the older set (age 43–52 in 1998) had a DB plan, more than the 29 percent of their younger counterparts (age 33–42 in 1998). Men are slightly more likely to have DB coverage than women, and baby boomers with income above $30,000 are nearly twice as likely to be covered by a pension plan. In fact, among older baby boomers with incomes above $30,000, almost half had DB coverage (Verma and Lichtenstein 2003). Thus we expect that the incentives in these plans will affect the retirement decision of boomers in 2010 and 2020.

Another factor that affects the timing of retirement is the availability of retiree health insurance. This is particularly a concern for pre-65 retirees who must purchase coverage in the retail marketplace. A recent Health Confidence Survey reported that 60 percent of workers said they would not retire before becoming eligible for Medicare, unless their employer provided retiree health benefits (EBRI 2002). Other evidence also confirms that retiree medical plans encourage older workers to retire early (Karoly and Rogowski 1994). Yet there is little consensus on the magnitude of these effects, perhaps because these studies suffer from data limitations regarding pension plan availability, pension plan incentives, measures of the value of retiree health insurance, and sample restrictions (Gruber and Madrian 2002).

Also the impact of retiree medical plans on future retirees may decline, since fewer companies are offering this benefit over time (McDevitt et al. 2002). Before 1980, employer-sponsored retiree health insurance often accompanied DB pension plans, and more than 80 percent of medium and large employers offered some form of retiree health insurance (Figure 7-2). By 2003, only 40 percent of medium and large firms offered a retiree medical plan to active employees. The nature of the retiree health benefit is also changing. Today's retiree health plans are more likely to have

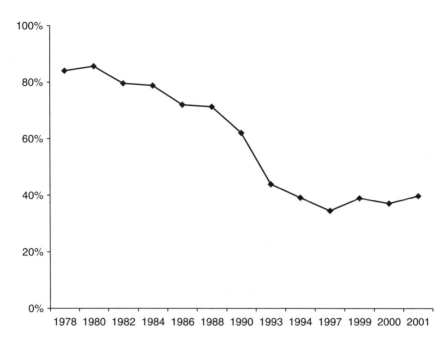

Figure 7-2. Percentage of medium and large firms offering a retiree health plan to active employees.
Source: Watson Wyatt Data Services (various years). These surveys were targeted at medium and large firms.

contribution caps, service-related contributions, and substantial retiree cost-sharing (McDevitt et al. 2002). While few empirical studies have accounted for these new plan design features, it is likely that these features will influence retirement incentives for the next generation of older workers.

Strategies to Retain Older Workers

Prior studies have found that early retirement pension provisions and retiree medical plans help induce early retirement, but the magnitude of these effects is, as yet, not firmly established. This is partly because of the difficulties inherent in separating the effects of pension incentives from retiree medical plans and other benefits.[9] Additionally, previous studies have been able to measure the existence of these plans, but they have not evaluated specific pension and medical plan designs. Finally, prior researchers have not accounted for the potential inter-relationships between work/life benefits and retirement incentives. These latter benefits, which include both formal and informal phased retirement arrangements and eldercare programs, may also influence retirement incentives.

To fill these gaps, we employ a unique dataset that combines personnel records with details about retirement plan design features. We have collected personnel files for forty-two large companies with DB pensions plans, representing nearly 300,000 active workers. Of these employees, 37,428 are age 55+, 72 percent of whom were eligible to retire. The datafiles include demographic information for all employees on age, sex, tenure, and salary; to this we have appended information on plan features and dollar values of each worker's pension and health benefits based on his age, salary, and tenure derived from Watson Wyatt's COMPARISON™ database. Using actuarial models, we compute the present value of each worker's pension benefit at the earliest age of eligibility or attained age, if later, as well as the worker's normal retirement age in the plan. Information is also available on the features of retiree medical plans if they were offered. Finally, we have information on work/life benefits including the existence of phased retirement programs and eldercare programs. Using these data, we explore three simulated scenarios.

Strategy 1: Reduce Economic Subsidies in Early Retirement Benefits. The vast majority (95 percent) of all DB plans offer some form of early retirement benefit (Mitchell 2003), with the size of the early retirement subsidy depending on the extent to which the normal retirement benefit is reduced, when calculating early benefits. The intent of the early retirement reduction factor is to adjust early benefits to account for the fact that benefits will be paid out over a longer number of years. As a rule of thumb, actuaries suggest that an early reduction factor of 60 percent is actuarially fair for a 55 year old; reductions of 40 percent and 30 percent, respectively, are roughly actuarially neutral for a 60 and 62 year old.[10]

We also point out the difference between an actuarially fair benefit and an economically fair benefit.[11] The actuarially fair reduction does not account for additional years and wage growth a worker would attain, if he or she delayed retirement until the plan's normal retirement age, whereas the economically fair benefit does. So even though an early retirement benefit is actuarially subsidized, it might not be seen as embodying an economic subsidy. That is, an economic subsidy exists if the present value of the early retirement benefit exceeds or equals the present value of the normal retirement benefit. In our sample, 28 percent of workers eligible to retire had an economic early retirement subsidy.

To estimate how an economic subsidy influences retirement, we created an indicator that equaled one when the present value of the early retirement benefit was greater than or equal to the present value of the normal retirement benefit. Results in Figure 7-3 show that the economic pension subsidy reduced the average retirement age by nearly 9 months for men and 10 months for women.

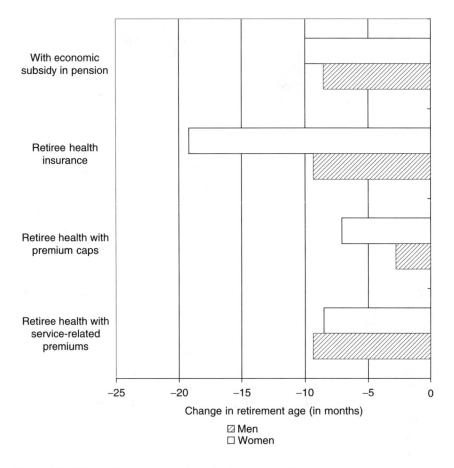

Figure 7-3. Effect of retirement plan provisions on retirement ages.
Source: Authors' estimates using coefficients presented in Table 7–A1.

Strategy 2: Change the Nature of Retiree Medical Benefits. As noted above, while having retiree health insurance boosts the likelihood of early retirement, there is little consensus on the magnitude of this effect.[12] For our sample of DB participants, 83 percent had retiree medical plans, which we find reduces retirement ages by 1.6 years for women and 9.4 months for men (although the effect is less statistically significant for men; Figure 7-3). If the prevalence of these plans falls in the future, this could significantly impact labor force participation rates. Of course, while the existence of the plan is important, the design features of plans are also important. In our sample, 28 percent of workers with retiree medical plans also faced capped employer premiums, and as this becomes more prevalent, employers will seek to pass on future retiree medical cost increases to the plan participants (McDevitt et al. 2002). This will have an impact on retirement ages according to our findings. If retiree medical insurance is available, but the plan has premium caps, this substantially offsets the tendency to retire early. For our dataset, for instance, retirement ages decline only by 2.7 months for men (6.6 months minus 9.9 months), and 7.2 months for women (1.0 months −1.6 months).

A second design feature of retire medical plans has to do with service-related premiums, by which we mean that employers link their premium contributions to the worker's tenure with the firm. In our dataset, 27 percent of firms with retiree medical plans had service-related premiums. If the retiree medical plan had such service-related premiums, retirement ages only declined by 8.5 months for women (versus 1.6 years if retiree medical coverage lacked service-related premiums). There is no significant effect of service-related premiums on men, perhaps because men in the sample had longer tenure. Philosophically, it makes sense to align retirement benefits with service which makes them more consistent with traditional DB pensions.

Strategy 3: Implement Work/Life Benefits Like Eldercare and Phased Retirement. While changing early retirement subsidies and retiree medical plans may help some employers achieve deferred retirement, some firms face pressure to preserve benefits for workers close to retirement. Consequently, there is a need for other ways to offer older workers incentives to remain on the job. Integral to these offerings is the element of time, since employees' time on the job competes against other demands including time spent with family, travel, volunteerism, and other activities.

A particularly time-consuming activity of much concern to older workers has to do with caregiving responsibilities for aging parents, grandchildren, or other relatives. It is estimated that 17 percent of the workforce is actively involved in providing care for an older family member or friend (National Alliance for Caregiving 2004). Caregivers report that they incur significant losses in career development, salary and retirement income, and substantial out-of-pocket expenses, as a result of their caregiving obligations (Metlife 1999). Approximately 10 percent of working caregivers retire early because they cannot successfully balance the demand of career and family (National Alliance for Caregiving 1997). In addition, we have calculated from the Current Population Survey that for women age 55–64 who exit the workforce, 23 percent report they left to take care of family.

To the extent that employers can help alleviate these caregiving responsibilities, they may free them up to work longer. One approach is to offer eldercare programs, which help employees identify, evaluate, and contact eldercare services. Some also provide a social worker to work with families to identify various alternatives given their work situations and incomes. When relatives need more intensive care, these services help locate home health aides and even help find high-quality nursing homes. In our datafile described above, one-quarter of older workers eligible to retire had access to eldercare programs.

Another way that employers can help their workers address caregiving needs is to develop phased retirement programs allowing them more time to care for an aging relative. Phased retirement programs allow workers to slowly transition into retirement and can include part-time work or flexible schedules. Our database suggests that 40 percent of employers provide flexible work schedules for their employees, and a separate Watson Wyatt survey found that 16 percent of large employers offer some type of formal phased retirement program.

While our analysis shows that eldercare assistance and phased retirement programs do encourage workers to delay retirement, the results differ by gender (see Figure 7-4). Men tend to be more responsive to eldercare programs but less to phased retirement programs, while women have the opposite response. This discrepancy reflects the fact that the nature of caregiving responsibilities often differs by sex (Metlife 2003); for instance, men are more likely to be long-distance caregivers and provide financial

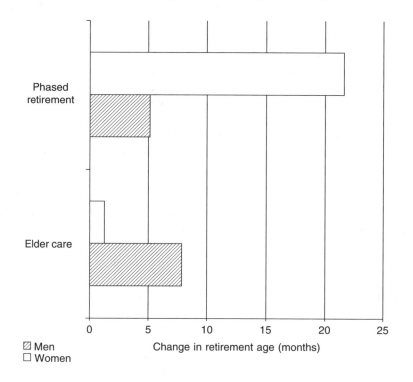

Figure 7-4. Effect of work/life benefits on retirement ages.
Source: Authors' estimates using coefficients presented in Table 7–A1.

support rather than actual personal care services. In addition, men tend to help more with nonpersonal caregiving events that can be scheduled around a workday. The services provided by eldercare assistance programs seem to meet those needs. In fact, our analysis shows that employer-provided elder care assistance programs increase the average retirement age of men by eight months, while the same programs increase the average retirement age of women by only one month. Women, on the other hand, are more likely than men to help with 'hands-on' personal care services like feeding, dressing, bathing, and transferring.

This is particularly relevant since a recent Metlife (2003) study found that women were more likely to report that they are leaving their jobs as a result of caregiving responsibilities (20 percent) compared with men (11 percent). Therefore, the flexibility offered by phased retirement programs often can addresses women's caregiving needs more effectively than do eldercare assistance programs. Overall, one-quarter percent of older workers appear to phase out of work (Quinn 1999), and women constitute the majority of phasers (Mulvey 2004). In addition, the desire to phase and the intensity of caregiving activities are related. Of workers who phased, 30 percent of female phasers provide care to a family member, while only 19 percent of male phasers have caregiving responsibilities.[13] Our analysis supports these trends and shows that the existence of a phased retirement program increases the average retirement age among women by 21 months. For men, phasing increased average retirement age by about 5 months.

To put each of these scenarios in perspective, we combine our analysis of labor supply and labor demand in Figure 7-5. This illustrates the predicted impact on the gap between labor supply and demand if employers were attempting to delay retirement ages for eligible workers by one, two, or three years. We find that a combination of these strategies might raise the average retirement age for men and women by nearly two years. This would have a measurable impact on the gap between labor supply and demand, of 11 percent in 2010, and 17 percent in 2020. It is possible that the remaining shortfall could be met by increasing labor force participation among workers age 65+ and among younger women. Indeed, Nyce and Schieber (2002) report that women's labor force participation rates would have to rise only about 3.5 percentage points in order to close the gap, assuming a productivity rate of two percent (naturally lower productivity growth rates would require a larger response).

Conclusions

Employer-sponsored pensions and retiree medical benefits remain an important source of retirement income, often providing incentives for workers to retire as early as age 55. At the same time, as baby boomers

Percent reduction in gap

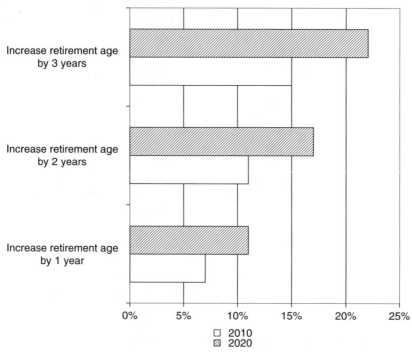

Figure 7-5. Effect of strategies on retirement ages.
Source: Authors' calculations assuming a 2 percent productivity growth rate for labor
gap estimates.

approach retirement, employers must confront an ever-tightening labor
market and some will want to keep older workers on the job. Unless
productivity growth is raised substantially, the productive sector must face
considerable staffing challenges.

Our work suggests that part of the gap can be filled by changing some of
the incentives built into programs for older workers. For instance, employers can continue to offer DB plans and retain their older workers by paring
early retirement subsidies. Modifying retiree health benefits can also have a
direct influence on retirement ages. Other strategies including the introduction of work/life programs can also have beneficial effects. Specifically,
the use of phased retirement and eldercare programs can provide positive
incentives for older workers to postpone retirement. We note that likely
responses to these programs differ by sex: men seem most responsive to
eldercare programs, while women are more responsive to phased retire-

ment programs. Combined with strategies to boost labor force participation among the elderly and women overall, such efforts could help to narrow the expected gap between labor supply and demand over the coming decades.

TABLE 7-A1   Analysis of Retirement Plan Designs and Work/Life Benefits on Retirement Age: Regression Results

	Men		Women	
	With pension only	*With pension and work/life*	*With pension only*	*With pension and work/life*
Intercept	58.58	57.7	57.53	57.18
Salary over $30,000	−0.38 *(−1.64)*	−0.51 *(−2.2)*	−0.83 *(−4.8)*	−0.74 *(−4.3)*
Age 62	3.35 *(21.58)*		3.1 *(12.0)*	
Economic Subsidy flag	−0.70 *(−5.4)*	−0.72 *(−5.6)*	−0.89 *(−3.4)*	−.838 *(−3.2)*
Ratio PV of early retirement benefit/PV of normal retirement benefit	0.16 *(6.13)*	0.016 *(6.3)*	0.031 *(9.12)*	.031 *(8.98)*
Retiree health available	−1.66 *(−3.72)*	−0.788 *(−1.7)*	−1.7 *(−7.8)*	−1.6 *(−5.46)*
Caps on retiree health premiums	0.87 *(8.10)*	0.556 *(3.2)*	0.74 *(3.28)*	1.01 *(3.58)*
Service related premiums	1.0 *(7.93)*	0.016 *(−0.19)*	1.21 *(4.8)*	0.891 *(2.98)*
Eldercare program available		0.65 *(3.44)*		0.105 *(0.4)*
Phased retirement available		0.42 *(3.7)*		1.8 *(2.55)*
Financial planning avail.		−.98 *(−4.65)*		−0.789 *(−2.57)*
Adj. R-square	0.1992	0.223	0.26	0.28
N	3,433	3,433	1,277	1,270

Endnotes

The authors wish to thank Michael Slover for his research assistance. The opinions and conclusions stated here are those of the authors and should not be construed to be those of Watson Wyatt Worldwide or any of its other associates.

1. GDP is not a perfect measure of improved standards of living across this period, in part because of the changing labor force behavior of women. For example, in 1946, fewer than half of working-age women in the USA were employed outside the home whereas nearly 80 percent were employed during 2000. As women entered the workforce, many tasks that were previously done by housewives and not measured in the government's calculation of GDP have been commercialized and are now included in measures of national output. GDP is also uninformative about changing life patterns and environmental factors that affect people's lives nor does it reflect the distribution of output from an economy across society.
2. Most projections begin with an estimate of the demand for goods and services based on the size and composition of various sectors of the economy. We have not developed our own macroeconomic projection model since there are several widely used in government and business planning.
3. The CBO only provides estimates of future GDP growth till 2014. To account for the last half of the next decade, our estimates assume that GDP will continue at the pace of the last projection year provided by the CBO.
4. Some have argued that we are embarked on a 'new' paradigm in productivity growth, but this conclusion has skeptics (Gordon 1999). It is unknown whether recent productivity improvements are sustainable; prudence suggests, however, that it is unwise to discount three decades of historical trend.
5. Our baseline projection assumes that current labor supply patterns at each age would persist into the future. For example, since 45 percent of women between the ages of 60 and 64 are in the labor force today, we assumed that 45 percent of women aged 60–64 would be in the labor force over the coming decade as well. In addition, we assumed that workers within each age group would continue working the same number of hours per year as they have in recent years. Applying current labor force participation rates and work patterns to the evolving population structure over the coming decade provides a reasonable estimate of the labor supply for each year as a baseline for the remainder of our analysis. By applying constant labor force participation rates in 2000 to population shares over the coming decade, our baseline labor force is projected to be 153.2 million in 2010. The BLS has made similar labor force projections for the 16+ civilian labor force through 2012; it projects the 2012 labor force to be 162.2 million, while our baseline labor force is projected to be 155.0 million (Toossi 2004; 48). The difference is caused by the BLS's expectations of a rather sizable increase in labor force participation rates for the 55+ age group.
6. We calculate FTE by dividing the total number of projected hours by a full-time employment level of 2,000 hours per year.
7. See Nyce and Schieber (2002) for a detailed discussion on the USA; Nyce and Schieber (2004) offer a broader look at other developed nations.

8. Every two years, the Bureau of Labor Statistics (BLS) publishes projections of labor force growth anticipated over the coming decade. As a result, that office must also estimate future changes in labor force participation rates. In their most recent estimates, labor force participation rates for persons age 55+ will rise from 34.5 percent in 2002 to 39.7 percent in 2012, equivalent to a 15 percent increase over the coming decade. In a separate analysis with our model, we find that participation rates would need to rise by 39 percent under the 1.5 percent productivity scenario, 26 percent under the 1.75 percent scenario and 15 percent under the 2 percent scenario. This indicates that, based on the BLS estimates of labor force growth, productivity rates would need to rise by an annual two percent between 2002 and 2012 in order to meet the output growth estimates set out by the Congressional Budget Office (Toosi 2004).
9. Gustman et. al. (1994) sought to disaggregate these effects but used only the existence of a subsidy, and not the size of the subsidy, as an independent variable.
10. The actual size of the factor for an actuarially fair adjustment depends on the specific discount and interest rates used.
11. Ippolito (1990) provides an excellent example of how these differ.
12. These studies suggest that retiree health insurance increases the probability of early retirement by 30 to 80 percent, and reduces the age at retirement by six to 24 months (cf. Gruber and Madrian 2002; Karoly and Rogowski 1994; Blau and Gilleskie 2001). In a related study, Johnson et al. (1999) found that the higher expected health insurance costs in retirement were the less likely a worker will retire.
13. Based on authors' analysis of Watson Wyatt Survey data on phased retirees.

References

Blau, David, M. and Donna B. Gilleskie (2001). 'Retiree Health Insurance and the Labor Force Behavior of Older Men in the 1990s', *Review of Economics and Statistics*, 83(1): 64–80.

Bureau of Labor Statistics, US Department of Labor (2004). 'National Compensation Survey: Employee Benefits in Private Industry in the United States, March 2003', Summary 04–02, April, Washington, DC: USBLS.

Clark, Robert L., Janemarie Mulvey, and Sylvester J. Schieber (2004). 'Effects of Nondiscrimination Rules on Pension Participation', in William Gale, John Shoven, and Mark Warshawsky (eds.), *Private Pensions and Public Policies*. Washington, DC: The Brookings Institution.

Coile, Courtney and Jonathan Gruber (2000). 'Social Security and Retirement', *NBER Working Paper* No. 7830, Washington, DC.

Coronado, Julia Lynn, and Phillip C. Copeland (2003). 'Cash Balance Pension Plan Conversions and the New Economy', Federal Reserve Board of Governors Working Paper, October.

Council of Economic Advisers (2004). *Economic Report of the President*, Washington, DC: USGPO.

Employee Benefit Research Institute (EBRI) (2002). '2002 Health Confidence Survey: Confidence & Satisfaction in Health Care System Show Little Change

Over Time, But Americans Still Worry About Its Future', News Release, September 25, 2002, Washington, DC: EBRI.

Foster, Ann C. (1996). 'Early Retirement Provisions in Defined Benefit Pension Plans', *Compensation and Working Conditions,* December: 12–17, Washington, DC.

Ghilarducci, Teresa (1992). *Labor's Capital: The Economics and Politics of Private Pensions,* Cambridge, MA: Massachusetts Institute of Technology.

Gordon, Robert J (1999). 'Has the "New Economy" Rendered the Productivity Slowdown Obsolete?' *http://www.econ.northwestern.edu/faculty-frame.html* Evanston, IL: Northwestern University.

Goodfellow, Gordon, Brendan McFarland and Janemarie Mulvey (2004). 'Workforce Realities, Not Cost, Drive Hybrid Conversions', Watson Wyatt Working Paper, Washington, DC, March.

Gruber, Jonathan and Brigitte C. Madrian (2002). 'Health Insurance, Labor Supply, and Job Mobility: A Critical Review of the Literature', NBER Working Paper No. 8817.

Gustman, Alan L., Olivia S. Mitchell, and Thomas L. Steinmeier (1994). 'Employer-Provided Health Insurance and Retirement Behavior', *Industrial and Labor Relations Review,* 48(1): 124–40.

Hustead, Edwin (1998). 'Trends in Retirement Income Plan Administrative Expenses', in Olivia S. Mitchell and S. Schieber (eds.), *Living with Defined Contribution Plans: Remaking Responsibility for Retirement,* Philadelphia, PA: University of Pennsylvania Press: 166–77.

Ippolito, Richard (1990). 'Toward Explaining Earlier Retirement after 1970.' *Industrial and Labor Relations Review,* 43(5): 556–69.

Johnson Richard, Amy Davidoff, and Kevin Perese (1999). *Health Insurance Costs and Early Retirement Decisions.* Urban Institute Report, August. *www.urban.org/url.cfm?ID=409207*

Karoly, Lynn A. and Jeannette A. Rogowski (1994). 'The Effect of Access to Post-Retirement Health Insurance on the Decision to Retire Early', *Industrial and Labor Relations Review,* 481: 103–23.

Lofgren, Eric P., Steven A. Nyce and Sylvester J. Schieber (2003). 'Designing Total Reward Programs for Tight Labor Markets', in Olivia S. Mitchell, David S. Blitzstein, Michael Gordon and Judith F. Mazo (eds.), *Benefits for the Workplace of the Future.* Philadelphia: University of Pennsylvania Press, pp. 151–77.

McDevitt, Roland D., Janemarie Mulvey, and Sylvester Schieber (2002). 'Retiree Health Benefits: Time to Resuscitate?', *Watson Wyatt Research Report,* 2002, Washington, DC, pp. 1–15.

MetLife Mature Market Institute (1999). 'The MetLife Juggling Act Study, Balancing Caregiving with Work and the Costs Involved', November, Westport, CT: Metlife.

—— —— (2003). 'The Metlife Study of Sons at Work: Balancing Employment and Eldercare', June, Westport, CT: Metlife.

Mitchell, Olivia S. (1982). 'Fringe Benefits and Labor Mobility', *The Journal of Human Resources,* 17(2): 286–98.

—— with Erica L. Dykes (2003). 'New Trends in US Pensions', in Olivia S. Mitchell, David S. Blitzstein, Michael Gordon and Judith F. Mazo (eds.), *Benefits for the Workplace of the Future.* Philadelphia: University of Pennsylvania Press, pp. 110–36.

Mulvey, Janemarie (2004). 'Phased Retirement: Aligning Employer Programs with Worker Preferences', Watson Wyatt Working Paper, February, Washington, DC: Watson Wyatt.

National Alliance for Caregiving and AARP (2004). 'Caregiving in the U.S'. Metlife Foundation, April. *http://www.caregiving.org/*

—— (1997). 'Family Caregiving in the U.S.: Findings from a National Survey'. *http://www.caregiving.org/*

Nyce, Steven A. and Sylvester J. Schieber (2002). 'The Decade of the Employee: The Workforce Environment in the Coming Decade', *Benefits Quarterly*, First Quarter.

—— —— (2004). 'Living Happily Ever After: The Economic Implications of Aging Societies', Report to the World Economic Forum Pension Readiness Initiative, January, Davos, Switzerland: Watson Wyatt.

Papke, Leslie E. (1999). 'Are 401(k) Plans Replacing Other Employer-Provided Pensions? Evidence from Panel Data', *Journal of Human Resources*, Spring, 34: 346–68.

Pension Benefit Guaranty Corporation (PBGC) (2004). *Pension Insurance Data Book 2003.* Winter 2004, Washington, DC: PBGC.

Quinn, Joseph F. (1999). 'Retirement Patterns and Bridge Jobs in the 1990s', Employee Benefit Research Institute Issue Brief, February, Washington, DC: EBRI.

Sass, Steven A. (1997). *The Promise of Private Pensions.* Cambridge: Harvard University Press.

Schieber, Sylvester J. (2003). *Pensions in Crises*, Watson Wyatt Insider, September, Washington, DC: Watson Wyatt.

—— (*Forthcoming*). 'The Employee Retirement Income Security Act: Motivations, Provisions, and Implications for Retirement', in William Gale, John Shoven, and Mark Warshawsky (eds.), *ERISA After 25 Years: A Framework for Evaluating Pension Reform.* Washington, DC: The Brookings Institution.

Social Security Administration (SSA) (2001). Unpublished projection series from the Office of the Actuary.

Toossi, Mitra (2004). 'Labor Force Projections to 2012: The Graying of the US Workforce,' *Monthly Labor Review*, February: 37–57.

Turner, John (1993). *Pension Policy for a Mobile Labor Force.* Kalamazoo, MI: Upjohn Institute.

Unicon Research Corporation (2003). *CPS Utilities, Annual Demographic and Income Supplement: March Files, 1988B–2000.* Santa Monica, CA: URC.

US Census Bureau (2000). *Projections of the Resident Population by Age, Sex, Race, and Hispanic Origin: 1999–2100.* January 13, NP-D1-A Washington, DC: Population Projections Program.

US Department of Commerce, Bureau of Economic Analysis (2004). 'GDP and Other Major NIPA Series, 1929–2003', *Survey of Current Business*, February 84(2).

US Congressional Budget Office (CBO) (2004). 'Budget and Economic Outlook: Fiscal Years 2005 to 2014', *ftp://ftp.cbo.gov/49xx/doc4985/AppendixE.pdf* January.

Verma, Satyendra K. And Jules H. Lichtenstein (2003). 'Retirement Plan Coverage of Baby Boomers and Retired Workers: Analysis of 1998 SIPP Data', AARP Public Policy Institute Working Paper #2003–10, July.

Waston Wyatt Data Services (1995–2002). *ECS Survey Report on Employee Benefits.* Washington, DC: Watson Wyatt.

—— (1993). *Employee Benefit Report.* Washington, DC: Watson Wyatt.

—— (1990). *Medical Benefits for Active and Retired Employees.* Washington, DC: Watson Wyatt.

—— (1978–1988). *Group Benefits Survey.* Washington, DC: Watson Wyatt.

Chapter 8

Developments in Phased Retirement

Robert Hutchens and Kerry L. Papps

Phased retirement is often seen as a way to encourage older workers to extend their time in the labor force. The essential idea of phased retirement is that employees then move from full-time work to part-time work without changing employers. One advantage is that older workers can reduce hours while maintaining existing skills and job relationships. However, a curious feature of phased retirement is that it sometimes occurs after employees have 'officially' retired. Even more curious is the fact that the time interval between official retirement and rehire is sometimes as short as a day. This seems odd, since there is no ready explanation for why working hours would be reduced in this way. That is, rehire with reduced hours might have just as easily occurred before official retirement.

In this chapter, we explore why employers might permit phased retirement only after employees officially retire. We address the question with the help of interviews conducted with close to 1,000 establishments regarding their phased retirement policies. Employers were asked whether they would permit an older worker to reduce hours, and, if so, whether they favored reduction in hours before or after official retirement. Using these data, we evaluate the extent to which employers actually do favor one or the other. Interestingly, we find that many employers do not indicate a strong preference; rather, they seem open to informally arranged reductions in hours, both before and after official retirement. We also use statistical methods to analyze what types of employers might permit hour reductions to occur before and/or after official retirement. Our findings suggest that the preference for retire/rehire is at the individual rather than the establishment level, often due to pension and other benefit plan inducements. We suggest that government policy could enhance work/retirement flexibility by clarifying the meaning of what constitutes retirement under tax and labor law.

Setting the Stage

Phased retirement appears to have many advantages for both the individual and the larger society, particularly given labor force aging (see Chapter 7). Not only might phased retirement provide a more satisfying path to full retirement, but also it could preserve specific human capital and thereby enhance productivity. In light of such potential benefits, it is somewhat disappointing that phased retirement is so rare. Research from the 1980s reported that fewer than 10 percent or a retiree cohort took phased retirement; instead, most older workers moved directly from full-time work to full-time labor force withdrawal (Quinn et al. 1990; Ruhm 1990). More recent data offer no evidence of a substantive change in the numbers (Chen 2003).

One plausible explanation for the low incidence of phased retirement is that employers may restrict opportunities for hours reductions. This suggestion is strengthened by surveys of older workers wherein respondents indicate a strong interest in phased retirement. For example, over half of the employed respondents aged 55–65 said they would prefer to gradually reduce their hours of work as they age according to the Health and Retirement Study (HRS; USGAO 2001). Similarly, Abraham and Houseman (Chapter 5) report that among older workers having retirement plans, many plan to cut back on work hours, instead of fully retiring. Hence it would appear that the low incidence of phased retirement may not be due to lack of worker interest.

There is an interesting contrast between the USA and Japan in this regard. Large Japanese employers often provide work opportunities for some fraction of their employees who reach the organization's mandatory retirement age (Rebick 1995). Typically, these post-career jobs involve reduced hours with the current employer or an affiliate of the current employer, so they are very similar to phased retirement. A striking feature of these post-career jobs is that while many employees indicate an interest in them,[1] employers are often quite selective about which workers have the opportunity to take them. Accordingly, high-performing employees are more likely to gain access to the jobs in Japan. In this sense, if we could show that US employers are targeting phased retirement opportunities to specific types of workers, they are not unique; in this they are similar to Japanese practice.

If US employers do limit opportunities for phased retirement, the question arises as to why. One explanation, advanced by Gustman and Steinmeier (1983), hypothesized that these limits might be more prevalent where firms impose minimum working hours constraints. This occurs when employees are required to work a minimum number of hours per week, month and/or year. Various explanations might rationalize such minimum hours constraints, including a production process that requires the presence of a team of workers; in any event, the point is that employees in these jobs can only reduce hours by quitting and taking a different job. In this case phased retirement (or, for that matter, part-time work at any age) would simply not be feasible.

An important alternative hypothesis for reluctance to offer phased retirement focuses on the role of defined benefit (DB) pension plans. As a rule, these pensions base benefits on a formula which rewards pay and service; as such they are distinct from defined contribution (DC) pensions where benefits are tied to the amount of money in an individual account at the time of retirement. Several analysts suggest that workers with DB pensions face formidable obstacles to phased retirement, as compared to those with DC pensions or no pension at all (Quinn et al. 1990; Hurd 1996; US GAO 2001).

DB pension plans may constrain phased retirement for several reasons. First, DB plans sometimes base pension benefits on earnings during the final few years before retirement. In this event, work at half-time or at partial-pay before retirement would potentially reduce all future pension benefits substantially, which in turn will discourage part-time work. The same issue does not arise as sharply in a DC plan, since the benefit formula is linked to the individual's account. Hence working half-time before retirement will not generate a similar loss in future pension benefits.[2]

A second concern is that Internal Revenue Service (IRS) tax regulations make it difficult for employees to combine salary income with pension benefits from the current employer's DB plan. Specifically, an *active* employee cannot receive DB benefits before the plan's normal retirement age (Purcell 2004). By implication, a worker who took phased retirement before a DB plan's normal retirement age (and thus stayed with the current employer) might not be able to supplement earnings with payments from that plan. This is less of a concern for a DC plan inasmuch as the IRS permits active employees to draw DC pension benefits, with the only major federal limitation requiring that the employee be over age $59\frac{1}{2}$.[3]

Our own previous work has also investigated the extent to which pensions and minimum hours constraints might influence phased retirement opportunities (Hutchens 2003; Hutchens and Chen 2004; Hutchens and Grace-Martin 2004). This research relies on an employer survey, to be described in more detail below; in short, we ask a sample of close to 1,000 employers about their views on phased retirement and what conditions might have to be in place to permit it. Several interesting results flowed from that research. One finding was that, generally, employers appear to prefer informal over formal arrangements. This is because many employers want to maintain control over which employees are offered the opportunity for phased retirement, the type of job they do as a part-timer, and when the work is performed (e.g. not during a period of diminished demand). In other words, employers are selective about who gets an opportunity for phased retirement (Hutchens and Chen 2004). We have also, in our earlier research, evaluated the effects of minimum hours constraints and pensions, and while we find support for the minimum hours constraints, there is virtually no support for the pension hypothesis (Hutchens and Grace-Martin 2004). In particular, employers with DB plans offer opportunities for phased retirement at roughly the same rate as do employers with DC plans. We also found that business conditions matter, a result that agrees with a Watson Wyatt (1999) survey where respondents indicated that 'hiring retirees for part-time and temporary work' is the most common phased retirement arrangement.

Our analysis further revealed that industries differ according to the opportunities for phased retirement: these were higher in the service sector and lower in public administration (excluding health, education, and social services). In addition, smaller organizations were more likely to permit phased retirement. And finally, if a large percentage of the white-collar workforce was unionized, establishments were less likely to permit phased retirement. These last two results were surprising since neither organization size nor unions were suggested as important factors in the previous literature. Nevertheless, we find that unions tend to prefer the codification of a contract, and large bureaucracies favor the consistency imposed by formal personnel policies. These preferences for codified and consistent policies and practices may then limit opportunities for phased retirement.

Why Hours Reductions Might Occur after Official Retirement

At first blush, there might seem to be no reason for employers to prefer workers to reduce their hour of work after, rather than before, 'official' retirement. Either way, the same employee works the same hours, and there is no obvious reason to favor one over the other if the only difference is that one precedes the retirement party while the other does not. On the other hand, phased retirement is an uncommon event, and there might be costs of setting up the formal structure. Accordingly, if employers minimize costs when accommodating a request for phased retirement, it would likely be easier if there are already temporary or contract workers in the establishment. Similarly, if an employer has policies involving flexible hours (e.g. the firm permits job-sharing or flexible starting times), then that employer should be more likely to permit phased retirement before official retirement because it is already a mechanism for accommodating nonstandard schedules. Accordingly we propose:

Hypothesis 1. Regarding existing employment arrangements: Other things equal, employers who permit flexible hours and job sharing are more likely to permit phased retirement before official retirement. Employers who use temporary, contract, or contingent workers are more likely to permit phased retirement after official retirement.

As noted above, it may also be true that the form and shape of the employer's pension offerings will influence whether phased retirement occurs before or after official retirement. One version of this argument focuses on the fact that some DB pensions base a retiree's pension benefits on earnings during the final few years before retirement, so such a pension would impose a major benefit penalty on the employee who shifted to part-time work. As Hurd (1996: 7) notes, 'a common way to avoid this problem is to have the worker retire, fixing the benefit, and then be rehired as a consultant or outside employee who has no benefits, and particularly no accrual of pension.'

In addition, the complex IRS regulations may make it difficult for active employees to receive benefits from their current employer's DB pension plan if they are younger than the plan's normal retirement age. In particular, the law is unclear about what constitutes a bona fide termination of employment, as noted by Penner et al. (2002: 82):

In many cases, employers, particularly small employers, are unaware of this technical requirement. Others take advantage of the absence of clear guidelines and bestow retiree status liberally. There is little risk of detection and even less risk of enforcement. Few employees would sue as the arrangement only benefits them, and federal regulators would become aware of the issue only through a detailed plan audit, if even then. On the other hand, the penalty for being caught—possible plan disqualification and loss of tax benefits for all plan participants—is severe.

Similar legal complications do not arise with DC plans. As long as the employee is over age $59\frac{1}{2}$, Federal law does not prohibit using benefits from a DC plan to supplement salary either before or after official retirement. It follows that establishments with only a DC plan would be expected to permit phased retirement both before and after official retirement. Accordingly we propose:

Hypothesis 2. Regarding pensions: Other things equal, employers with only a DB plan will tend to provide opportunities for phased retirement after official retirement. Employers with only a DC plan will tend to provide opportunities for phased retirement both before and after official retirement.[4]

The Survey and the Key Questions

To test these hypotheses empirically, we analyze a survey of 950 establishments with 20+ more employees.[5] An establishment is defined as a single physical location at which business is conducted or services or industrial operations are performed; it may or may not be part of a larger organization (e.g. General Motors has hundreds of establishments). The survey focused on white-collar workers, and the sample was restricted to nonagricultural establishments with twenty or more employees and at least two white-collar employees who are aged 55+.[6] This latter restriction ensures that questions about phased retirement are relevant to the establishment's current situation. The focus on white-collar workers is due to the need to conduct reasonably brief interviews.

The telephone survey was undertaken between June 2001 and November 2002 by the University of Massachusetts Center for Survey Research. The Center first contacted the establishment and asked for the person who was best able to answer questions about flexible work schedules and employee benefits (e.g. a human resource manager or benefits manager). In larger establishments, especially those that were part of a complex organization, it was sometimes necessary to rely on multiple respondents.[7] Our overall response rate was 61 percent, with most nonresponse arising when screening establishments for eligibility (e.g. all had to have at least two white-collar employees age 55+); selection thus occurred before respondents knew the purpose of the survey. Interviews were completed for 89 percent of the establishments that were successfully screened, a rate comparable to other establishment-level telephone surveys.[8]

After asking a series of question about the characteristics of the establishment and its human resource and pension policies, the interviewer posed the following question:

Question 1. Think of a secure full-time white-collar employee who is aged 55 or over. One day that person comes to you and says that at some point in the next few years he/she may want to shift to a part-time work schedule at this establishment. Could this person's request to shift to part-time employment be worked out in a way that would be acceptable to your establishment?

If the response was 'yes' or 'in some cases,' then additional questions were asked about how this could be worked out. For example, the respondent was asked to explain what he or she meant by part-time: part-week, part-year, or something else.[9] There was also a question about the preferred timing of the phased retirement. Specifically:

Question 2. If the employee did shift from a full-time to a part-time work schedule, could he/she shift to part-time work *before official retirement,* would he/she have *to officially retire first,* or *could he/she do either?*

Results from both questions are tabulated in Table 8-1,[10] and they indicate that almost 70 percent of the establishments were willing to permit phased retirement, while a further 15 percent allowed it in some cases.[11] Only 14 percent of establishments would not permit phased retirement at all. Of the 779 establishments that said 'yes' or 'in some cases' to Q1, the great majority indicated that the reduction in hours could take place either before or after official retirement. Only 15 percent reported that full-time employees could only move to a part-time schedule before retirement, and 7 percent said that part-time was only possible after official retirement. The fact that so many establishments can accommodate phased retirement either before or after official retirement suggests that establishment characteristics may be less important than individual characteristics in influencing the timing of phased retirement.[12]

TABLE 8-1 Responses to Questions about Availability and Timing of Phased
Retirement

Whether phased retirement is available	When phased retirement may occur in relation to official retirement				
	Before	After	Either	Not specified	Total
Yes	119	48	435	39	641
In some cases	25	15	81	17	138
No	—	—	—	—	131
Not specified	—	—	—	—	40
Total	144	63	516	56	950

Source: Authors' calculations.

One issue we seek to evaluate is whether employers who *claim* that they
would permit phased retirement *actually do so* in practice. Accordingly, the
survey included a question about whether, in the last three years, a white-
collar worker age 55+ had actually shifted from a full-time to a part-time work
schedule. For those employers who said that something could be worked out
before official retirement, fully 36 percent said 'yes,' someone had made that
shift before official retirement. For those who indicated that something
could be worked out after official retirement, 22 percent said 'yes,' it had
happened in the last three years. As one would expect, these percentages
increase with size of establishment.[13] Thus, when these employers claim that
something can be worked out, there is reason to believe them.

If a respondent indicated that hours could be reduced after official retirement, the interviewer then sought to learn more about how this would be
implemented. One question dealt with the nature of the employment relationship. As indicated in Figure 8-1, employers favor hiring white-collar
retirees as part-time workers for a specific project or a specific length of
time. Interestingly, however, the second most-favored option is to place the
older employee into a regular part-time position; least favored is independent contractor. Only 22 percent of the establishments report that it is not at
all likely that the person would be hired as an independent contractor.

Figure 8-2 examines the waiting period between official retirement and
return to work. Most employers do not require a waiting period, and
among those that do, the majority require fewer than two months.
Even among employers with DB plans, the majority reported no waiting
period. Workers can and do retire on Friday and return to the same
employer as a part-timer on Monday. Finally, Figure 8-3 examines the
form of part-time work that employers prefer for rehired retirees. There
is a preference for part-week over part-year or part-day. Still, there is a
significant degree of flexibility here. At some establishments one can
work out either a part-year or part-week arrangement.

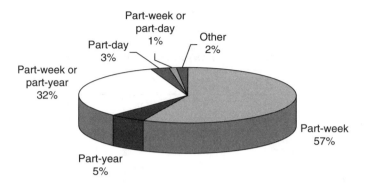

Figure 8-1. Nature of the employment relationship in establishments that rehire retirees as part-time workers.
Source: Authors' calculations.

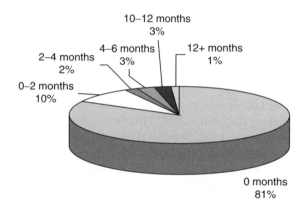

Figure 8-2. Minimum time between retire and rehire: establishments that rehire retirees as part-time workers.
Source: Authors' calculations.

To gain a better understanding of the results, Table 8-2 tabulates characteristics of employers who responded in different ways to Q2. Establishments in column 1 only allow phased retirement before official retirement, those in the third column only allow phased retirement after official retirement, and those in column 5 permit either type of phased retirement. For example, the first entry in column 1 indicates that of those establishments that only allowed phased retirement *before* official retirement, three percent were in the construction industry. Similarly, the first entry in column 3 indicates that of those establishments that only allowed phased retirement *after* official retirement, one percent was in the construction industry. By implication, the industry percentages in column 1 sum to 100 percent as do the industry

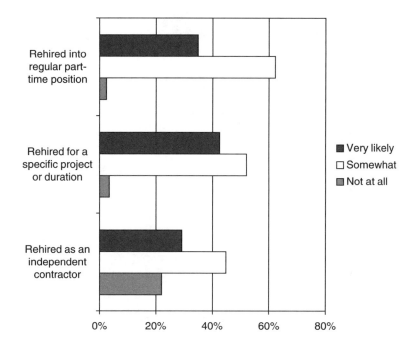

Figure 8-3. Possible employment arrangements for rehired retirees.
Source: Authors' calculations.

percentages in columns 3 and 5. Looking at the remaining industries, we see that industrial composition is quite similar across the three columns. The major exception is the service sector. In health, education, and social services, phased retirement is more likely to only be permitted before official retirement. The opposite is true in other services, where establishments tend to prefer what we shall term 'retire-rehire'. The asterisk next to the column 1 entry indicates that for both of these service industries, the difference between the averages in columns 1 and 3 is statistically significant at a 5 percent level. Table 8-2 also reveals an interesting regional pattern. Establishments in the South tend to be particularly likely to offer retire/rehire, while those in the West lean toward reduced hours before official retirement. Such results make one wonder whether this phenomenon is more a matter of taste than economic fundamentals.

The results on establishment and organization size strongly suggest that the phenomenon is not simply a matter of taste. The size composition of the establishments in columns 1 and 3 are similar (none of the differences are statistically significant at a 5 percent level), but results in column 5 reveal that small establishments are more likely to say that phased retirement is allowed, both before and after phased retirement. As establishment size increases, employers move away from this 'anything goes' response.

TABLE 8-2 Response to Questions About Timing of Hours Reduction Relative to Official Retirement

| | When phased retirement may occur in relation to official retirement | | | | | |
| | Before | | After | | Either | |
Variable	Mean (1)	S.D. (2)	Mean (3)	S.D. (4)	Mean (5)	S.D. (6)
A. Industry of establishment						
Construction	0.03	0.01	0.01	0.01	0.02	0.01
Manufacturing	0.12	0.03	0.14	0.04	0.15	0.02
Transportation, communications, and utilities	0.03	0.02	0.02	0.02	0.04	0.01
Wholesale and retail trade	0.11	0.03	0.06	0.03	0.14	0.02
Finance	0.03	0.02	0.04	0.02	0.07	0.01
Health, education, and social services	0.18*	0.03	0.04	0.02	0.17	0.02
Other services	0.39	0.04	0.64*	0.06	0.36	0.02
Public administration	0.11	0.03	0.06	0.03	0.05	0.01
B. Region of establishment						
East	0.19	0.03	0.13	0.04	0.18	0.02
Central	0.31	0.04	0.36	0.06	0.30	0.02
South	0.24	0.04	0.40*	0.06	0.30	0.02
West	0.26*	0.04	0.11	0.04	0.22	0.02
C. Size of establishment						
Fewer than 50 employees	0.27	0.04	0.34	0.06	0.46	0.02
50–99 employees	0.29	0.04	0.29	0.06	0.24	0.02

	(1)		(3)		(5)	
100–249 employees	0.21	0.03	0.20	0.05	0.19	0.02
250–999 employees	0.15	0.03	0.13	0.04	0.08	0.01
1,000 or more employees	0.07	0.02	0.04	0.02	0.04	0.01
D. Other establishment characteristics						
Establishment is part of a larger organization	0.43	0.04	0.61*	0.06	0.28†	0.02
With fewer than 1,000 employees	0.14	0.03	0.33*	0.06	0.11	0.01
With 1,000 or more employees	0.30	0.04	0.28	0.06	0.17	0.02
Establishment is non-profit	0.58	0.04	0.65	0.06	0.44†	0.02
E. Pension type						
DB only	0.32	0.04	0.34	0.06	0.20†	0.02
DC only	0.36	0.04	0.29	0.06	0.51†	0.02
Both DB and DC	0.16	0.03	0.25	0.05	0.10	0.01
No pension, NA	0.16	0.03	0.12	0.04	0.18	0.02
F. Characteristics of workforce						
Proportion of employees that are white collar	0.63	0.03	0.68	0.04	0.62	0.01
Proportion of white collar that are union	0.23	0.03	0.25	0.05	0.12†	0.01
Proportion of white collar that work part time	0.08	0.01	0.11	0.02	0.11	0.01
G. Human resource policies						
Flexible starting time is possible	0.63*	0.04	0.40	0.06	0.73†	0.02
Job sharing is possible	0.46	0.04	0.42	0.06	0.51	0.02
Uses temp, contract, or contingent workers	0.51	0.04	0.59	0.06	0.43	0.02

Source: Authors' calculations.

* indicates that the mean in column 1(3) is greater than the mean in column 3(1) at a 5 percent significance level.
† indicates that the mean in column 5 is different from both the column 1 and 3 means at a 5 percent significance level.

Perhaps bureaucracy plays a role in the results: that is, effective functioning of large establishments may require formal rules and procedures, whereas small establishments may have more flexible policies and thereby be more likely to permit hour reductions either before or after official retirement.

This idea gains support from the data on organization size. Organization size differs from establishment size because, as noted above, an establishment may belong to larger organizations, for example, a school building may belong to a larger school district. Fully 61 percent of the column 3 establishments are part of a larger organization, while only 28 percent of the column 5 establishments belong to a larger organization. As indicated by the dagger (†) to the right of the 0.28 entries, this column 5 average is statistically different from both the column 1 and column 3 average. Thus, establishments that are part of a larger organization are less likely to say 'anything goes.' Such evidence is certainly consistent with the idea that bureaucracy plays a role in these results; establishments that are part of larger organizations are presumably more likely to have formal rules and procedures governing the path into retirement.

Part E of Table 8-2 examines pensions. Since pensions have been thought to be a key determinant of employer phased retirement policy, considerable effort was devoted to obtain accurate pension information. Respondents were asked whether older white-collar workers were covered by a traditional DB plan, a cash balance plan, a DC plan, or something else. In addition, respondents were given a list of possible pension types (401 (K), ESOP, etc.). We used this information to assess whether the establishment had a DB or DC pension. For example, if the respondent told us that the pension was a cash balance plan, then regardless of what the respondent said about the type of plan, the pension was classified as a DB pension. Since many firms have multiple plans (e.g. a traditional DB as well as a 401 (K)), the interviewers also sought information on each of the plans. Some respondents were able to provide detailed answers; others had difficulty remembering their establishment's pension but we pursued these where possible.[14]

From the second hypothesis, we expect retire rehire to be more likely in establishments with DB plans. In fact, columns 1 and 3 are quite similar. While 34 percent of the 'after' establishments in column 3 had a DB plan and no DC plan, 32 percent of the 'before' establishments had this arrangement. In contrast, a significant difference appears in column 5 where only 20 percent of the 'before or after' establishments were classified as having only a DB plan. A mirror image of this result is found for establishments that only had a DC plan; once again the column 1 and column 3 results are roughly similar while a significantly larger 51 percent of the column 5 'before and after' establishments have only a DC plan. Thus, DC plans are evidently associated with greater flexibility in the timing of phased retirement. Of course, this could be related to the results on establishment and organization size. DC plans are often found in small establishments and organizations.

Part F of Table 8-2 examines selected characteristics of the establishment's workforce. The percentage of all employees who are white-collar is roughly the same across the three columns as is the percentage of white-collar workers who are part-time. That is not, however, the case for the percentage of white-collar workers who are covered by a collective bargaining agreement. For the 'before' establishments in column 1, an average of 23 percent of the white-collar workers were covered by a collective bargaining agreement. This number is almost the same (25 percent) for the column 3 'after' establishments.[15] It is, however, only 12 percent for the 'before or after' establishments in column 5. This is, of course, quite similar to the results for DB pensions; it may simply reflect the fact that unions often negotiate DB pensions.

It is reasonable to expect flexibility in the timing of phased retirement to be associated with flexibility in the timing of when people come to work. Both types of flexibility imply an openness to alternative work schedules. Part G of Table 8-2 examines selected human resource policies of the establishment, where the data show that establishments where white-collar workers have flexible starting times are particularly likely to indicate that phased retirement can occur either before or after official retirement (column 5). Further, they are much less likely to indicate that phased retirement can only occur after official retirement. One might similarly expect establishments that permit job sharing to be flexible in the timing of phased retirement. In fact, although the results on job sharing exhibit the same basic pattern as those for flexible starting times, the differences in column averages are not statistically significant. Finally, the survey asked whether in the last 12 months, the establishment has used temporary, contract, or contingent workers in white-collar positions. In line with the first hypothesis, it is reasonable to expect such establishments to be more open to retire-rehire. In such cases the employee can essentially return to the establishment as a temporary worker. While the Table 8-2 data are consistent with this, once again the differences in column averages are not statistically significant.

To evaluate whether these univariate results are robust to controls for other variables, we also estimated three Probit models with different dependent variables.[16] Specifically, we examine whether the employer only allows phased retirement before official retirement; whether the employer allows phased retirement both before and after official retirement; and whether the employer only allows phased retirement after official retirement.[17] Our goal is to understand why some employers prefer that phased retirement occur before or after official retirement, so we focus on establishments that answered 'yes' or 'in some cases' to Q1.[18]

Rather than focusing on specific results, here we summarize findings and provide detailed estimates in the Appendix for interested readers. One interesting finding pertains to whether the establishment is part of a larger organization; other things equal, the probability that an establishment *only* allows phased retirement before (after) official retirement is particularly high when the establishment is part of an organization with more than 1,000 (fewer than 1,000) employees. If an establishment is not part of a larger organization, then it is more likely to respond that phased retirement can occur *either* before or after official retirement. Another finding is that the economic and organizational environment within which the establishment operates are relatively unimportant; indeed most are not statistically significant at conventional significance levels.

Table 8-3 presents simulated probabilities for key variables assuming a base case where the establishment is not part of a larger organization and all other explanatory variables are set at the sample means. In this case, the probability that the establishment requires that phased retirement occur before official retirement is 15.5 percent, requires that phased retirement occur after is 5.1 percent, and permits both before and after is 76 percent.[19]

Now suppose this establishment were integrated into a larger organization with fewer than 1,000 employees. According to Table 8-4, this change would increase the 'before' probability from 15.5 to 16.6 percent, the 'after' probability from 5.1 to 13.8 percent, and decrease the 'either' probability from 76 to 63.2 percent. In essence the establishment moves away from an 'anything goes' attitude toward rules governing the timing of phased retirement. If the organization had more than 1,000 employees, then the increase in the 'before' probability would be even greater. This supports the view that very large organizations tend to be bureaucratic with employment regulated through a set of formal rules. Not only do such organizations avoid phased retirement (Hutchens and Grace-Martin 2004), but also the procedural requirements that surround hiring of new workers may lead them to avoid rehiring retired workers.

We also explore variables that represent minimum hours constraints. We expect establishments with flexible starting times and job sharing to be

TABLE 8-3 Simulated Effects of Organization Size from Probit Models

| | *Probability of phased retirement* | | |
	Only before official retirement	*Before and after official retirement*	*Only after official retirement*
Establishment is not part of a larger organization	0.155	0.760	0.051
Establishment is part of a larger organization:			
With fewer than 1,000 employees	0.166	0.632	0.138
With 1,000 or more employees	0.247	0.674	0.052

Source: Authors' calculations.

TABLE 8-4 Simulated Effects of Part-Time Percentage from Probit Models

	Probability of phased retirement		
	Only before official retirement	Before and after official retirement	Only after official retirement
Percentage of White Collar that Work Part Time:			
0 percent	0.224	0.680	0.061
10 percent	0.148	0.754	0.064
20 percent	0.106	0.803	0.061
30 percent	0.086	0.833	0.052
40 percent	0.080	0.848	0.039
50 percent	0.088	0.850	0.026

Source: Authors' calculations.

more open to hours reductions before official retirement, and establishments that use temporary workers to favor retire-rehire outcomes. However, our estimated models suggest a somewhat different relationship: thus we find that establishments with flexible starting times are more likely to offer phased retirement *either* before *or* after official retirement. Further, after controlling for other variables, there is a nonlinear relationship between the percentage of employees working part-time and the timing of phased retirement. In other words, establishments with only a few or no part-time workers tend to favor hour reductions *before* official retirement, but as the percentage of part-time workers rises, the establishment tends to become more open to hours reductions either before or after official retirement. Table 8-4 depicts this relationship, using the same simulation approach employed in Table 8-3.[20] This unanticipated finding may be explained by the view that establishments with few part-time workers are willing to have retirees return to work but not as part-timers. Since most work schedules in the establishment are full-time, a retiree who wants to return will have to work a full-time schedule. If such an establishment were to accommodate an hour reduction by an older worker, then it will either do so before official retirement or not at all.

We also explore the type of pension offered by establishments and link it to key outcomes of interest. As we expected, establishments with DB benefit pensions (regardless of whether they have a DC pension) were more likely to offer opportunities for reduced hours after official retirement. This result is only statistically significant for establishments that combine DB and DC plans. Table 8-5 illustrates the magnitudes using methods similar to Tables 8-3 and 8-4. The majority of establishments with only DC plans allow phased retirement both before and after retirement, and those establishments with DB plans are more likely to offer phased retirement only after

TABLE 8-5 Simulated Effects of Pensions from Probit Models

	Probability of phased retirement		
	Only before official retirement	*Before and after official retirement*	*Only after official retirement*
Defined contribution only	0.165	0.761	0.044
Defined benefit only	0.193	0.720	0.051
Both DB and DC	0.202	0.615	0.138
Cannot classify pension	0.166	0.821	0.010
No pension	0.155	0.700	0.113

Source: Authors' calculations.

retirement. Curiously, these establishments are also more likely to require that hour reductions occur before official retirement; this effect is not statistically significant but it is interesting. In an establishment with a DB plan, workers can reduce hours before they officially retire if (*a*) they supplement salary with pension benefits and are older than the DB plan's normal retirement age, or (*b*) they do not supplement salary with pension benefits. Perhaps these establishments with DB plans are avoiding the legal conundrum of deciding what constitutes a bona fide retirement. In effect, one either takes phased retirement before official retirement or not at all. And if salary is to be supplemented with pension benefits, then the worker simply must have reached the normal retirement age in the pension. While this simple rule avoids the above noted legal issues associated with paying pensions to rehired retirees, it probably also has the effect of discouraging phased retirement.

In summary, our key empirical finding is that many employers are open to hours reductions both before and after official retirement. This 'anything goes' position is particularly likely in establishments that are not part of a large organization, do not have unions, and have DC pensions. Of course, we suspect that that does not really mean 'anything goes;' rather, employers may have clear preferences when it comes to phased retirement options for specific workers. By this argument, employer preferences about the timing of phased retirement pertain to a specific individual doing a specific job. What matters less is the establishment characteristics and what matters more, the characteristic of the individual worker, the pension, and the job.

Our two hypotheses provide a partial explanation for what is going on in the multivariate analysis. Both pensions and existing employment arrangements influence the timing of hour reductions relative to official retirement, but not in precisely the way anticipated by the hypotheses. Moreover, we found that establishments with few part-timers and that are part of large organizations tend to prefer that phased retirement occur before official retirement.

Conclusions

This chapter asks why firms might only permit phased retirement after its workers officially retire. Our answer proves complicated. First, those employers who permit some form of phased retirement do not usually restrict it to rehiring of retirees. In fact, most employers say they are open to informally-arranged hours reductions both before and after official retirement. Second, we were surprised to find that neither univariate nor multivariate statistical methods provide strong support for the claim that either pensions or existing employment arrangements drive an establishment level preference for retire-rehire. Also surprising was the result on organization size; all indications are that if an organization with more than 1000 employees permits some form of phased retirement, then it will tend to *not* prefer retire/rehire.

These results, along with the fact that employers favor informal arrangements, lead us to suspect that the real preference for retire/rehire is at the individual rather than the establishment level. In many establishments, both pensions and existing employment arrangements differ across jobs. Some workers are covered by DB plans while others are not. Some workers are in jobs that employ temporary and contingent workers, while others are not. For this reason, it might not make sense to have an establishment-wide preference for retire/rehire. Rather, employers and employees may be interested in reducing hours in ways that meet their job and worker-specific needs. This could mean reduced hours before official retirement for one worker, but after official retirement for another.

It is likely that such individually negotiated arrangements will become an ever-more important element of the evolving retirement paradigm. Like Japanese employers, Western employers often want to be selective about which older workers have an opportunity for continued work at reduced hours. This selectivity has the advantage of producing employment relationships beneficial to both employers and employees. It might also have the disadvantage of perceived inequity; thus a given employer might grant apparently similar workers very different opportunities for continued work.

Government policy might enhance this labor market flexibility by clarifying the meaning of a bona fide retirement. As noted above, it is legal for workers to retire, begin receiving DB pension benefits, and then be rehired by their former employer as long as he had reached the plan's normal retirement age. Further, even if he were younger than this age, the transition would be legal so long as the worker's retirement was bona fide. Unfortunately the IRS provides no clear definition of what constitutes a bona fide retirement, and employers might fear penalties for an incorrect interpretation of the regulations. Clarifying these rules could reduce uncertainty and thereby facilitate efficient transactions, a result of potentially large importance for large organizations likely to be targets of government scrutiny.

TABLE 8-A1 Probit Analysis of Employer Response to Question About Timing of Hours Reduction Relative to Official Retirement (Dependent variable equals 1 if response is 'Only Before')

Variable	Model 1		Model 2		Model 3		Model 4	
Industry of establishment								
Manufacturing	0.172	(0.30)	0.114	(0.20)	0.224	(0.38)	0.154	(0.26)
Transport, communication, and utilities	−0.155	(0.24)	−0.126	(0.19)	−0.102	(0.16)	−0.085	(0.13)
Wholesale and retail trade	0.005	(0.01)	0.048	(0.08)	0.061	(0.10)	0.085	(0.14)
Finance	−0.687	(1.00)	−0.570	(0.82)	−0.598	(0.86)	−0.503	(0.72)
Health, education, and social services	0.250	(0.43)	0.319	(0.55)	0.335	(0.56)	0.378	(0.64)
Other services	−0.263	(0.44)	−0.155	(0.26)	−0.191	(0.32)	−0.103	(0.17)
Public administration	0.167	(0.27)	0.249	(0.40)	0.213	(0.34)	0.287	(0.45)
Region								
Central	−0.211	(1.13)	−0.249	(1.31)	−0.219	(1.17)	−0.254	(1.32)
South	−0.230	(1.18)	−0.340	(1.68)	−0.236	(1.20)	−0.343	(1.69)
West	0.013	(0.06)	0.006	(0.03)	0.011	(0.06)	0.008	(0.04)
Establishment size								
50–99 employees	0.195	(0.98)	0.230	(1.13)	0.199	(1.00)	0.236	(1.15)
100–249 employees	0.243	(1.32)	0.269	(1.40)	0.241	(1.30)	0.270	(1.41)
250–999 employees	0.322	(1.59)	0.350	(1.64)	0.303	(1.48)	0.345	(1.61)
1,000 or more employees	0.157	(0.52)	0.179	(0.56)	0.122	(0.40)	0.161	(0.50)
Establishment is part of a larger organization								
With fewer than 1,000 workers	0.140	(0.57)	0.063	(0.25)	0.116	(0.47)	0.046	(0.18)
With more than 1,000 workers	0.378	(2.34)*	0.346	(2.11)*	0.358	(2.20)*	0.331	(2.01)*
Other establishment characteristics								
Establishment is non-profit	0.332	(1.74)	0.356	(1.80)	0.293	(1.51)	0.323	(1.60)

	(1)		(2)		(3)		(4)	
Prop. that are white collar (WC)	0.001	(0.32)	0.001	(0.30)	0.001	(0.22)	0.001	(0.25)
Prop. of WC that are union	0.002	(0.89)	0.001	(0.45)	0.002	(0.82)	0.001	(0.41)
proxies for minimum hours constraints								
Prop. of WC that work part time			−0.033	(2.98)†			−0.033	(2.90)†
Square of prop. part time			0.000	(2.83)†			0.000	(2.77)†
Permits job sharing			−0.052	(0.37)			−0.046	(0.32)
Permits flexible start time			−0.313	(2.08)*			−0.317	(2.09)*
Uses temporary, contract, or contingent workers			0.156	(1.08)			0.137	(0.94)
Pensions								
DB only					0.165	(1.02)	0.106	(0.64)
Both DB and DC					0.151	(0.75)	0.140	(0.67)
Cannot classify pension					0.047	(0.15)	0.005	(0.02)
No pension, NA					−0.072	(0.32)	−0.042	(0.18)
Constant	−1.214	(2.01)*	−0.915	(1.51)	−1.284	(2.08)*	−0.965	(1.56)
Number of observations	552		552		552		552	
Likelihood ratio chi-squared test (P-value)	32.50	(0.03)	49.05	(0.00)	34.10	(0.06)	49.87	(0.01)
Pseudo R-squared	0.059		0.089		0.062		0.091	

Source: Authors' calculations. The excluded industry is construction, the excluded region is East, the excluded establishment size is 20–49, and the excluded pension is defined contribution. Absolute value of z-statistic shown in parentheses.

* denotes significance at the 5 percent level;
† denotes significance at the 1 percent level.

TABLE 8-A2 Probit Analysis of Employer Response to Question About Timing of Hours Reduction Relative to Official Retirement (Dependent variable equals 1 if response is 'Either Before or After')

Variable	Model 1		Model 2		Model 3		Model 4	
Industry of establishment								
Manufacturing	−0.017	(0.03)	0.038	(0.08)	−0.062	(0.13)	0.002	(0.00)
Transport, communication, and utilities	0.346	(0.62)	0.362	(0.64)	0.290	(0.52)	0.297	(0.53)
Wholesale and retail trade	0.279	(0.55)	0.235	(0.47)	0.238	(0.47)	0.203	(0.40)
Finance	0.679	(1.19)	0.532	(0.92)	0.588	(1.03)	0.430	(0.74)
Health, education, and social services	0.126	(0.25)	0.072	(0.14)	0.053	(0.11)	0.020	(0.04)
Other services	0.257	(0.50)	0.188	(0.37)	0.165	(0.32)	0.097	(0.19)
Public administration	0.088	(0.16)	0.030	(0.05)	0.028	(0.05)	−0.042	(0.08)
Region								
Central	0.017	(0.10)	0.038	(0.21)	0.006	(0.03)	0.025	(0.14)
South	0.017	(0.09)	0.139	(0.74)	0.019	(0.10)	0.145	(0.76)
West	−0.044	(0.23)	−0.041	(0.21)	−0.055	(0.29)	−0.053	(0.27)
Establishment size								
50–99 employees	−0.064	(0.35)	−0.086	(0.45)	−0.081	(0.44)	−0.105	(0.55)
100–249 employees	−0.185	(1.11)	−0.178	(1.02)	−0.183	(1.09)	−0.183	(1.04)
250–999 employees	−0.499	(2.75)†	−0.486	(2.56)*	−0.503	(2.74)†	−0.510	(2.66)†
1,000 or more employees	0.059	(0.21)	0.076	(0.25)	0.126	(0.43)	0.120	(0.39)
Establishment is part of a larger organization								
With fewer than 1,000 workers	−0.445	(2.07)*	−0.402	(1.81)	−0.408	(1.88)	−0.371	(1.65)
With more than 1,000 workers	−0.295	(1.96)	−0.279	(1.83)	−0.267	(1.76)	−0.257	(1.67)

	(1)		(2)		(3)		(4)	
Other establishment characteristics								
Establishment is non-profit	−0.249	(1.42)	−0.305	(1.68)	−0.181	(1.01)	−0.249	(1.34)
Prop. that are white collar (WC)	0.000	(0.10)	0.001	(0.35)	0.001	(0.25)	0.001	(0.43)
Prop. of WC that are union	−0.003	(1.46)	−0.002	(1.03)	−0.003	(1.36)	−0.002	(0.93)
Proxies for minimum hours constraints								
Prop. of WC that work part time			0.024	(2.37)*			0.024	(2.42)*
Square of prop. part time			−0.000	(1.91)			−0.000	(1.88)
Permits job sharing			0.163	(1.26)			0.164	(1.25)
Permits flexible start time			0.392	(2.83)†			0.403	(2.87)†
Uses temporary, contract, or contingent Workers			−0.263	(2.00)*			−0.232	(1.73)
Pensions								
DB only					−0.201	(1.33)	−0.127	(0.83)
Both DB and DC					−0.431	(2.32)*	−0.419	(2.21)*
Cannot classify pension					0.095	(0.32)	0.209	(0.67)
No pension, NA					−0.131	(0.65)	−0.187	(0.89)
Constant	0.793	(1.54)	0.425	(0.81)	0.921	(1.77)	0.520	(0.99)
Number of observations	552		552		552		552	
Likelihood ratio chi-squared test (*P*-value)	38.46	(0.01)	61.33	(0.00)	44.89	(0.00)	67.69	(0.00)
Pseudo *R*-squared	0.058		0.092		0.068		0.102	

Notes: See Appendix Table 8-1.

TABLE 8-A3 Probit Analysis of Employer Response to Question About Timing of Hours Reduction Relative to Official Retirement (Dependent variable equals 1 if response is 'Only After')

Variable	Model 1		Model 2		Model 3		Model 4	
Industry of establishment								
Manufacturing	−0.170	(0.28)	−0.231	(0.38)	−0.195	(0.32)	−0.270	(0.44)
Transport, communication, and utilities	−0.341	(0.49)	−0.475	(0.67)	−0.322	(0.46)	−0.422	(0.60)
Wholesale and retail trade	−0.612	(0.95)	−0.653	(1.01)	−0.625	(0.96)	−0.672	(1.03)
Finance	−0.294	(0.42)	−0.301	(0.42)	−0.227	(0.32)	−0.202	(0.28)
Health, education, and social services	−0.847	(1.28)	−0.896	(1.35)	−0.842	(1.27)	−0.917	(1.38)
Other services	−0.016	(0.02)	−0.082	(0.13)	0.059	(0.09)	0.012	(0.02)
Public administration	−0.490	(0.67)	−0.531	(0.73)	−0.539	(0.73)	−0.570	(0.76)
Region								
Central	0.392	(1.49)	0.439	(1.60)	0.446	(1.65)	0.492	(1.73)
South	0.440	(1.63)	0.410	(1.45)	0.457	(1.64)	0.419	(1.42)
West	0.125	(0.43)	0.154	(0.51)	0.160	(0.53)	0.185	(0.59)
Establishment size								
50–99 employees	−0.235	(0.88)	−0.245	(0.88)	−0.189	(0.69)	−0.195	(0.68)
100–249 employees	−0.034	(0.15)	−0.109	(0.46)	−0.030	(0.13)	−0.105	(0.43)
250–999 employees	0.407	(1.74)	0.337	(1.38)	0.472	(1.96)	0.428	(1.70)
1,000 or more employees	−0.550	(1.12)	−0.636	(1.26)	−0.668	(1.27)	−0.724	(1.36)
Establishment is part of a larger organization								
With fewer than 1,000 workers	0.564*	(2.28)	0.547*	(2.14)	0.562*	(2.22)	0.547*	(2.09)
With more than 1,000 workers	−0.010	(0.05)	−0.004	(0.02)	−0.009	(0.04)	0.007	(0.03)

	(1)		(2)		(3)		(4)	
Other establishment characteristics								
Establishment is non-profit	−0.059	(0.23)	0.021	(0.08)	−0.128	(0.48)	−0.017	(0.06)
Prop. that are white collar (WC)	−0.003	(0.89)	−0.003	(1.14)	−0.003	(1.06)	−0.004	(1.30)
Prop. of WC that are union	0.003	(1.17)	0.003	(1.09)	0.003	(0.99)	0.003	(0.87)
Proxies for minimum hours constraints								
Prop. of WC that work part time			0.009	(0.54)			0.006	(0.33)
Square of prop. part time			−0.000	(0.91)			−0.000	(0.87)
Permits job sharing			−0.306	(1.67)			−0.351	(1.86)
Permits flexible start time			−0.212	(1.14)			−0.248	(1.28)
Uses temporary, contract, or contingent workers			0.288	(1.63)			0.264	(1.44)
Pensions								
DB only					0.126	(0.60)	0.070	(0.32)
Both DB and DC					0.622	(2.58)†	0.617	(2.48)*
Cannot classify pension					−0.414	(0.78)	−0.612	(1.08)
No pension, NA					0.397	(1.44)	0.497	(1.73)
Constant	−1.349	(2.09)*	−1.137	(1.73)	−1.522	(2.34)*	−1.249	(1.88)
Number of observations	552		552		552		552	
Likelihood ratio chi-squared test (*P* value)	34.46	(0.02)	44.35	(0.01)	43.77	(0.01)	55.26	(0.00)
Pseudo *R*-squared	0.101		0.130		0.129		0.163	

Notes: See Appendix Table 8-1.

Endnotes

1. See *http://www.asahi.com/english/business/TKY200406100152.html* We thank Olivia Mitchell for pointing out this article.
2. This is not to say there will be no effect; the half-time worker usually contributes less to the account and thereby accrues a smaller pension asset than an equivalent full-time worker.
3. This is the essence of the key regulations, but they are quire complex. For example, in one type of DC plan (a money purchase plan) benefits are treated just as are traditional DB benefits. For a more complete treatment see Fields and Hutchens (2002) and Penner et al. (2002).
4. Hypotheses 1 and 2 are formulated at the establishment level, but they could just as easily apply to the individual. For example, if temporary and contract workers take on tasks similar to those of a current employee, then phased retirement by that employee may more easily be accommodated after official retirement. Similarly, different workers in the same establishment can have different types of pension coverage; some may be covered by a 401(k) plan, others by a traditional DB pension, and still others by both plans. In such a situation, the employer might prefer that some workers move to part-time before official retirement, while other workers make a similar shift after official retirement.
5. The sample universe was the Dun and Bradstreet Strategic Marketing Record for December 2000. These data primarily come from credit checks, although information is also obtained from the United States Postal Service, banks, newspapers, yellow pages and other public records. In order to ensure adequate numbers of large establishments, the sample was stratified by establishment size; most of the results are weighted to ensure representative samples.
6. The 1999 Census Bureau County Business Patterns indicates that, excluding government, railroads and the self-employed, approximately 15 percent of all establishments have 20 or more employees and 75 percent of all employees work in establishments with 20 or more employees.
7. Interviews were conducted with a Computer Assisted Telephone Interviewing (CATI) system, thereby permitting an interview to be completed over several telephone calls. The median number of telephone calls required to complete an interview was 10, with 10 percent of the interviews requiring 30 or more calls to complete.
8. The response rate was 64 percent in the Educational Quality of the Workforce National Employers Survey administered by the United States Bureau of the Census as a telephone survey in August and September 1994 to a nationally representative sample of private establishments with more than 20 employees (see Lynch and Black 1998). The response rate was 65.5 percent in Osterman's (1992) telephone survey of establishments with more than 50 employees (see Osterman (1994). Holzer and Neumark (1999) reported a response rate of 67 percent for establishments that were successfully screened in a telephone survey undertaken between June 1992 and May 1994.
9. If the respondent said that part-time could not be worked out, the survey made certain by asking whether part-year might be possible.
10. Application of weights has virtually no effect on these numbers.

11. These numbers differ from those in Hutchens (2003) because Table 8-1 includes respondents in the 'not specified' category.

12. Our results indicate more availability of phased retirement than the Watson Wyatt (1999) study. We have no ready explanation for the difference, though the two surveys undoubtedly ask different questions and the samples are surely distinct (our sample appears to have more smaller organizations). The American Association of Retired Persons (AARP) (2000) also suggests that their response rate may have been low.

13. Small establishments may employ only a handful of people over 55, so if no one was interested in phased retirement, the right answer to the question would be 'no' regardless of the opportunity. This is less likely in large establishments with more workers age 55+. In fact, for establishments with 500 or more employees, the comparable percentages are 67 percent of the 'before' employers and 71 percent of the 'after' employers.

14. For example, one respondent told us that the pension was the Arkansas teacher retirement plan. In that case we checked with Arkansas to find out whether the plan was a DB or DC plan.

15. Health insurance may also play a role. Therefore employers who required that phased retirement occur after official retirement were, in contrast to those who required that it occur before official retirement, particularly likely to provide retiree health insurance and particularly unlikely to provide health insurance to part-timers. These differences were not statistically significant but the pattern suggests that employers who practice retire-rehire tend to provide health insurance in a way that reinforces the practice.

16. Results using an ordered Probit model indicated that the data did not follow the hierarchical structure imposing by the ordering so we rely on the simple Probits here.

17. As is the case with any survey, some respondents did not answer all of the questions. In our multivariate work we use listwise deletion of observations with missing data. As a result, the analysis is based on 552 rather than 723 observations. See Allison (2002) for a discussion of the advantages of listwise deletion. Hutchens and Grace-Martin (2004) uses multiple imputation to address missing data issues in this survey. Those results indicated that missing data does not seriously bias coefficients.

18. In statistical terms, this can be viewed as a problem involving a marginal and conditional probability. Thus, $Pr(Y_{2i} = k) = Pr(Y_{2i} = k|Y_{1i} = 1)Pr(Y_{1i} = 1)$, where $Pr(Y_{2i} = k)$ is the probability that Y_{2i} equals k with $k = 0,1,2$ (the three answers to Q2) for establishment i; $Pr(Y_{2i} = k|Y_{1i} = 1)$ is the probability that Y_{2i} equals k conditional on Y_{1i} equals 1 (the 'conditional probability'), and $Pr(Y_{1i} = 1)$ is the probability that Y_{1i} equals 1 (the 'marginal probability'), where Y_{1i} equals 1 when the answer to Q1 is 'yes' or 'in some cases.' This paper estimates the conditional probability, while Hutchens and Grace-Martin (2004) estimate the marginal probability.

19. For purposes of this illustration, probabilities are predicted with the 'before' and 'either' Probit, and the 'after' probability calculated as a residual. Computations were done this way because the 'before' and 'either' categories have

larger sample sizes. If we use the 'after' Probit for predictions, qualitative results are similar.
20. The table stops at 50 percent part-time because very few establishments in the sample exceed that percentage.

References

AARP (2000). *Easing the Transition: Phased and Partial Retirement Programs: Highlights 1999.* AARP Report. Washington, DC: AARP.

Allison, Paul D. (2002). *Missing Data*, California: Sage Publications.

Chen, Jennjou (2003). 'The Part-Time Labor Market for Older Workers', Working Paper, Cornell University.

Fields, Vivian and Robert Hutchens (2002). 'Regulatory Obstacles to Phased Retirement in the For-profit Sector', *Benefits Quarterly*, (18): 35–41.

Gustman, Alan L. and Thomas L. Steinmeier (1983). 'Minimum Hours Constraints and Retirement Behavior', *Contemporary Policy Issues*, (3): 77–91.

Holzer, Harry and David Neumark (1999). 'Are Affirmation Action Hires Less Qualified? Evidence from Employer-employee Data on New Hires', *Journal of Labor Economics*, (17): 534–69.

Hurd, Michael D. (1996). 'The Effect of Labor Market Rigidities on the Labor Force Behavior of Older Workers', in David A. Wise (ed.), *The Economics of Aging*. Chicago: University of Chicago Press, pp. 11–56.

Hutchens, Robert M. (2003). 'The Cornell Study of Employer Phased Retirement Policies: A Report on Key Findings', Working Paper. Ithaca, NY: School of Industrial and Labor Relations, Cornell University.

—— and Jennjou Chen (2004). 'The Role of Employers in Phased Retirement: Opportunities for Phased Retirement Among White-Collar Workers', Working Paper. Ithaca, NY: School of Industrial and Labor Relations, Cornell University.

—— and Karen Grace-Martin (2004). 'Who Among White-Collar Workers Has an Opportunity for Phased Retirement? Establishment Characteristics'. Ithaca, NY: School of Industrial and Labor Relations, Cornell University.

Lynch, Lisa M. and Sandra E. Black (1998). 'Beyond the Incidence of Employer-provided Training', *Industrial and Labor Relations Review*, (52): 64–81.

Penner, Rudolph G., Pamela Perun and C. Eugene Steuerle (2002). 'Legal and Institutional Impediments to Partial Retirement and Part-time Work by Older Workers'. Urban Institute Research Report. Washington, DC: Urban Institute.

Osterman, Paul (1992). 'How Common Is Workplace Transformation and Who Adopts It?', *Industrial and Labor Relations Review*, (47): 173–88.

Purcell, Patrick (2004). 'Older Workers: Employment and Retirement Trends', Pension Research Council Working Paper, The Wharton School.

Quinn, Joseph F., Richard V. Burkhauser and Daniel A. Myers (1990). *Passing the Torch: The Influence of Economic Incentives on Work and Retirement*. Kalamazoo: W. E. Upjohn Institute.

Rebick, Marcus E. (1995). 'Rewards in the Afterlife: Late Career Job Placements as Incentives in the Japanese Firm', *Journal of the Japanese and International Economies*, 9(1): 1–28.

Ruhm, Christopher J. (1990). 'Bridge Jobs and Partial Retirement', *Journal of Labor Economics*, 8 (4): 482–501.

United States General Accounting Office (USGAO) (2001). *Older Workers: Demographic Trends Pose Challenges for Employers and Workers.* Report to the Ranking Minority Member, Subcommittee on Employer-Employee Relations, Committee on Education and the Workforce, House of Representatives, GAO-02–85. Washington, DC: USGAO.

Watson Wyatt Worldwide (1999). *Phased Retirement: Reshaping the End of Work.* Bethesda, MD: Watson Wyatt Worldwide.

Part III
Managing the Retirement Promise

Chapter 9

Educating Pension Plan Participants

William J. Arnone

Individuals who do not understand financial mathematics, expected rates of return on investments, and the level of income needed to meet consumption expectations in retirement, are very likely to have considerably less retirement income than they desire. Better financial education is necessary if workers are to achieve their retirement objectives, and financial literacy is key to informed retirement saving decisions. A central issue worthy of debate is who should pay for financial education and how it should be provided.

A growing awareness of the need for pension education is partly due to the rise of defined contribution (DC) plans. As Mitchell and Schieber (1998) note, 'pension education is becoming increasingly important to sponsors of DC plans. Participants vary according to the types of information they need and can process regarding investment risk, return and related issues. Examining alternative approaches to pension education reveals that the way pension education is presented can have a large impact on pension plan members' investment behavior.' But education is also urgently needed for participants in defined benefit (DB) plans, as they must determine if their pensions are sufficient to meet retirement needs, or if they should contribute to supplemental retirement plans and save outside of tax-deferred plans.

It is my contention that firms and plan sponsors have an obligation to provide financial education in conjunction with their retirement plans. A practical definition of employer-sponsored participant education is a program that helps employees develop skills to make informed decisions and take action to improve their financial well-being in retirement. This definition incorporates: the responsibility to help individuals based on their status as employees of an organization; provide recipients with skill development, which may include either new competencies or the enhancement of existing competencies; enable participants to make decisions about issues; provide a basis of accurate, unbiased information for such decisions; take an action-oriented stance and thereby attempt to affect behavior; and seeks the long-term result of improved financial well-being.

What Types of Programs Have Employers Provided?

Employer-sponsored education programs for plan participants are an out-growth of pre-retirement planning programs that were offered by many large (i.e. at least 1,000 employees) employers in the 1980s. Pre-retirement planning programs were typically limited to employees who were within a few years of being able to retire under their employer's DB pension plan. The primary goal of these programs was to help employees identify their basic retirement goals and start planning for their departure from the workforce. The focus of pre-retirement planning programs was on project-ing income sources in retirement (e.g. pension plans, savings plans, social security, personal investments, part-time employment), matching these to projected income needs, and deciding on a retirement date that was consistent with this savings behavior.

The emphasis in such programs was on saving behavior and on payout options. Some programs included small components of nonfinancial con-cerns, such as health, housing, life adjustments, and other financial issues, such as estate planning. Employers that offered pre-retirement planning seminars to employees reported that the most common reactions by parti-cipants were that the seminars were one of the best 'benefits' ever provided to them as employees and that the employer should have provided similar programs much earlier in the employee's career when planning horizons were much longer.

Employer-sponsored education for employees at younger ages followed the significant shift from DB to DC plans that began to occur in the 1980s. As 401(k) and other DC plans became more prevalent, employees had to assume more responsibility for making retirement financing decisions. Some leading employers recognized the need to provide employees with the tools and resources to meet this new responsibility. Employee success in achieving financial security became an objective of human resource divi-sions of many large companies. These employers recognized the strategic importance of pension plans and quality educational programs in recruit-ing, retaining, and motivating a committed, productive workforce. While the scope of some employer educational efforts was broad and accompan-ied a life-events approach to benefits communications, most employer-sponsored education programs were narrowly focused on investing in company-sponsored 401(k) or other DC plans.

Participant investment education did not, however, achieve main-stream status until the US Department of Labor (USDOL) issued guide-lines under Section 404 (c) of the Employee Retirement Income Security Act (ERISA) of 1974. These guidelines, issued in 1992, clarified the 'suffi-cient information' requirement for a plan sponsor to claim 404(c) protec-tion against participant claims due to investment losses in participant-directed accounts. In 1993, for example, the Institute for International

Research (IIR) sponsored a conference on 'Designing and Implementing Investment Education Programs for 401(k) Plan Participants', in what was billed as 'the first forum dealing with the most critical issue facing human resource, employee benefits and trust investment professionals' (IIR 1993).

In 1995, the USDOL launched a national pension education program with the objective of attracting workers' attention to the necessity of taking personal responsibility for their retirement security. This campaign featured the slogan 'Save! Your Retirement Clock is Ticking.' At this time, it was estimated that 88 percent of large employers offered some form of financial education, more than two-thirds of which added these programs after 1990 (Bernheim 1998). In 1996, the USDOL gave further impetus to participant education when it issued Interpretive Bulletin 96–1. This document clarified this type of education from investment advice as defined by the ERISA. At that time, plan sponsors were extremely concerned about crossing a legal line and being charged with providing investment advice. Today, many employers realize that the risk of offering advice may be less than the risk of not offering it.

Surveys vary widely in their estimates of the proportion of employers that offer financial education and advice. According to the Profit Sharing Council of America (PSCA) (2002), 22 percent of its 141 member companies made investment advice available to plan participants in 2002. Investment advice methods can be divided into three categories:

1. *Advice Directly from Plan Providers with Disclosures.* The Retirement Security Advice Act, sponsored by Rep. John Boehner (R-Ohio), has passed the House of Representatives in each of the past three years. Although it has had the ongoing support of the Bush Administration, it has been unable to pass the Senate. Under this bill, a plan sponsor may authorize a plan provider to take on the role of investment advisor under ERISA. The advisor may be a provider or manager of plan investment funds, but must disclose to participants relevant fees and potential conflicts of interest. The provider would be able to give advice directly to participants without using independent sources of advice.

2. *Advice from Plan Providers Using Independent Sources.* USDOL issued advisory opinion 2001–09A in December 2001 to SunAmerica, allowing a financial institution to offer advice to plan participants, but only if the source of the advice is independent of the institution as plan provider. This opinion also allows participants to delegate investment decisions to professional advisors who in effect take over the management of their 401(k) accounts. The opinion defines 'independent' as receiving no more than 5 percent of revenues from a source related to the financial institution.

3. *Advice from Independent Sources Only.* The Independent Investment Advice Act, introduced by Sen. Jeff Bingaman (D-New Mexico), would protect plan sponsors who offer investment advice from liability, but only if the advice is given by independent firms that do not provide or manage plan funds. Similar legislation introduced by Sens. Edward Kennedy (D-Mass.) and John Kerry (D-Mass.) reflects this approach.

Until further action is taken by Congress or the USDOL, many plan sponsors have expressed concern about the extent to which they might be liable for losses with respect to investment advice they make available to participants. The most recent federal initiative to promote financial education has come from the US Treasury Department's Office of Financial Education (OFE 2004). In January 2004, it released the first issue of its on-line, quarterly newsletter entitled *The Treasury Financial Education Messenger.* The inaugural issue contains a message from Treasury Secretary John Snow stressing the importance of financial education and highlighting eight elements of a successful financial education program.

Employee financial education programs have by and large been vaguely defined. Most surveys have accepted employer statements that they have such programs without subjecting such statements to independent scrutiny. For example, a Towers Perrin TP Track survey of 122 companies reported in August 2002 found that 33 percent of responding firms educated their employees 'constantly' about investments (Plan Sponsor.com August 2002). Other respondents limited educational activities to plan enrollment periods (32 percent) or to employee requests (24 percent). Typical program deliverables include generic print publications (e.g. newsletters, guides, workbooks); personalized print items (e.g. individual benefit statements, retirement projections); group learning settings (e.g. live workshops/seminars, on-line sessions); individual learning (e.g. CDs, videotapes, audiotapes, Web-based self-study modules); telephone counseling; face-to-face counseling, and web-based tools. Few employers to date have awarded these programs such a high priority that they established positions in their human resources or benefit functions devoted in whole or in part to education. One employer who did so was Xerox, which created the position of 'Manager, Benefits Education' (Barocas 1993).

Based on my experience, a high-quality employer-paid program should be available all year round, during employees' working hours, and it should include education both custom-tailored to an employer's specific benefit plans and individualized to each employee. To date, I estimate that fewer than one fifth of large employers have such a program. The vast majority of participants in 401(k) plans remain on their own, when it comes to obtaining financial planning assistance. This dearth of suitable financial education will become an increasing concern to employees, their employers, and to society.

What Impact Have Employer-Sponsored Financial Education Programs Had on Participant Behavior?

Meaningful evaluations of employee financial education activities must clearly indicate the objectives of the program and how these goals can be measured. In addition, program evaluation will occur throughout the life of the program and at specific milestones. Good evaluation should also assess changes in the actual impact of various educational activities over time, utilizing both quantitative and qualitative measures. Few if any programs have been the subject of this level of evaluation to date. Given their expense, it is likely that employers will need to establish financial education programs, evaluate them carefully, and then amend the programs to successfully prepare workers for retirement.

In early work on this theme, Bernheim (1998) noted that a great deal of the evaluation evidence regarding workplace retirement education relies on qualitative surveys and case studies. The few that have attempted to provide quantitative evidence of the effects of such education lacked good descriptions of program structure and content. Furthermore, virtually all assessments of financial education programs have been based on participant statements of satisfaction with program deliverables. These responses have been typically obtained by questionnaires immediately following their participation, and are based on expressions of intent to take action. No reported attempts have been made thus far to track actual changes in participant behavior as a result of participation in employer-sponsored education programs.

A successful program needs a baseline of data from which to measure progress. In view of technological advances in plan recordkeeping, more data on employee 401(k) and other benefit plan activities are now available to identify patterns that may have serious long-term retirement security consequences. Such data will be more meaningful if supplemented with qualitative assessments of different employee population segments. Sources of data include surveys, individual interviews, and focus groups. Employees may be segmented in many different ways, including demographic cuts (e.g. age, years of service, gender, income, education), job (e.g. business unit, location, function, pay level), financial sophistication (e.g. basic financial literacy, interest in money management, investment savvy, retirement confidence) and learning styles (e.g. self-study vs. instructor-led, group learning vs. individual counseling, live vs. Web-based, text vs. graphics).

Overall, plan sponsors do not appear to be satisfied with their current employee financial education programs. A recent survey by investment education provider ICC Plan Solutions found that only 11.9 percent of plan sponsors said they were satisfied with their current programs, while 73.8 percent said that their participants needed help with basic investing knowledge. Employers are also seeing evidence of increasing financial difficulties on the part of their employees through such vehicles as employee assistance programs. For example, a Chicago-based employee assistance provider covering about 25 million people worldwide found that 40 percent of all work-life calls made by workers were related to financial help, up from 26 percent a year earlier.

Today many plan sponsors seem most concerned with five patterns of participant behavior that run the risk of jeopardizing their future financial well-being. These include: non-participation in pension plans; low rates of pension plan contribution; questionable investment allocations; high levels of loans from the pension accounts; and distributions upon termination. To each we address some brief comments.

Participation. The average participation rate in large 401(k) plans is approximately 70 percent, according to Fidelity Investments (2003). Not only is participation less than universal, but also there appears to be a downward trend in participation rates over time. For instance, Hewitt Associates (2002) reported that the average plan participation in 2002 was only 68.2 percent.

Several authors have tried to figure out what induces workers to participate in an offered 401(k) plan, and how much they contribute to the plan once they do participate. Munnell et al. (2000) found that, in addition to being positively associated with a worker's age, income, education, and length of service, participation was greater among employees whose planning horizon was four years or more. The authors interpreted this result to suggest that educating employees on the importance of planning for retirement would boost saving rates. That research also indicated that the amounts employees contributed were positively related to income and wealth, long planning horizons, employer matching contributions, and the ability to borrow from the plan.

There have been direct attempts to measure the impact of employee education on plan participation. Clark and Schieber (1998) considered various levels of plan communications, all of which involved the provision of written information (e.g. enrollment forms, statements of account balances, generic newsletters, custom-tailored materials). They found that enhancing the quality of communications significantly boosted participation rates. For example, providing generic materials in addition to forms and statements increased the probability of participation by 15 percentage points. Using custom-tailored information increased the probability by another 21 percentage points over only providing forms and statements. To isolate the impact of such materials, the match rate was held constant. Indeed, one of their most important findings was that improving communications had nearly as important impact on participation as did raising the employer match rate. They also found that workers tended to make their participation decisions in response to education programs instituted some time earlier. A key determinant of education impact is apparently frequency. According to Bernheim (1998), low-frequency education enhanced plan participation by only about half the rate as high-frequency education.

More recently, a study was conducted of one-hour financial education seminars provided by TIAA-CREF at educational institutions and other nonprofit organizations. As reported by Clark and d'Ambrosio (2002), surveys were given to seminar participants at the start, immediately after, and three months following the seminars. The primary behavioral focus of the research was to measure the impact of the seminar on participants' retirement goals, particularly their planned retirement ages. The first round of surveys covered 270 respondents, and results found that nearly 10 percent stated that they had increased their retirement age and nearly 18 percent decreased their retirement income objective. In addition, many seminar attendees said that they intended to become more active in saving for retirement thereafter.

Contributions. Evidence from a range of sources suggests that plan participants do not save at very high rates. For instance, the PSCA found that 401(k) deferrals averaged 5.2 percent in 2002, and Hewitt Associates reported an average contribution rate of 7.8 percent. Both represent inadequate contribution rates, especially by participants who rely on their 401(k) plan as the primary retirement funding vehicle and their only form of long-term saving. EBRI (1997) noted that fewer than one-third of workers reported contributing the maximum allowed to their company's 401(k) plan.

Low plan contribution rates also mean that many workers fail to earn the full employer match in many cases. In this light, Clark and Schieber (1998) reported that certain types of participant communications had a considerable positive impact on contribution rates. Specifically, tailored plan information resulted in an increase in the annual contribution rate by 2 percentage points.

Investments. Many plan participants appear to be engaged in questionable investment behavior in their DC plans. These ranges from the failure to rebalance funds periodically, to fund selections that fail to diversify retirement assets in general and over investment in employer stock in particular. Fidelity Investments (2003) found in one survey that a quarter of DC plan participants held only a single investment asset in their 401(k) plans. Hewitt Associates (2002) notes that 41 percent of plan participants held only one or two funds in 2002. There is also some evidence of choice overload in plans leading to dubious participant decisions, including nonparticipation (Iyengar et al. 2004). Other data show that more than 8 million 401(k) participants held more than 20 percent of their plan assets in company stock (VanDerhei 2002). Overall, company stock still dominates many pension plan accounts, averaging 42 percent of balances among participants holding *any* company stock (Hewitt Associates 2002).

Investment advice providers have only recently begun to report on internal evaluations of participant use of their programs. The International Society of Certified Employee Benefit Specialists (ISCEBS) (2002) surveyed employers who provided advice to their employees and reported that 18 percent of participants shifted asset allocations as a result of their use of on-line advice services. Overall, however, 70 percent of employers either did not measure the impact or did not know. None reported using independent third party assessments.

Loans. A loan provision is a common feature in most 401(k) plans and approximately 20 percent of plan participants have outstanding loans at any one point in time. Since loan features are often desired by workers, firms must carefully consider whether to include this option or restrict its use in an effort to increase retirement saving. The problem is that few participants appear to understand the true cost of loans and their negative impact on long-term retirement funding. No reported program evaluations have focused on this aspect of participant behavior.

Distributions. Many participants in 401(k) plans take lump sums on terminating employment, instead of deferring distributions or rolling them over to individual retirement accounts or other employer plans. As a result, there is widespread 'leakage' of retirement funds and workers may have insufficient funds at retirement.

A New Policy Paradigm in Investment Education

To date, there has been too little research on the effectiveness of the few programs that have arisen, though a new project is now underway. Working with the Employee Benefit Research Institute (EBRI), a client of Ernst & Young's employee financial education practice is initiating a means of tracking actual employee 401(k) plan behavior. The goal is to correlate changes in behavior and employee participation in live workshops on saving, investing, and retirement planning, employee viewing of a videotaped workshop, and employee use of an on-line modeling tool. With a sample size of some 25,000 participants, participant behaviors can be studied, including changes in plan participation, plan contribution rates, and plan investment selections.

This study, and others like it, is driven by the realization that more workers are being required to take greater responsibility for their own retirement saving than ever before. They will need more and better financial education, and employers can help provide this, as long as it is reviewed, monitored, evaluated, and modified when needed. To date, most employers, even the very large ones, lack high- quality financial education programs supportive of their firm's retirement plans and policies. In the future, companies will need to evaluate how to allocate resources to educational programs so as to better prepare their employees for retirement.

References

Barocas, Victor S. (1993). *Benefit Communications: Enhancing the Employer's Investment.* A Conference Board Report. New York: The Conference Board.

Bernheim, Douglas (1998). 'Financial Literacy, Education and Retirement Saving', in Olivia S. Mitchell and Sylvester J. Schieber, (eds.), *Living with Defined Contribution Pension Plans.* Philadelphia: University of Pennsylvania Press, pp. 38–68.

Clark, Robert L. and d'Ambrosio, Madeleine B. (2002). 'Financial Education and Retirement Savings', Society of Actuaries, San Francisco, CA, June.

—— and Schieber, Sylvester J. (1998). 'Rates and Contribution Levels in 401(k) Plans', in Olivia S. Mitchell and Sylvester J. Schieber (eds.), *Living with Defined Contribution Pension Plans.* Philadelphia: University of Pennsylvania Press, pp. 69–97.

Employee Benefit Research Institute (EBRI) (1997). 'The Reality of Retirement Today', Issue Brief, Washington, DC: EBRI, January.

Fidelity Investments (2003). *Building Futures*, A Fidelity Report, December. Boston, MA: Fidelity.

Hewitt Associates (2002). 'How Well Are Employees Saving and Investing in 401(k) Plans'. Lincolnshire, IL: Hewitt Associates.

Institute for International Research. (IIR) (1993). 'Designing and Implementing Investment Education Programs for 401(k) Plan Participants'. New York: IIR.

International Society of Certified Employee Benefit Specialists (2002). 'New Kid on the Block: Financial Planning as an Employee Benefit'. Reported in Employee Benefit Plan Review, February.

Iyengar, Sheena S., Wei Jiang and Gur Huberman (2004). 'How Much Choice is Too Much: Contributions to 401(k) Retirement Plans', in Olivia Mitchell and Stephen Utkus (eds.), *Pension Design and Structure: New Lessons from Behavioral Finance*, Oxford: Oxford University Press, pp. 83–96.

Mitchell, Olivia S. and Sylvester J. Schieber (eds.) (1998). *Living with Defined Contribution Pension Plans.* Philadelphia: University of Pennsylvania Press.

Munnell, Alicia H., Annika Sundén, and C. Taylor (2000). 'What Determines 401(k) Participation and Contributions?' Working Paper 2000–12, Center for Retirement Research, Boston College, Chestnut Hill, MA, December.

Plan Sponsor.com. (2002). 'Did You Know? Investment Education', August.

Profit Sharing Council of America (2003). *46th Annual Survey of Profit Sharing and 401(k) Plans.* Chicago, IL: Profit Sharing Council of America.

US Department of the Treasury (2004). Office of Financial Education. Washington, DC: US Treasury.

VanDerhei, Jack (2002). 'The Role of Company Stock in 401(k) Plans', Testimony for the Subcommittee on Employer-Employee Relations, Committee on Education and the Workforce, US House of Representatives, Washington, DC, February 13.

Chapter 10

Changes in Accounting Practices Will Drive Pension Paradigm Shifts

Douglas Fore

The long bull market for equities in the 1990s permitted many firms with defined benefit (DB) pension funds to dramatically scale back, and in many cases even eliminate, required annual contributions to these plans. This occurred because equity allocations in the pension trusts grew so significantly, as to more than keep pace with growth in plan liabilities. In short, the stock market did all of their heavy lifting for them. Some firms, in fact, were able to turn their pension plans into profit centers that contributed in a nontrivial way to the firms' quarterly income growth. As we shall show below, especially in the USA but to some extent in Europe as well, the accounting rules for pension plan asset allocation featured an odd disconnect insofar as risk and return were concerned, which permitted heavy equity allocations to pension plans.

This phase in pension profitability came to an abrupt end with the bursting of the stock market bubble and the onset of the bear market in March 2000. Making matters worse, interest rates then fell sharply, thus boosting the present value of DB pension liabilities. Erosion in DB plan funding status was sharp and dramatic. For firms in the S&P 500, approximately 70 percent of which offered DB plans, these plans were, in aggregate, roughly $300 billion overfunded in 1999, the last full year of the bull market (Morgan Stanley 2003). By mid-2003, analysts estimated that DB plans in the S&P 500 were underfunded by $340 billion. Furthermore, many of the S&P 500 firms have a relatively older workforce, as well as large numbers of annuitants, and they are rapidly approaching the day when they will begin paying out large pension cash flows on a sustained basis. This abrupt shift in DB plan funding status raises the question of whether pension accounting rules are consistent with the principles of pension finance.

This volume examines proposed changes in US and international pension accounting standards and the rationales for such changes. One finding is that convergence is on the way, and this is probably a good thing in terms of fundamental principles of finance though the journey could be a bumpy one. Another finding is that convergence will probably change the way pension investments are managed. Plan sponsors must become more aware of these changes in the accounting arena and the impact they will have on pension as well as corporate finance.

Setting the Rules for Pension Accounting

In the USA, the Financial Accounting Standards Board (FASB) is the designated organization in the private sector that determines standards of financial accounting and reporting. The standards set by FASB are officially recognized as authoritative by the Securities and Exchange Commission (SEC) for all firms listed on US exchanges. Officially, the SEC has the authority to override FASB and establish standards, but it has been SEC practice to rely on the private sector for standard setting. One of the missions of FASB is to keep standards current to reflect changes in the economic environment, and at any given time a dozen or more projects may be underway to improve and update standards, of which several may be on convergence-related topics. For example, the recently released SFAS 132, *Employers' Disclosures about Pensions and Other Postretirement Benefits*, was motivated partly with convergence in mind, partly by an awareness that the existing pension accounting framework was antiquated, and partly in response to concerns expressed by users of financial statements about the need for more and clearer information.

The parallel private-sector standard-setting body in the UK is the Accounting Standards Board (ASB). At present, it is leading a movement to fair value accounting standards, with the intention of serving as a global model. In FRS 17 *Retirement Benefits*, the ASB (2000: 6) summed up key objectives in this area:

- Financial statements should reflect at fair value the assets and liabilities arising from an employer's retirement benefit obligations and any related funding.
- The operating costs of providing retirement benefits to employees should be recognized in the accounting period(s) in which the benefits are earned by the employees, and the related finance costs and any other changes in value of the assets and liabilities are recognized in the accounting periods in which they arise.
- The financial statements should contain adequate disclosure of the cost of providing retirement benefits and the related gains, losses, assets and liabilities.

The International Accounting Standards Board (IASB) is an independent, privately funded standard-setter based in London, whose mission is to develop a single set of high quality, understandable, and enforceable global accounting standards. The IASB cooperates with national standard-setters such as FASB to achieve convergence around the world. As we will see, standards for retirement benefits developed by the IASB bear the influence of ASB, with certain Continental European influences as well. The standards also show the influence of the new disclosures issues by FASB.

Pension Accounting in the USA

The main reason that pension accounting rules are so critically important in the DB context is that these plans have very long time horizons, both with regard to the accumulation and the payout phases. An employer sponsoring a DB plan is not only responsible for providing sufficient cash flows to meet not only this year's service and interest contributions, but also he must meet obligations at far distant points in time. Consequently, for funding purposes, actuarial projections must be made over long time horizons involving such factors as future mortality experience and assumptions regarding asset returns.

From 1986 through 2003, the prevailing US standard for pension accounting was SFAS 87. This embodied a smoothing methodology to dampen fluctuations in pension assets and liabilities from one year to the next. Under SFAS 87, liabilities were essentially treated as fixed-income instruments and discounted at a specified long-term interest rate. There were a variety of rules governing permissible actuarial assumptions when measuring a plan's accumulated liabilities. It is important to note, however, that the discount rate used to measure plan liabilities never depended on the plan's participant demographic structure. That is to say, the rules insisted that the proper discount rate was invariant to expected cash flows actually payable by DB plan sponsors. For example, in the case of an old-line industrial firm with many workers nearing retirement age, the DB plan would face the prospect of having to pay out large sums to these workers as they began to retire in large numbers. Finance experts would have recommended that these plan liabilities should be discounted with a set of interest rates that matched the timing of required cash flows. But SFAS 87 required a single interest rate unrelated to the place on the yield curve that a plan sponsor might need to discount benefit payments using finance methodology.

SFAS 87 also required that the projected unit credit (PUC) method be used to measure plan liabilities. The PUC takes both present-day benefit accruals and their likely future values into account, in addition to benefits earned by vested terminated employees.[1] Given the lack of portability in DB plans, this last can constitute a significant portion of the total obligation. The accumulated benefit obligation is the present value of benefits accrued to date, by each vested employee in the plan at the start of each year. An additional minimum liability must be recognized if the accumulated benefit obligation exceeds the fair value of plan assets. The present value of benefits accrued by employees during the course of the year is referred to as the plan's service or normal cost. Service cost can be amortized over a period of several years. The present value of the liabilities of the plan at the beginning of the year multiplied by the plan's discount rate is referred to as the interest cost of the plan. The interest cost is the cost of financing the plan for a year. Future liabilities which long-term employees in the plan are expected to earn is called the projected benefit obligation (PBO); this is measured as the actuarial present value of benefits earned by an employee under the pension benefit formula to a certain date. This is computed using assumptions about future compensation levels, and it also takes into consideration the design of the pension benefit formula (i.e. final-pay, final-average-pay, or career-average-pay plans).

Under the Employee Retirement Income Security Act (ERISA) of 1974, benefits earned in corporate DB plans in the past may not be changed. Nevertheless, it is possible to change the formula for future benefits, an outcome that sometimes produces tension between employees and employers. This is particularly true with a DB plan that is backloaded in its benefit formula. Backloading means that a high percentage of the DB pension value accrues during the last few years of employment.[2] The fact that future benefits can be changed of course implies that the PBO is not an ironclad measure of total plan liabilities. Instead, the measure will vary from firm to firm, and it depends on such factors as union agreements, whether the plan is part of a multi-employer arrangement, the funding status of the plan, and so on.[3]

In the summer of 2003, the FASB released an Exposure Draft of Statement 132. This was part of a project with the IASB, motivated by widespread dissatisfaction with US pension accounting. After receiving comments, FASB moved with unaccustomed speed to issue the final version of SFAS 132 in December 2003. During deliberations, the Board considered but rejected, requiring additional disclosures that would have enabled users of financial statements obtain a better understanding of the timing of cash flows associated with the demographic structure of DB pension plans. Most importantly, such a requirement would have permitted analysts to assess whether a plan's portfolio of assets matched its liabilities in terms of duration. This information could be helpful in formulating assessments of a firm's liability structure and the magnitude of cash flows payable over time. Duration disclosures could also help those seeking to conduct sensitivity analysis and test key assumptions about the firm's asset management strategies and stress-test the firm's liability immunization strategy. Unfortunately the FASB eventually excluded these requirements from the final Statement.

Under the previous versions of SFAS 87 and 132 (in effect from 1986–2003), a single rate of return assumption was used for accounting for plan assets, and returns were smoothed over a period of years. This had the very powerful effect of making actual volatility virtually unrelated to the rate of return assumption selected by the plan sponsor. Further, during that period, plan sponsors were not required to disclose volatility assumptions for asset returns. As a result, the accounting rules embedded a strong pro-equity bias; some argue that pension assets were managed with such a 'tilt' that it appeared as if they had a beta of zero in financial terms (Gold 2001; Ambachtsheer Chapter 11).

It is our contention that the accounting rules explain why the equity share in pension portfolios has remained so high for the past several decades, despite changes that should have encouraged a shift to fixed income investment to better match changes in the liability structure (particularly demographic aging). These rules produced a situation where pension returns were decoupled from pension risks. Anticipated returns could be booked on the income statement today, but the risks could be smoothed on the balance sheet over a period of several years. This led some to raise anticipated return assumptions, boost the share of the portfolio devoted to equities, and 'hope for the best.' This strategy worked as long as the market continued to defy gravity during the bull market experienced in the USA over the 1990s. Eventually, however, the bubble burst and analysts undertook more detailed examinations of balance sheets. At that time, the smoothing strategy was recognized as problematic and worse: indeed when the market fell for three straight years post-2000, the smoothing strategy was revealed to have a built-in negative reinforcement mechanism. DB plans that appeared comfortably overfunded in 1999 became dramatically underfunded by 2003, and now they face the prospect of many years of deficit-reduction contributions.

Several authors have recently characterized the traditional DB accounting system as one which encouraged an 'opaque' model of asset allocation (Gold 2001; Coronado and Sharpe 2003). Another way to frame the debate is to say that during a bull market, users of financial statements tended to focus more on firm income statements and less on the footnotes. But when times grow difficult and firms are more likely to be in distress, analysts focus more heavily on the footnotes and the balance sheet. Coronado and Sharpe (2003) confirm this hypothesis empirically, finding that users of financial statements used pension accrual data from income statements rather than information regarding the market value of the DB plan assets and liabilities reported in the footnotes. In a related study, Amir and Benartzi (1997) found that firms raised their fixed-income allocations between 1988–94 to avoid recognizing additional minimum DB plan liabilities. In addition, they found that plans with high proportions of younger workers had higher equity weightings in their plan portfolios.

Another surprising fact is that DB plan asset allocation patterns have been relatively invariant over the last several years, despite repeated and sometimes violent market shocks. Asset allocations remained quite stable despite the market bubble in which standard measures of valuation such as price to book and price/equity ratios were seen by many as 'otherworldly'. And despite the now-extended bear market for equities and strong bull market in at least some sections of the fixed-income market, asset allocations still remained quite stable. As a result, DB plan funding deteriorated dramatically and the duration of their liabilities shortened as well.

One explanation for the puzzle of the stability of DB plan asset allocation may be the fact that senior plan sponsors have strong incentives to argue the case for equities. For instance, a chief financial officer (CFO) who reduced his plan's equity weighing would likely have to boost plan contributions indefinitely. This CFO would have to report to the chief executive officer (CEO) and Board that not only would next quarter's earnings would be reduced, but also earnings over more reporting horizons than the length of the CFO's contract. Perhaps a CFO with great credibility could escape with his stock price intact, but most would anticipate a negative market reaction. This reality discourages the incentive to reduce equity allocations despite changing circumstances.

Instead of requiring disclosure of the expected rate of return by individual asset category, the revised SFAS 132 requires only a narrative description of the investment strategies employed by the DB plans. FASB now requires only an explanation of the basis used to determine the overall expected rate of return on assets, but it did not specify which significant factors should be included when determining the long-term rate of return on assets assumption. The Board did say, however, that the disclosure should explain the general approach taken, which historical data were used in forming the long-term rate of return assumption, and information on factors as whether adjustments were made to historical data. As a result, assumptions can still vary from one plan sponsor to the next.

Pension Accounting in the United Kingdom

The UK moved to the forefront of the fair value accounting movement in 2000, when the UK Accounting Standards Board issued Financial Reporting Standard (FRS) 17. In a nutshell, fair value approach to accounting represents a conscious effort to move away from smoothing techniques, toward the use of market prices to value assets and liabilities.

The evolution of FRS 17 indicated an important shift within the UK actuarial community regarding the proper way to measure DB plan assets and liabilities. Initially, actuaries and the ASB were opposed to fair valuation of plan assets, preferring instead the more traditional actuarial valuation approach. By the end of the decade, however, it appeared clear that the actuarial approach to assets valuation would be viewed as weak both inside Europe and outside, and would probably not be adopted by other standard-setters. As a result, they moved to DB plan market valuation, and in so doing, they went a step farther than did the USA with SFAS 87. For instance, under the US approach, plan asset values can still be smoothed over a period of up to five years. In the UK, under FRS 17, gains and losses must be immediately recognized.

The ASB also indicated a strong preference for market valuation of DB plan liabilities. In some ways, this debate mirrors the discussion concerning the accounting treatment of long-dated insurance liabilities which continues to cause controversy between the IASB and life insurance firms around the world.[4] Acknowledging the lack of an active market in long pension liabilities, the ASB considered alternative actuarial methods for discounting plan liabilities. Ultimately, it determined that under the prospective benefit method the total cost that accrues, including interest, is spread evenly over the time of service of an employee. The ASB argued that this did not represent economic reality where the cost of providing a DB pension increased as an employee approached the retirement date.

The old Statement of Standard Accounting Practice 24 (SSAP 24) permitted plan sponsors to discount liabilities at the same rate as the expected return on DB plan assets. This produced biased incentive effects, leading firms to raise the rate of return assumptions and the discount rate at the same time. Aware of this problem, the ASB in its deliberations considered a variety of approaches for setting the discount rate for plan liabilities. One issue was whether the DB annuity payment was fixed in nominal terms, or adjusted for inflation., and the Board realized that, in many cases, inflation-adjustment of DB annuities had participating elements. In other works, annuitants sometimes shared in the investment performance of the DB plan's assets, and in other cases they shared in temporary mismatches of the plan's asset-liability mix. The Board considered whether index-linked bonds were the best instruments to discount the liabilities, index-linked government bonds having been in use in the UK for far longer than in the USA. In addition, the ASB considered whether a discount rate that reflected the returns of a weighted portfolio consisting of both equities and fixed-income investments would be preferable for DB plans that based benefits on final salary accrual patterns. In SSAP 24, plan sponsors had considerable discretion with regard to the choice of actuarial and other assumptions, and one of the principal changes in the switch to FRS 17 was the reduction in the degree of discretion allowed.

All this discussion took place against the backdrop of research in pension finance, which was focused on the question of what instrument might offer the best long-term match against wage growth. Final salary plans, in particular, link benefits to pay levels, so many plan sponsors have felt that equity investment was a decent hedge against the benefit promise in such formulas. Plans which continue payments for the length of retirees' lives (as opposed to contracting out the annuities to an insurer) also must be aware that the time horizon for choosing a security or securities to match liabilities is not the worker's retirement date but rather the retirees' life expectancy.[5] Looked at in this way, the question of portfolio choice for expected cash flows soon proves to be far more complicated than commonly thought. Nevertheless, the ASB ultimately decided to simplify and adopt a single discount rate, the rate on AA corporate bonds, for discounting plan liabilities. In coming to this conclusion, it explicitly noted that part of the rationale for this decision was to bring about convergence in standards.

One criticism of fair value accounting for pensions is that it introduces excessive volatility into financial statements for little or no apparent benefit. Another is that it makes accounting regulations drive economic and financial decision-making. In rebuttal, the Board argued that recognizing year-to-year fluctuations in asset values in the financial statements was similar to recognizing revaluation gains and losses on fixed assets. It stated (ASB 2000: 71):

The Board regards actuarial gains and losses as similar in nature to revaluation gains and losses on fixed assets. In relation to the assets in the pension scheme, they are held with a view to producing a relatively secure long-term return that will assist in financing the pension cost. The length of the term, coupled with the options available to the employer to restrict the liability in extreme circumstances, mean that much of the fluctuations in market values does not affect the relatively stable cash flows between the employer and its pension scheme. Market fluctuations are incidental to the main purpose of the pension scheme just as the revaluation gains and losses on a fixed asset are incidental to its main operating role. They are therefore best reported within the statement of total recognized gains and losses.

It is interesting that many felt that the move to full fair value accounting had profound implications for financial statements for UK firms with DB plans. The fact that sponsors could no longer smooth returns meant that they (and their parent firms) now had to recognize the stochastic nature of asset returns. Plan sponsors could no longer act as if returns and risks were unrelated, or to put it another way, plan sponsors could no longer assume that equities had a financial beta value of zero.

This result did not necessarily mean that the Board took a stance with regard to pension portfolio choice. In other words, the fact that plan sponsors had to acknowledge the existence of volatility was not evidence that the Board's sought to shift asset allocation patterns away from equities and toward fixed-income securities. Nevertheless, critics of FRS 17 argued that this regulation was responsible for causing (or at the very least providing incentives for) many firms to terminate their DB plans. They contended that terminating the DB plans removed the volatility which had to be reported by FRS 17. Empirical evidence on this point is, as yet, still mixed. Klumpes et al. (2003) followed ninety UK firms of which thirty-seven terminated their DB plans after switching from SSAP 24 to FRS 17;

they found no support for the view that the change in the discount rate mandated by the switch to FRS 17 was a statistically significant predictor of plan termination. They did, however, find that firms which terminated their DB plans were more likely to be highly leveraged. This tends to suggest that firms which terminated their DB plans did so in part due to the adverse impact of FRS 17 on their of the balance sheets.

The importance of the leverage issue may be a cautionary tale for standard-setters and policymakers in other countries, inasmuch as it indicates the issues in accounting reform when weak industries are involved. For example, in the USA, an immediate shift to a complete fair market value accounting regime could be problematic under today's financial market conditions. Firms with underfunded plans and/or highly leveraged capital structures might quickly terminate their DB plans if forced to undertake a rapid transition to a fair market value accounting; companies might also fall in violation of their debt covenants. The problem, then, is that in view of the poor funding status of many US plans, adoption of a FRS 17-style rule is probably not feasible in the near term. Over the longer term, however, it is probably inevitable.

Implementation of FRS 17 in the UK and Ireland was delayed, in part, by the desire of various stakeholders to make the change from old UK accounting standards to the new international rules in 2005. As of 2001, UK firms have had to disclose FRS 17 numbers in the notes to their financial statements. While the Board urged all firms to switch to FRS 17, it realized that firms would have to adopt IASB standards in 2005; consequently the full implementation of FRS 17 was delayed to 2005. The IASB Board's project on pension accounting is in most respects convergent with FRS 17.

Financial analysts in London welcomed the change to FRS 17, even if implementation was partial at the outset. In a research study on UK pension underfunding, Morgan Stanley (2003) noted that its analysis could not have been done using SSAP 24 disclosures. Its analysis of a group of fifty-seven UK firms revealed that the disclosures were strong predictors of cash flow; that is, there was a positive relationship between the pension plans' service cost and contributions paid. Also it reported that contributions were higher if a plan's funding status was weaker. Overall, DB underfunding for sample firms reduced shareholder equity by approximately 5 percent, with a wide dispersion. The variability was considerable from year to year due to the very high equity allocations in UK plans. Average equity allocations in UK plans were between 60 and 70 percent, with some even higher. There is one famous exception worth noting, however: after the new rule, the Boots pharmacy firm cut its DB pension equity exposure to zero and shifted entirely into bonds. Interestingly, that study found no relation between funding status and equity allocation, or between equity allocation and the maturity status of the plan.

The high average equity allocations in UK plans caused a dramatic reversal of fortune in terms of aggregate funding status, when the equity market began to fall sharply as of 2000. By the end of 2002, DB plan underfunding was reported in the range of £160–300 billion (CBI 2003). Fund managers and plan sponsors complained that they were prohibited from building up a 'rainy day' reserve during the bull market of the 1990s by the regulation that funds in excess of 105 percent were subject to taxation at a rate of 35 percent (Blake 2003). This regulation was in force during the era of SSAP 24, however, when the actuarial rules were sufficiently loose that plan sponsors who wanted to save for a rainy day could have done so if they were worried that the market was building into a bubble and that things would eventually end badly. Instead, many plan sponsors maintained high equity allocations and took extended contribution holidays during the 1990s. It is true, however, that an additional tax regulation working to the detriment of full funding was the end to the right to reclaim imputed taxes on dividend income. This exacerbated the funding problem at the same time that the present value of liabilities was being forced dramatically up by the switch from SSAP 24 treatment to FRS 17 treatment, with further pressure on present values coming from the fall in the yield curve.

The dramatic deterioration in UK pension funding levels, at the time that more stringent FRS 17 standards came into effect (at least in the notes to the statements), meant that DB plan sponsors faced immediate and in many cases prolonged calls for additional plan contributions. Some blamed this for the fact that, by year-end 2002, approximately half of all UK DB plans had closed to new entrants while the remaining active members continued to accrue benefits (Blake 2003). This does not mean that new employees were denied pension coverage, since old plan closures in many cases resulted in a substitution of new DC plans. Of course, the shift to DC plans offers the advantage of portability and probably signals that the UK will experience the same shift as has the USA for the last thirty years.

Convergence in International Pension Accounting

All these changes also have implications for financial reporting by foreign multinational firms, though the picture is still complex. For example, a firm might need to adopt several different methods in accounting for its pension obligations and when filing statements: it would have to use national standards for its domestic reports, IAS standards for international reports (e.g. on the London Stock Exchange), and FASB standards for US listings. If the firm was a multinational insurer listing in the USA, it would also have to meet SAP standards for statutory reporting in fifty states and the District of Columbia. The problem is that multiple reporting can introduce inadvertent mistakes and increase costs, and also perhaps confuse analysts.

To bring convergence to reality, the IASB and the FASB have recently signed a memorandum on convergence committing them to convergence in global accounting standards in as many areas as their respective boards have judged feasible. One area in need of improvement is clearly pension accounting, and the IASB Board added a project on convergence on accounting for retirement benefits to its active agenda in June 2002. It has made substantial progress since then, influenced heavily by FRS 17 but also by the recent issuance of SFAS 132. It has incorporated certain of its disclosure rules into the forthcoming exposure draft of the revised IAS 19, and it appears that the revised IAS 19 will be a very large step in terms of convergence (IAS 2004).

IAS 19 proposes to be based on a fair value accounting framework. Assets in the plan will be valued using market prices wherever possible. Pension plan liabilities will be discounted using high-grade corporate bonds. The rules do not specify the exact grade or type of security, as in FRS 17, but the intent of the standard is clearly convergence with both FRS 17 and SFAS 87. Pension plan liabilities must be valued using the projected unit credit method. In addition to the formal terms of the plan, indexation agreements and future salary increases must be taken into account when valuing liabilities. In addition, 'constructive' obligations must be taken into account. An example of a constructive obligation is a regular practice such as regular annual wage and salary increases at a certain rate. This shows the influence on IASB thinking of FRS 17 and also of other actors (such as social partners in Europe) regarding the valuation of long-dated liabilities.

Under this framework, actuarial gains and losses must be recognized immediately, outside the income statement, in a statement of total recognized income and expenses, and they also must be included immediately in retained earnings. Previously, the old standard had a 10 percent corridor around the full funding level, and changes in surplus of that amount (in absolute value) did not have to be reflected on the plan sponsor's balance sheet. In addition, actuarial gains and losses above or below this level could be amortized over the working lives of employees, a view reflective of the SFAS 87 approach. The new standard eliminates this corridor entirely as well as the spreading and amortization approach to valuing actuarial gains and losses, and it adopts the FRS 17 approach of recognizing them immediately.

In terms of disclosures, convergence has also been achieved by requiring disclosures adopted from SFAS 132, principally those concerned with how plan sponsors and fund managers determine the expected return on DB plan assets. Assets held by the plan must be disclosed according to their major asset classes and as a percentage of the total fair value of the plan's assets. Of particular importance, the disclosure must include a description of the assumptions and logic used to determine the overall expected rate of return on assets as well as the previously agreed disclosure of the expected rate of return for each major asset class. Some elements of convergence did not cross the Atlantic, however. In SFAS 132, the disclosure requirements include a description of investment policies and strategies. As of this writing, the IASB has only flagged this as a question for the exposure draft, but no resolution is yet known.

In terms of contributions and benefits, the required disclosure is an estimate of contributions, if any; the plan sponsor expects to pay into the plan in the next fiscal year after the balance sheet date. In SFAS 132, the disclosure requirements for benefits the plan sponsor expects to pay must be listed by line item for the next five fiscal years, and in aggregate, for the five fiscal years following. The IASB will resolve this difference in its final ruling.

Consistency with the Economics of Pension Finance

Pension accounting rules in the past can be, and have been, justly criticized for divorcing real world assumptions about asset returns from their distributions. This built in a bias, in terms of asset allocation, and for this reason, accounting rules can be said to have had a systematic impact on economic decision-making. The bias may, in fact, have been large enough to have contributed to the US stock market bubble in a significant way (Coronado and Sharpe 2003). Further, when the bubble burst, DB pension plan overexposure to equities exacerbated the shock sustained by plan portfolios. If plan portfolios had been properly immunized at the onset of the market decline, the damage sustained and the subsequent degree of underfunding would have been much less.

The new accounting rules are an attempt to rectify perceived problems caused by past smoothing, and they are part of a larger international movement toward fair value accounting standards. Proponents of the new standards believe that moving to the more transparent world of fair value accounting, and away from actuarial smoothing of gains and losses, will prevent periodic funding crises by highlighting small problems before they can grow into large problems. Opponents of the new standards argue, conversely, that introducing fair value accounting into a system of long-dated commitments introduces excessive volatility for too little benefit. They point to the large-scale closure of DB plans to new entrants in the UK as vindication of their position. They further argue that this is a case where accounting rules not only drive decision-making but also affect the lives of active employees.

In the USA, with many underfunded plans and financial distress in several sectors of the economy, an immediate move to fair value accounting standards would have serious consequences. Among them would probably be violations of debt covenants, immediate plan terminations, closures of plans to new entrants, and removal or sharp reductions in retiree health insurance coverage. Yet a case can be made that a true reading of the financial situation of troubled firms would indicate that they are already in violation of their debt covenants; many probably plan to terminate their plans in the near future anyway. Congress and the Administration are attempting to craft legislative transition rules to buy time until plan sponsors can restore full funding levels. It is unclear whether they this will be more successful with this strategy than similar efforts were with regard to the savings and loan industry in the 1980s.

Our discussion also raises questions about proper investment strategies for DB plans. Most DB accrual plans have some form of final salary formula as the arrangement of choice. In addition, annuitants generally can be assumed to be married at the time of retirement, with joint and survivor annuities the default, so that the receipt of income will be statistically longer than for a single life annuity. This means that plan sponsors and asset managers must design an immunization strategy matched against nominal wage growth and employee demographics during employees' active years, and against the terms of the two-life annuities during the payout years. In addition, the immunization strategy must account for the pension rights of those who have separated from employment but are vested and will eventually receive annuities.

Concerning the first part of the immunization problem, no sovereign or high-grade private entity currently issues securities with coupons and maturities that match expected wage trajectories of employees in a corporate or public sector DB plan. This is especially true for younger employees, who are most likely to leave the plan. Inflation-indexed government bonds are the asset class that comes the closest, but if this asset were to constitute the entire portfolio it would in turn imply high contribution rates and lower earnings for the plan sponsor.

This is an important point that reformers should take seriously. Calling for sharply increased contributions by the plan sponsor could backfire on the very people the reform is intended to benefit. If plan sponsors or Boards of Directors decide that the cost of fully funding and immunizing a DB plan with inflation-linked bonds is too high, they could decide to terminate the plan altogether.

Conclusions

This volume focuses on the trend toward international convergence in pension accounting. We devote special emphasis to recent changes in UK accounting standards since that country's rule-setting Board is acting as the model for global changes. In addition, we ask whether some of the recent accounting changes may result in changes in DB plan design and asset management.

We show that standard-setters are moving toward international convergence, and it seems clear that this trend will continue. On the whole, we argue that the new accounting paradigm is an improvement over the old accounting paradigm, with its emphasis on smoothing and its decoupling of risks from returns. Opponents of fair value standards have argued that switching to these will import introduce excessive volatility to financial statements for little or no benefit to users and issuers of statements. These arguments continue, yet the standards are set for adoption in Europe from 2005.

In the USA, the DB funding situation is far from positive: even with a reasonably good economy, it will be some time before the system as a whole is restored to full solvency. Immediate application of a fair value framework would run the risk of massive DB plan terminations, yet improved disclosure rules will aid users of financial statements, and they in turn will make their voices heard concerning the quality of information disclosed.

Convergence will probably change the way DB plan investments are managed. Fixed-income investment strategies will probably pay more attention to immunization and duration than was the case previously. In the USA where so many DB plans have relatively old demographic structures, plan sponsors and investment managers may concentrate more on investment strategies attuned to the timing of retirement benefit cash flows. An argument can be made that the old accounting conventions encouraged DB plan sponsors and fund managers to invest too much in equity. But similarly, some will claim that the new standards will encourage too much fixed income in pension fund portfolios. Ultimately, accounting rules work best when they are neutral with respect to economic decision-making, when they acknowledge that returns are coupled with risks of a long-term nature.

Endnotes

1. For a discussion of pension funding terminology see McGill et al. (2004).
2. The fact that some DB formulas were backloaded explains some of the controversy over some firms' switch from a traditional DB to a cash balance or hybrid plan (Schieber 2003).
3. We note that public sector plan practice often differs; cf. Anderson and Brainard (Chapter 12).
4. Whether the switch to fair value accounting may change corporate economic decision making has been raised recently in the context of accounting for life insurance (Fore 2003).
5. Of course, if the promise is a joint and survivor annuity, as is typically the case, then this adds several more years to the payment promise.

References

Accounting Standards Board (ASB) (2000). *Financial Reporting Standard 17: Retirement Benefits*. Accounting Standards Board, November.

Amir, Eli, and Shlomo Benartzi (1997). 'Accounting Recognition of Additional Minimum Liability Affects Pension Asset Allocation: Empirical Evidence', Paine Webber Working Paper 97–11, November.

Blake, David (2003). 'The UK Pension System: Key Issues', *Pensions* 8(4): 330–75.

Confederation of British Industry (CBI) (2003). 'Focus on Investment: The Impact of Pension Deficits', *Economic Brief,* July.

Coronado, Julia Lynn and Steven A. Sharpe (2003). 'Did Pension Plan Accounting Contribute to a Stock Market Bubble', *Brookings Papers on Economic Activity.* 1: 323–71.

Financial Accounting Standards Board (2003). *Statement of Financial Accounting Standards No. 132* (revised), *Employers' Disclosures about Pensions and Other Postretirement Benefits.*

Fore, Douglas (2003). 'The Impact of Fair Value Accounting Standards on the Portfolio Composition of Life Insurance Companies', TIAA-CREF Institute Working Paper, 13-050103, May.

Gold, Jeremy (2001). 'Accounting/Actuarial Bias Enables Equity Investment by Defined Benefit Pension Plans', Pension Research Council Working Paper 2001–5, The Wharton School.

International Accounting Standards Committee Foundation (2004). *Post-Employment Benefits Convergence, 2004.*

Klumpes, Paul, Yong Li, and Mark Whittington (2003). 'The Impact of UK Accounting Rule Changes on Pension Terminations', Warwick Business School Working Paper, August.

McGill, Dan, Kyle Brown, John Haley, and Sylvester Schieber (2004). *Fundamentals of Private Pensions,* 8th edn. Oxford: Oxford University Press.

Morgan Stanley (2003). *Yawn or Yell on Pensions: An Update.* Global Valuation and Accounting Group, July 8.

Schieber, Sylvester (2003). 'The Shift to Hybrid Pensions by US Employers: An Empirical Analysis of Actual Plan Conversions', *Pension Research Council Working Paper* 2003–23, The Wharton School.

Van Bezooyen, Jeroen (2002). *FRS 17 Revisited—A Statistical Analysis.* Morgan Stanley: Global Pensions Group, November.

Chapter 11

Why Pension Fund Management Needs a Paradigm Shift

Keith Ambachtsheer

A paradigm is a lens through which to see the world. The lens through which the institutional investment community has heretofore seen the defined benefit (DB) pension fund management world has three facets. First, stocks have outperformed bonds by about 5 percent per annum on average in the past. Looking ahead, many DB plan managers believe that this 5 percent equity risk premium will also be available in the future, as long as one is patient enough. Second, many DB plan managers believe that a 60:40 equity-bond mix provides sufficient diversification over the shorter term to create long-term sustainability, while still providing a 3 percent risk premium as compared to a 100 percent bonds-only policy. They see this as a good reward/risk 'deal'; in fact, the experience of the 1990s persuaded many that even a more aggressive 70:30 mix could pass the prudence test. Given the first two assumptions, resources allocated to managing pension funds can mainly focus on generating additional net return relative to a passively implemented 60:40 (or 70:30) policy portfolio.

The fundamental questions we address in this chapter flow from these assumptions. Is this traditional lens a good one through which to see the pension fund management world in the future, and if not, why not? What would a better lens impart? Our approach is inductive, beginning with a thorough examination of 'old' paradigm pension fund management practices and the results they have produced. We unearth material flaws in current practices and suggest better ways to manage pension funds.

Performance under the Old Paradigm

It is well known that what gets measured, gets managed; hence it is not surprising that the measurement of pension fund performance has historically focused on the third facet of the 'old' paradigm enunciated above. Specifically, managers have been alert to how the fund has performed relative to simply implementing the chosen asset mix policy passively. In other words, managers ask was additional return produced, and at what cost and risk? Answers to this question are available from the Cost Effectiveness Measurement (CEM) database containing 10 years of pension performance data.[1] The database includes information on 256 funds (142 American [\$1.5 trillion], 90 Canadian [C\$374 billion], and 12 each European [€328 billion] and Australian [A\$70 billion]); of these, 114 were corporate, 113 public sector, and 29 industry/other funds. Average fund size was \$9 billion versus a median size of \$2 billion.

In the reported results that follow, all available performance data over the ten-year period was employed including information on funds with less than a full ten-year history. Specifically, all possible calculations were made on the measure equal to [(annual total fund return) − (annual fund policy portfolio return) − (annual total operating costs)]. The resulting 2,671 fund 'net implementation value-added' (NIVA) metrics were analyzed. Figure 11-1 reveals the results: the average NIVA was +11 basis points (bps), with a respectable t-value of 1.8, suggesting that active management did add value over the 1993–2002 period. Even more interesting is the split of total NIVA into its three components. Average 'gross in-category value-added' was an even more impressive +69 bps ($t = 11.2$), while 'mix value-added' subtracted an average −21 bps ($t = -5.9$). Operating costs brought total fund performance down a further average −37 bps.

These findings lead to two further important conclusions. First, operating with a 100 percent passive implementation style costs money, so the proper benchmark against which to evaluate the +11 bps NIVA finding is not 0 bps, but the cost of pure passive implementation including all relevant overheads. This consideration reduces the benchmark NIVA from 0 basis points to, say, minus 9 bps. Consequently, a more realistic estimate of average NIVA experience of the pension funds in the CEM database, relative to a pure passive alternative in the 1993–2002 period, was +20 basis points. Second, the observed average NIVA of +20 bps would have more than doubled, had it not been for the calculated negative ten-year 'mix' effect of −21 bps. This effect resulted from the funds doing something other than following the standard database protocol of rebalancing the asset mix weights back to those of the stated asset mix policy on January first of each year. Below, we address the question of why actual rebalancing strategies systematically underperformed, as compared to the standard rebalancing protocol over the period.

The Asset Class 'Alphas': Good News and Bad News

Also worth investigating further is the question of which asset classes produced the greatest 'in category' net value added, and whether we can identify structural pension fund characteristics that are statistically associated with positive NIVA performance. Figure 11-2 displays the 'in-category selection alphas' for seven major asset classes for all US funds in the CEM database. These 'in-category alphas' are calculated by subtracting from the annual asset class return, the return on a relevant asset class benchmark

Excess
Return

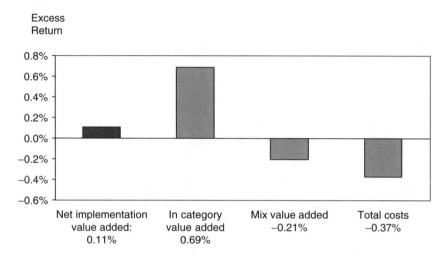

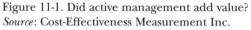

Figure 11-1. Did active management add value?
Source: Cost-Effectiveness Measurement Inc.

Excess Return

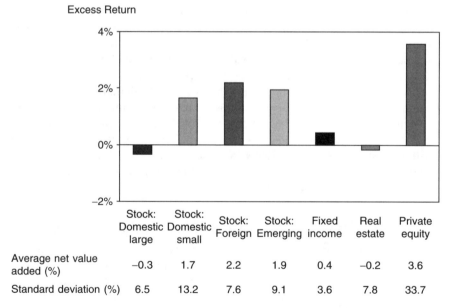

	Stock: Domestic large	Stock: Domestic small	Stock: Foreign	Stock: Emerging	Fixed income	Real estate	Private equity
Average net value added (%)	−0.3	1.7	2.2	1.9	0.4	−0.2	3.6
Standard deviation (%)	6.5	13.2	7.6	9.1	3.6	7.8	33.7

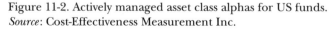

Figure 11-2. Actively managed asset class alphas for US funds.
Source: Cost-Effectiveness Measurement Inc.

portfolio selected by the participating fund. Note also that the direct costs associated with managing investments within each of the seven asset classes (i.e. either external fees or allocated internal costs) have been netted out.

In evaluating Figure 11-2, one should be mindful that the averages and standard deviations were calculated from very large actively managed samples over the 1993–2002 period. For example, the domestic large cap stocks category statistics are drawn from a sample of 1,770 annual observations. Even the real estate and private equity sample sizes are 1,466 and 1,221 respectively. So from the perspective of standard tests of statistical significance, all the calculated average asset class net alphas easily pass the null hypothesis test, except for real estate. That leaves us with five positive asset class alpha results, and only one negative one. That is the good news.

Having said that, the results also confirm that individual fund asset class alpha outcomes vary greatly: this is the bad news. From a reward/risk ratio perspective, none of the average asset class alpha performances are exciting. The attractiveness of average selectivity within foreign stock investing in developed markets scores best with an average reward/risk ratio of 0.3 (i.e. 2.2/7.6), and we suspect this success largely represents the systemic under-weighting of Japan by most US pension funds over the 1993–2002 period. The very modest average 0.1 reward/risk ratio generated by the private equity asset class provides a very sober view of selectivity risk here. The 33.7 percent standard deviation suggests that being right on the asset class is not enough. It means that, even though private equity as an asset class may perform well, one can still end up with terrible results in the fund. The implication is that, unless a fund has enormous confidence in its own private equity manager selection skills, it had better pay careful attention to manager diversification.

Of course, the observed great variance in private equity results could be given a more positive spin. The results suggest that good manager selection skills in this asset class have a very large payoff. Figure 11-2 statistics suggest that similar conclusions (both negative and positive) apply to the domestic small cap stocks and foreign emerging markets stocks asset classes.

The Negative Mix-Related Alpha Question: Is 'Excess Cash' the Culprit?

We next focus on the highly statistically significant −21 bps average annual loss due to asset mix-related reasons over the ten-year period displayed earlier in Figure 11-1. Further research points to a likely contributor: in the eight individual years when average fund policy returns were positive (i.e. 1993–2000), the average asset mix–related alphas were negative in each year. In contrast, in the two individual years when the average fund policy returns were negative (i.e. 2001 and 2002), the average asset mix–related alphas were positive in both years.

What does this year-by-year breakdown of the ten-year average −21 bps result imply? It suggests that the holding of excess cash in relation to the policy asset mix may be a culprit, a hypothesis consistent with the average asset mix–related alpha being negative in each of the eight positive policy return-years (average mix alpha was −32 bps), and being positive in each of the two negative policy return years (average mix alpha was +28 bps). The discovery that holding 'excess cash' may reduce the typical fund's incremental return by one-third sends a powerful message. Decisive steps should be taken to minimize the negative impact of excess cash on total fund long-term performance.

Is There Also a Pay-off from Actively Managing Pension Fund Costs?

Figure 11-1 indicated that investment-related total operating costs captured in the database averaged 37 bps annually over the ten-year period. Table 11-1 provides important additional information, where we note that the database spans annual cost experience from a miniscule 1 bp to a hefty 236 bps (based on 2,450 observations). Indeed, the 10–90 percentile experience still encompasses a broad 15–58 bps range. This wide-ranging operating cost experience prompts an important question: is there an 'excess cost' performance drag, in the same way that the analysis above suggested there was an excess cash performance drag, over most of the 1993–2002 period?

The simplest way to address this question is to regress fund performance (NIVA) against total operating costs. If there was an excess cost performance drag embedded in the data, it would show up as a statistically significant negative cost coefficient—a hypothesis that seems to be the case. The statistically significant cost coefficient was −0.48 ($t = -2.2$), implying that one basis point of additional operating cost reduced NIVA by an average −0.48 bps over the 1993–2002 period. While this is an important finding, it raises three important further questions. First, pension fund management

TABLE 11-1 Annual Total Operating Costs (bps)

Low	1.1
10th percentile	14.5
1st quartile	23.1
Median	33.9
3rd quartile	46.7
90th percentile	58.4
High	236.2

Source: Cost-Effectiveness Measurement Inc.

should experience significant economies of scale; what happens when we adjust for this scale factor? Second, certain types of investment policies are much more expensive to implement than others; what happens when we adjust for this investment policy factor? Third, operating cost structures may to some degree be country-specific; what happens when we adjust for this country factor?

All three questions have interesting answers. First we find that the scale effect averaged −19 bps. For every tenfold increase in fund asset value in the database (total range $100 million–$150 billion), total operating costs declined an average −19 bps. Thus large funds have a material cost advantage over small funds. Second, the incremental cost coefficients for domestic stock, foreign stock, real estate, and private equity mandates were +38, +62, +88, and +199 bps. These metrics indicate average total operating cost increases by shifting a fund out of bonds into domestic stocks, foreign stocks, real estate, and or private equity respectively. Thus investment policy choices do materially impact cost experience. Finally, adjusted for scale and mix factors, Canadian funds experienced operating costs an average −11 bps lower than their US counterparts. It appears that Canadian funds generally chose simpler investment management structures and faced lower domestic external management fee structures. Out of the total cost variance (measured by a standard deviation of 19 bps for the full sample), these three cost drivers explained about one-half of the cost variance.

Next we examine whether the three systematic cost drivers are responsible for the measured 'excess cost' performance drag coefficient of −0.48 bps. This is assessed by reestimating the fund NIVA performance versus fund operating costs relationship, but now using fund cost experience adjusted for differences in scale, asset mix, and country. If the 'excess cost' coefficient remains statistically significantly negative, it would indicate that—regardless of fund size, mix, or country—eliminating excess costs, like eliminating excess cash, has a positive performance payoff. The new excess cost coefficient is, in fact, negative and significant [−0.54; $t = -1.9$]. Thus every basis point of additional scale-mix-country-adjusted excess cost reduced NIVA by an average −0.54 bps over the 1993–2002 period. This suggests that managing costs by ensuring that they have a positive payoff matters, which is the essence of cost-effectiveness.

Two Cost-Effectiveness Strategies

What might specific examples of such 'cost-effectiveness' strategies be? The CEM database offers two examples. First, there is no statistical difference between the gross alphas of comparable externally and internally managed investment mandates. However, internal management is on average 30 bps less costly and hence that strategy outperformed external management by an average 30 bps on a net basis. Second, every 10 percentage point increase in passive management was statistically associated with nine bps of additional NIVA. This suggests that significant exposure to very low-cost passive management, together with concentrated active management, was generally a cost-effective, value-producing combination over the period.

These findings add up to two important lessons. In assessing the attractiveness of within-asset class active management, it is first important to distinguish between average experience, and the variability of that experience. For example, over the 1993–2002 period, active management was on average successful in five out of seven major asset classes. However, with that average success came significant potential for individual funds to reduce return rather than enhance it. Second, a much surer way to increase fund NIVA is to carefully manage excess cash and excess costs. The value of having neither was easily worth as much as the total average value of active management, but without its downside exposure, suggesting that there may, after all, be something akin to the proverbial 'free lunch'.

The Common Performance Driver: Organizational Effectiveness

Our findings in turn beget broader questions. For instance, can we identify a common driver of good (or bad) 'alpha' performance? What can we learn about the attributes of high performance pension funds? Research during the 1990s provides interesting answers to these questions. For instance, anthropologists William O'Barr and John Conley (1992) caused quite a stir with their book on pension fund management drawn from close observations of nine pension fund organizations over the 1990–1 period. These evaluations led them to conclude that fund organizational structures were the result of the funds' historical origins, rather than from the disciplined application of good governance and management practices. They also found that deflecting responsibility and shifting blame seemed to be important motivators in the funds' decision-making processes. For instance, close relationships with outside services suppliers (e.g. money managers, consultants, investment dealers, custodians) seemed to be an extraordinarily high priority for pension fund trustees and executives.

The pension community of the day reacted with shock and outrage to these allegations, but when, two years later, fifty pension fund CEOs were asked what they estimated their 'excellence shortfall' to be (i.e. annual return shortfall due to internal governance and management problems), the median response was a hefty 66 bps. When they characterized the nature of their internal problems, most mentioned poor structure and decision processes (forty-nine mentions), almost half mentioned inadequate resources (twenty-four mentions), and almost half spoke of lack of focus and mission clarity (twenty-two mentions). This feedback suggested that perhaps O'Barr and Conley had found factors that did actually make a difference.

Logically then, the next step in the performance driver discovery process was to establish a statistical relationship between pension fund performance and the quality of governance and management practices. In an initial study, Ambachtsheer et al. (1998) used 1993–6 NIVAs from the CEM regressed on metrics representing the quality of a pension fund's governance and management practices. These were calculated from the survey responses of eighty participating pension fund CEOs. The heart of the survey was forty-five statements related to a fund's governance, management, and operations practices. The CEOs were invited to give each of the statements a ranking between one and six, depending on their assessment how well the statement reflected reality inside their own organization. Each statement was designed so that a six represented perceived best practice and a one perceived poor practice. In each case, the average of the forty-five statement rankings in each survey was designated as the 'CEO Score' for that survey. Thus in all, eighty 'CEO Scores' were calculated from the eighty completed surveys.

The eighty CEO Scores were interesting: for instance, scores ranged from a low of 3.0 to a high of 6.0, with both mean and median scores at 4.8. This meant that overall, the eighty raters felt pretty good about their organizations (not one was below three at the low end, and one wag assigned his organization a perfect six on forty-five counts). Having said that, an overall three to six score spread is a good statistical range to work with. Also, of the eighty CEOs, fifty-one represented corporate funds and twenty-nine noncorporate (mainly public sector). The average corporate CEO Score was 4.9 versus a 4.7 average for noncorporates; the difference was not statistically significant though it suggested that corporate fund CEOs had, on average, a somewhat higher opinion of their fund's organizational competence than did noncorporate fund CEOs of theirs. This finding fits nicely with our earlier observation that corporate funds had somewhat higher average NIVA performance over the 1993–2002 period (12 bps) than did noncorporate funds. The statistical relationship between the CEO Scores and fund investment performance, the data indicated a 'CEO Score' coefficient of 0.4 with a significant t-value of 2.9, using 1993–6 performance data. This meant that an additional point of CEO Score in 1997 translated into an additional average 40 bps of annual return over the 1993–6 period. A two-point 'CEO Score' increase, say from 3.5 to 5.5, was associated with 80 bps of annual incremental performance. This finding fitted nicely with the median 66 bps excellence shortfall estimate of the fifty CEOs at the 1994 New York gathering.

We have now updated the analysis to 2000, as reported in Table 11-2. Arguably, finding a statistical relationship between the CEO Scores and

TABLE 11-2 New Results: Fund Performance vs. 'CEO Scores'

	'CEO score' coefficient	t-value
Pre-survey period		
4-year period (1993–6)	+0.4	2.9
Post-survey period		
1-year period (1997)	+0.8	2.7
2-year period (1997–8)	+0.6	1.9
3-year period (1997–9)	+0.7	1.7
4-year period (1997–2000)	+0.3	1.0

fund performance in this post-survey period would provide further confirmation that good governance and management matter most. First we replicate previous findings for the 1993–6 period, and then we set out the new results for 1997 only, then for 1997–8, then for 1997–9, and finally for the full 1997–2000 period.

The evidence shows that funds with high CEO Scores were able to maintain their average performance edge, relative to funds with low CEO Scores, even after immediately after the survey was conducted in 1997. It was only in the fourth year after the rankings were completed that there was a material reduction in the performance edge of high CEO Score funds relative to the low scoring funds. Note that the post-survey period coefficients were higher than the pre-survey coefficient of 0.4, until the year 2000 was included in the performance results. So it appears that a careful study of governance and management practices can help in understanding and hence improving pension fund performance.

Good Governance and Management Related to NIVA Performance

We should recall that the 'CEO Scores' were composites of forty-five individual statement rankings: approximately one-third of these statements related to governance practices, one-third to management practices, and one-third to operations. A test to determine which of the forty-five statement scores correlated most closely with fund performance showed that only eleven had significant positive correlation with fund performance. Of these, six were governance-related and five management-related.

The statistically significant governance statements in the survey related mainly to effective fiduciary behavior and selection processes, clarity in delegation of authority, and a high level of trust between the governing and managing fiduciaries. The statistically significant management statements related mainly to clear strategic positioning and to the effective development and execution of the fund's strategic plan. These findings represent a noteworthy convergence between what are deemed to be generally good governance and management practices in the for-profit and not-for-profit sectors as a whole, and what we now find is important in the governance and management of pension funds.

An interesting issue is why the performance edge of the high CEO Score funds began to diminish in the fourth year after the scores were captured. Perhaps the high scoring funds of 1997 failed to work hard enough to maintain a competitive advantage beyond 1997. Certainly, we find that maintaining a competitive advantage requires as much work as it took to achieve that advantage in the first place. This question deserves further research.

Assessing Pension Fund Risk

Until this point, the discussion has not considered the risk side of the pension fund management task. Figure 11-3 plots the net alphas (NIVAs)

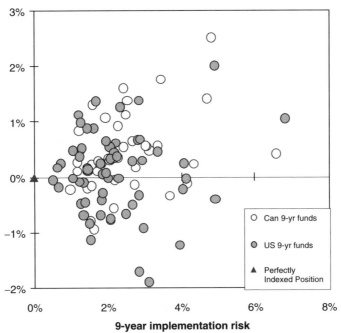

Figure 11-3. Implementation value added vs. implementation risk.
Source: Cost-Effectiveness Measurement Inc.

of all eighty US and Canadian funds with ten years of continuous data against their implementation risk (i.e. the volatility of fund returns relative to their respective policy portfolio returns). This implementation risk can be thought of as the additional risk contributed by active management. As noted above, the average NIVA realization was marginally positive. Now we also see that the measured implementation risk for these funds ranged from a low of virtually zero, to a couple of outliers in the six percent range. Nevertheless, the bulk of measured experience was around two percent. Statistically, the NIVA/Tracking Error Volatility coefficient was a positive 0.12, with a *t*-value of 1.9. So on average, funds garnered a marginal amount of additional net alpha for a modest amount of additional 'active' risk. Thus our previous conclusion continues to hold: in an old paradigm context, pension fund management was on average modestly successful over the ten-year period ending 2002.

Next we explore the behavior of the fund return components that can be attributed to the funds' choices of asset mix policy. In the CEM data file, these choices are represented by passively implemented 'policy portfolios'. Specifically, we are interested in the behavior of these policy portfolios relative to the liability return requirements of each fund.[2] These requirements are estimated in each case by calculating the return on a bond portfolio (i.e. the 'liability portfolio') that mimics a fund's liabilities in terms of duration and inflation-sensitivity. Figure 11-4 addresses this ques-

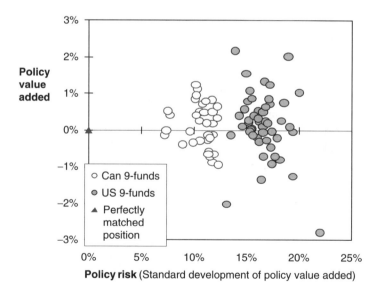

Figure 11-4. Policy value added vs policy risk.
Source: Cost-Effectiveness Measurement Inc.

tion and it tells a much less positive story. In comparison with Figure 11-3, for instance, nothing much changes on the vertical axis. Over the observation period, policy portfolio returns over/underperformed their respective 'liability portfolio' returns in a narrow +2% to −2% range (i.e. Policy Value Added). However, looking along the horizontal axis (i.e. Policy Risk), one notes that the policy mismatch volatility metrics for the Canadian funds are now in the 7–12 percent range. For the US funds, the range is more like 15–20 percent. Further, there is no correlation between the liability-relative excess returns and liability relative policy risks. So we derive two important conclusions: first, the 'policy' risk of US funds dominated their 'active' risk by a factor of about eight to one over the ten-year observation period. Second, this outsized exposure to policy risk received, on average, no compensation.

The database also provides direct evidence that, consistent with 'old' paradigm thinking, fund managers of late have made no measurable effort to take into account the financial characteristics of their liabilities when structuring their fund policy portfolios. A test was devised to compare the asset mix policies of the 50 percent of US funds with the most inflation-sensitive liabilities (82 percent inflation-sensitive, on average) with the 50 percent with the least inflation-sensitive liabilities (31 percent inflation-sensitive, on average). It turned out that the two subuniverses had, on average, identical asset mix policies: 63 percent equities, 32 percent fixed income, and 5 percent inflation-sensitive investments. Even if the two subuniverses had the same appetite for equity risk, one would expect that the most inflation-sensitive half of the universe would favour inflation-sensitive investment over fixed income investments. The reverse should be true with the less inflation-sensitive subuniverse. Remarkably, this was not the case.

The bottom line is that, when both recent bull market and bear market experiences are included in the measurement period, and when we benchmark the realized policy returns against marked-to-market liability portfolio requirements, the policy portfolios of DB pension funds generated very little excess return for a highly material amount of balance sheet mismatch risk in the ten years ending in 2002. (Thus, Figure 11-4 showed that most US funds had policy risks in the 15–20 percent range.) Of course under 'old' paradigm behavior, these findings should not be surprising. We know, for example, that 'old' paradigm typically behavior produces very similar policy asset mixes without regard for differences in liability structures. We also know that the observation period included the three-year 'perfect pension storm' period (i.e. 2000–2), when both equity prices and bond yields fell together; this led to massive marked-to-market funded pension ratio declines in the 25–50 percentage point range. The profound question raised by these findings is whether the 'old' fund management paradigm indeed is the best lens through which pension fiduciaries should see their world.

Why the 'Old' Lens Distorts

The old lens is not the best lens for pension fiduciaries to use today for at least three reasons. First, the prospective equity risk premium will not always be 5 percent, even over long periods: it can be predictably high, normal, or low, with 'normal' about 2.5 percent rather than 5 percent. Second, a 60:40 (or 70:30) asset mix policy is not always a good reward/risk 'deal' for the stakeholders in pension plans. This is because such a policy will not always offer sufficient reward per unit of properly defined risk; further, in some situations, such a policy is just absolutely too risky, regardless of whether the prospective reward is sufficient or not. Third, devoting the bulk of a fund's resources to attempt to generate a modest amount of policy portfolio-relative 'net alpha' for a modest amount of policy portfolio-relative additional risk may no longer be prudent.

To confirm that the equity risk premium is indeed predictably high, medium, or low, we point to Figure 11-5 which plots almost 200 years of equity risk premium predictions on the horizontal axis, against on the vertical axis what actually happened (i.e. the actual excess return of equities

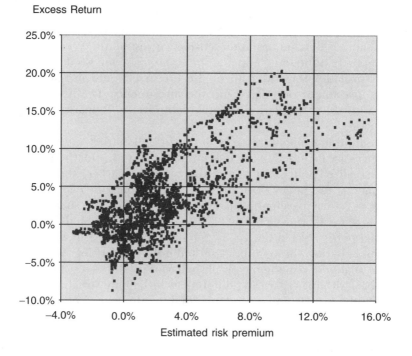

Figure 11-5. Equity risk premium & subsequent ten-year excess returns, 1810–1991. *Source*: Arnott and Bernstein (2002).

relative to bonds) over the ten-year period after the predictions were made. The figure uses the simple rule of thumb that the ERP at any point in time equals the current dividend yield plus the prior ten years earnings growth minus the current long bond yield. Note the predictions on the horizontal axis range from minus three percent to +15 percent. The actual ten-year outcomes on the vertical axis range from minus eight percent to +20 percent (Arnott and Bernstein 2002).

The key issue is whether there is a positive relationship between the equity risk premium predictions and the subsequent ten-year outcomes purely random. The data show that this was indeed the case. Generally, high predictions produced high outcomes, and low predictions low outcomes. The rule of thumb equity risk premium prediction calculation today works out to about +1.5 percent.[3] The figure says that when the prediction is +1.5 percent, the historical ten-year outcome range has been about −7 percent to +10 percent. There are no good reasons that we know of why this range should not also frame ten-year equity-bond return prospects today. If it does, the case for placing most of the risk chips in pension funds on a policy portfolio with 60–70 percent equity exposure is questionable.

Figure 11-5 also makes clear that even if the rule of thumb produced an expected equity risk premium today higher than 1.5 percent, a policy portfolio with 60–70 percent equity exposure might still be too risky, in some situations. Pension funds of DB plans sponsored by corporations struggling with poor operating results and weak balance sheets come to mind. The figure also shows that in a world of varying equity risk premium prospects, and varying abilities of fund stakeholders to withstand disappointing outcomes in five to ten year timeframes, focusing largely on alpha games, where the realistic stakes are a net 0.5 percent of extra return for two percent of extra risk, makes little sense.

A New Lens

So pension fund managers need a new lens. Here are its three facets. First, *a set of investment beliefs* grounded in good theory and confirmed by real world experience. An important element of such a beliefs set should be the notion of a predictably varying equity risk premium. Other elements will reflect views on the return generation processes in various capital market sectors and the predictability of those processes. Second, *an integrative investment model* is needed that directly links a varying return opportunity set to stakeholder income needs and risk tolerances. The essence of a successful model is to capture the linkages between fuzzy expectations, transactional friction, and stakeholder needs. Third, *a decision-making protocol* must be designed that can dynamically integrate components one and two into 'value' for fund stakeholders. The essence of a successful protocol is effective human interaction. Thus its foundation must be alignment of economic interests, good governance, and good organization design.

The implications of seeing pension fund management through this new three-component lens can be best understood by being mindful of Einstein's observation that solving significant problems requires a higher level of thinking than used to create them. For example, while Keynes' 1936 opus *The General Theory* was meant to address the economics of depression, it contains a very powerful chapter on investment beliefs (Keynes 1961 Chapter 12). With some restatement, Keynes believed that capitalism embodies two distinct types of investment processes. 'Long horizon' investing is about the projection and valuation of future cash flows. 'Short horizon' investing is about zero-sum, adversarial trading in financial instruments. The mistake many pension funds make is to try and blend these two radically different investment processes together. In the 'old' paradigm, 'long horizon' strategies are assumed to have pre-determined long term, static expected rates of return. 'Short horizon' strategies, on the other hand, require 'smart' active managers capable of producing positive net alpha. So, for example, most 'active' investment mandates today continue to be defined in the context of static 'long horizon' benchmark portfolios, to which active managers are to add some 'alpha' through over/underweighting strategies.

This is a highly restrictive, suboptimal delegation strategy, if two plausible conditions hold. The first condition is that the expected returns on 'long horizon' investment strategies are not static but variable, and to some degree predictive. The second condition is that successful 'active' strategies can be identified before the fact. These two conditions logically lead to the internally controlled, dynamic, integrated 'new' paradigm reward/risk management process further described below. Why is the long horizon/short horizon distinction so important in this? Because there is persuasive evidence that the returns on 'long horizon' investments are intrinsically predictive, to some degree. In contrast, whether the returns on 'short horizon' investment processes (most efficiently packaged as bundles of active market-neutral strategies) are predictive, is in the eyes of the beholder. But what may be true for some can't possibly be true for all.

There is no place for static 'policy portfolios' in this 'new' investment paradigm. The integrative investment model sketched out in Figure 11-6 makes clear why. The only relevant benchmark now is the risk-minimizing portfolio that looks most like the liabilities the pension fund is meant to cover. Moving to the right on the horizontal axis implies taking on increasing mismatch risk relative to this liability portfolio. In the 'new' paradigm, all mismatch risk is 'active' risk. It no longer matters whether its source is 'long horizon' risky strategies, 'short horizon' risky strategies, or some blend of the two. The vertical axis measures increasing amounts of expected or realized excess return relative to the return of the risk-minimizing portfolio. The 10 percent on the horizontal axis might

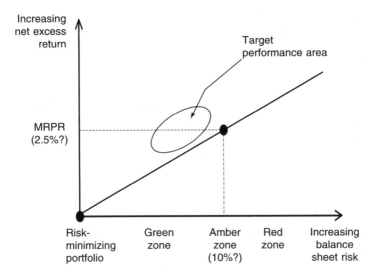

Figure 11-6. Integrative investment model.

represent the 'mismatch risk budget' that a fund management must work within. The 1.5 percent on the vertical axis might represent the minimum required price of risk (MRPR) that should be earned with a 10 percent risk budget. The ellipse indicating the target performance area suggests that now all that matters are balance sheet–relative results, and not policy portfolio–relative results. Thus that is also what should be measured.

Earlier in the chapter, we provided statistical evidence that good governance and organization design matter. Such human system-based disciplines lead to mission clarity, delegation clarity, effective strategic planning and execution, and a high level trust within the pension fund organization. These factors in turn drive superior organization performance, and getting them right is just as important as getting the investment beliefs and the investment model right. Specifically then, these factors become important in actually moving the organization from the 'old' to the 'new' paradigm, and in setting up the necessary infrastructure to run a 'new' paradigm pension fund organization.

If this is the new standard against which to evaluate the practices of today's institutional investment community, how does it measure up? Unfortunately, most of the discussions we hear at various institutional investment forums continue to fit the 'old' investment paradigm far better than the new. Nevertheless, there are glimmers of light, since some pension fund executives are observing that they are being pressed by their boards 'to become more tactical'. We take this to mean that some boards are beginning to understand there is no such thing as a single policy portfolio for all seasons. Instead, the emerging view is that balance sheets should be managed dynamically, sensitive to changing socioeconomic and capital market conditions.

Another encouraging sign is the fact that conference agendas have been giving greater attention to the importance of good fund governance and organization design. Pension boards and investment executives themselves have begun to pay more attention to these organizational factors. Pension consultants are becoming more open to the possibility of a paradigm shift. Investment managers with confidence in their investment skills are beginning to see their world through a lens that splits investment strategies as being either 'long horizon' or 'short horizon' based.

Conclusions

Pension fund management has been guided by a paradigm that appeared to work well during the 1980s and the 1990s. It seemed to be a good lens through which to see the world. The equity risk premium was generally positive, as assumptions suggested it should be. Equity market dips were short, and soon reversed themselves. Nothing happened that a 60–40 asset mix policy apparently couldn't deal with. In addition, our research confirmed that over the ten-year 1993–2002 period, a typical fund generated a modest amount of 'net alpha' by taking a modest amount of 'implementation' risk relative to its policy portfolio. Under the 'old' paradigm, this was an important accomplishment.

Then, during the three-year 'perfect pension storm' of 2000–2, the 'old' lens developed serious cracks. The surpluses on DB balance sheets turned to serious deficits. With the benefit of hindsight, it became clear that the asset mix policies of the 1990s exposed the stakeholders of DB balance sheets to material mismatch risk. This experience has led many pension boards and executives to ask if that material mismatch risk has now receded. Alternatively, could pension balance sheet stakeholders withstand the financial pain if a 2000–2 type shock were to occur again a few years hence. Related issues are how much compensation in terms of additional expected return is sufficient for these risks to be undertaken, and what the sources of that addition return will be in the future. Any pension organization that thinks these questions are important can no longer be guided by the 'old' paradigm. It needs a new lens through which to see the world.

Endnotes

1. Cost-Effectiveness Measurement Inc. (CEM) benchmarks the organizational performance of many of the world's largest DB and DC pension plans, both on the investment and benefit administration sides of the pension 'business'. The author is a Founding Partner of the firm, located in Toronto, Canada.

2. CEM estimates the 'liability returns' of participating DB pension plans by first creating a bond portfolio that reflects the inflation sensitivity and the duration of plan liabilities, and then estimating the marked-to-market annual return on that portfolio.
3. The current stock dividend yield is about 1.5 percent. The referenced Arnott-Bernstein paper (2002) suggests a good dividend real growth rule of thumb is 2 percent. The current yield on long TIPS is about 2 percent. So using the simplified Gordon formula, we are looking at a current equity risk premium estimate of $\{1.5\% + 2\% - 2\% = 1.5\%\}$.

References

Ambachtsheer, Keith, Ronald Capelle and Tom Scheibelhut (1998). 'Improving Pension Fund Performance', *Financial Analysts' Journal*, 54/6:15–20.

Arnott, Robert and Peter L. Bernstein (2002). 'What Risk Premium is Normal?', *Financial Analysts' Journal*, 58/2: 64–85.

Keynes, John Maynard (1961). *The General Theory of Employment, Interest and Money*. New York: St. Martin's Press.

O'Barr, William and John Conley (1992). *Fortune and Folly: The Wealth and Power of Institutional Investing*. Homewood, IL: Business One Irwin.

Chapter 12

Profitable Prudence: The Case for Public Employer Defined Benefit Plans

Gary W. Anderson and Keith Brainard

US public sector plans covering employees of state and local governments have grown to comprise a substantial segment of national pension assets and membership. Participants include more than 14 million workers—10 percent of the national workforce—and six million retirees as well as other annuitants; all are members of more than 2,000 retirement systems sponsored by a state or local government (US Census 2002). These systems have combined assets of more than $2 trillion and they distributed over $110 billion in pension and other benefits (Board of Governors 2004; US Census 2002); this volume exceeded the entire economic output of twenty-two states and the District of Columbia (US Dept. of Commerce 2003).

In recent years, public sector pensions have diverged from the private sector pension trend, in that the percentage of public employees participating in a defined benefit (DB) plan has held steady at around 90 percent, while the fraction of private sector workers with a DB plan has plummeted to around 20 percent (BLS 2002). Against the backdrop of thirty years of private pension experience with the Employee Retirement Income Security Act (ERISA) of 1974, it is useful to note that US public sector pensions evolved before, and outside the purview of, this federal legislation. This different experience makes it invaluable to not only learn what effects state and local government pensions have on stakeholders—including participants, public sectors employers, and taxpayers—but also to glean lessons that the public pension experience may offer to private industry.

A Brief History of Public Pensions

Public DB plans have engaged in substantial efforts to reinvent themselves in recent years, adding elements that increase their flexibility and portability. Nevertheless, public plans retain the core attributes of a traditional DB model: that is, the employer bears investment risk and the plan pays lifelong benefits according to a specified formula. Against this backdrop, it remains the case that each of the over 2,000 public retirement systems has its own unique plan design, benefit structure, and governance arrangement, set forth in a vast assortment of state constitutions, laws, and administrative rules. This mosaic of structures and features reflects each state's rich variety of legal, political, economic, and demographic cultures and history, as well as its political subdivisions. In other words, state and local government plans are creatures of state constitutional, statutory, and case law. As such, public pensions are accountable to each state's legislative and executive branches, independent boards of trustees which often include employee representatives and ex officio publicly elected officials, and ultimately, the taxpayers of that jurisdiction.

Although some US public pensions date to the late Nineteenth century, most public plans were established between the 1920s and 1940s. These were mainly of the DB variety. Municipal governments led states and the federal government in providing pension coverage for their workers, largely because the first groups to be covered—police, firefighters, and teachers—were established at the local level, by cities, towns, and school districts. As Clark et al. (2003) point out, these plans were initially financed from employee contributions, as a form of 'forced saving plans,' although over time, employers gradually took on greater responsibility for plan financing.

Because public employees initially had their own plans, the US Social Security system initially excluded state and local government workers due to uncertainty about whether the federal government could legally tax state and local employers. In 1950, Congress amended the Social Security Act to allow states to voluntarily provide Social Security coverage for their employees, if the state entered into an agreement with the Social Security Administration (Mitchell and Hustead 2001). Today, the majority of state and local government employees participate in Social Security; the remaining nonparticipants are teachers and public safety personnel though most public employees in seven states do not participate (Alaska, Colorado, Maine, Massachusetts, Louisiana, Nevada, and Ohio). Where employees are exempt from social security contributions, the pension benefit and contribution levels are typically higher.

The passage of ERISA and subsequent amendments were watershed events in the evolution of private industry pensions, but these had little impact on public pensions which remained largely untouched by federal regulation. As Metz noted (1988: 4):

Governmental plans are specifically exempt from all of the substantive qualification requirements added to the (Internal Revenue) Code by Title II of ERISA (with the exception of the Section 415 maximum limitation on benefits), including those relating directly to participation, vesting, funding, prohibited transactions, joint and survivor annuities, plan merger and consolidation, alienation and assignment of plan benefits, payment of benefits, certain social security benefit increases, and withdrawal of employee contributions. In addition, governmental plans are exempt from ERISA's other major provisions, including reporting and disclosure requirements (Title I) and plan termination insurance (Title IV). Although government plans are not subject to ERISA's participation, vesting, funding and fiduciary rules, they are, nonetheless, covered by comparable although not as restrictive rules as stated in the Internal Revenue Code before ERISA's enactment.

In the private sector, ERISA's impact was to impose a relatively uniform and comprehensive set of regulations and standards to the pension sector; by contrast, public retirement systems' diverse nature would not be possible if they had been governed in a like manner. This is not to say that the federal government has not tried, as noted by the GFOA (1992):

Since passage of ERISA, in 1974... Congress has deliberated over federal involvement in the setting of conforming standards for state and local government retirement systems. In 1978, the Pension Task Force Report, issued by the House Committee on Education and Labor, recommended federal regulation of PERS. Legislative proposals have been introduced in each successive Congress to establish federal rules for state and local government retirement systems. However, during this period PERS have made great strides in funding future pension obligations, following prudent investment policies, disseminating information and implementing administrative and operational discipline. These advances have been made without the intervention of the federal government.

Public versus Private Sector Plan Differences

Since the passage of ERISA, the percentage of private sector workers with a DB plan as their primary retirement benefit has fallen steadily, while coverage has risen by defined contribution (DC) plans (primarily of the 401(k) variety). A recent Bureau of Labor Statistics (BLS 2003) study found that only 58 percent of full-time private sector workers participated in an employer-sponsored retirement plan, and only 10 percent of private sector employers nationwide provided a DB plan. By contrast, virtually all full-time public sector employees participate in a retirement plan, and the vast majority (90 percent) is in a DB plan. Here benefits are usually expressed as a percentage of salary for a designated period just before retirement, multiplied by years of service credit (Findlay 1997).

What accounts for the divergence in pension coverage and type, when comparing private industry and the public sector? Several reasons have been offered for the loss of ground by DB plans in the private sector: increased private-sector government regulation; changes in the private-sector workplace, including growing employee and employer appreciation of DC plans; changes in business awareness regarding risk associated with funding DB plans; falling firmsize; greater global competition boosting the need for more flexibility in plan design; and successful marketing efforts of consultants and DC plan service providers (Rajnes 2002).

Nevertheless, there are also less appealing consequences of relying on DC plans as the primary retirement benefit (CBO 2003). For instance, DC plans are seen as an unreliable vehicle for ensuring financial security in retirement to the extent that investment risk is borne solely by individual participants; this is exacerbated when plan participants are poor investors. A study prepared for the Nebraska Public Employee Retirement System (PERS) found that from 1983–99, that system's DB plans generated an average of 11 percent annually, but the system's DC participants paid returns of only 6 percent (Buck Consultants 2000). This occurred despite ongoing efforts by the PERS to educate participants on the importance of proper asset allocation. Nebraska PERS also found that a large percentage of terminating DC participants cashed out their retirement saving rather than retaining them in a retirement account. One explanation for why public DC plan returns lag professionally invested DB portfolios is that the DC asset allocations are often quite conservative. For instance, approximately half of all assets held in 403(b) and 457 plans (primarily and exclusively used by public employees, respectively) were held in the form of annuity reserves at life insurance companies (ICI 2004).

Another concern with DC plans as the primary retirement benefit is termed the 'leakage' problem, a term applied to describe a variety of circumstances when retirement assets are spent by plan participants before retirement. For example, leakage occurs if an employee chooses to spend his retirement assets after leaving a job, rather than rolling them over to an Individual Retirement Account or to a new employer's retirement plan. Leakage also occurs when workers borrow against their retirement plan assets and then fail to repay the loans. A recent study by Brainard (2003:7) addressed the issue of leakage as follows:

A good example of terminating participants spending, rather than saving, their retirement assets are in Nebraska, where state and county government employees historically have participated in a DC plan. A study of the Nebraska Public Employees Retirement System, conducted by a national actuarial consultant, found that 68% of terminating participants cashed out their assets rather than rolling them over to another retirement plan. This finding is consistent with a Hewitt Associates study which found that more than two-thirds of participants terminating from DC plans cash out their lump sum distributions rather than rolling them to other retirement accounts.

In what follows, we outline the key advantages of DB plans to public sector employees and employers, seeking to illustrate how this paradigm for retirement provision is well-situated to meet retirement needs of the future.

Benefits to Employees

The ideal mix of retirement income sources has long been described as a 'three-legged stool,' with one leg each representing Social Security, an employer pension, and individual savings. As a rule of thumb, financial planners recommend replacing approximately 70–80 percent of one's working income in retirement. Public sector DB plans help achieve this goal by linking employee salary and retirement income: thus a Social Security–eligible employee retiring with twenty years of service in a typical public pension plan can expect the benefit to replace 35–40 percent of his salary. Combined with Social Security and personal saving, the retiree then finds the 70–80 percent target within reach. Retirees and beneficiaries of public DB plans received annual benefits of over $18,000 in fiscal year 2002 (Brainard 2004).[1] In addition to the basic DB plan, many public employers today also offer a voluntary, supplemental retirement saving plan which enables workers to save on their own for retirement. The most popular public employer-sponsored supplemental savings plans are 457 plans, also known as deferred compensation plans, and 403(b) plans, commonly referred to TSA's or tax-sheltered annuities.

Retiree financial independence relies heavily on the guaranteed income replacement concept provided by a DB plan, and it also relies on the central concept that the retiree will continue to receive benefits until death. Further, most public DB plans provide joint and survivor annuity options, to ensure that spouses and other named beneficiaries will continue to receive a benefit even in the event of the death of the retiree (Mitchell and Hustead 2001). By contrast, DC plans do not guarantee access to a life annuity nor joint and survivor benefits.

A factor receiving increasing attention in recent years is the point that public DB assets are held in trust for participants; the assets are normally administered by a governing board whose members are legal fiduciaries. Unlike private industry DB plans, which can be curtailed in the event of the plan sponsor's bankruptcy, public pension benefits generally cannot be reduced. That is, ERISA protects only private sector DB benefits that have already accrued, while it does not protect the right to future benefit accruals. Constitutional provisions governing contract and property rights are generally interpreted as protecting not only accrued benefits but also future benefit accruals. This practice varies from state to state, with some state constitutions explicitly protecting pension benefits, while in other cases, statutes and case law expressly forbid cutting pension benefits. By contrast, state and local laws generally afford participants far greater protections, prohibiting public employers from diminishing the benefit formula, often with respect to future accruals. Another advantage of public plans is that most provide some form of protection against inflation. Since the median life expectancy of a 65-year-old woman is 22 years in the USA, inflation of just 2 percent will cut purchasing power by more than one-third over the retirement period. Public plans offer several mechanisms for adjusting benefits post-retirement, including with periodic adjustments subject to legislative approval, automatic increases linked to the inflation rate, and annual automatic increases of a flat percentage or dollar amount (Brainard 2003).

Benefits to Employers

Pensions were introduced in the public sector to help public administrators attract and retain quality workers, to provide them with performance incentives, and to retire them in an orderly fashion (Eitelberg 1997). It is worth recognizing that governments, in their dual roles as both employers and policymakers, are uniquely situated to promote retirement financial security and serve as models for private industry, in their capacity as employer to more than one in ten working Americans.

The diversity of the public sector workforce has few, if any, peers in private industry, and attracting and retaining such a workforce requires a concerted and ongoing effort. For instance, just a few of the numerous positions maintained by US public employers include game wardens and garbage collectors, school teachers and environmental scientists, elected officials and insurance analysts, psychiatrists and custodians, historians and police officers, prison guards and firefighters, and college professors, among others. Each of these positions requires a different set of skills, knowledge, and abilities; exhibits differing demographic features and career patterns; and has unique requirements for recruitment, retention, salary, and compensation. As Mitchell and Hustead (2001: 15) note:

One reason why pension plans differ (from those in private industry) is that they cover employees with different employment characteristics. For instance, because police work and fire fighting are physically demanding occupations, retirement benefits for public safety workers typically allow retirement at earlier ages, in part to maintain a younger workforce. Consequently, the retirement benefits available to police and firefighters are usually different from those provided to teachers or to general employees.

Similarly, pensions for judges typically are intended to reflect that, as a group, judges are older than most other employees when entering their positions, and they often forgo larger salaries in private industry to serve as judges. Since protecting and educating its citizens is generally considered to be a government's core responsibilities, it should be no surprise that more than half of all public employees work in positions classified by the US Bureau of Labor Statistics (2002) as either Education or Protective Service. More than nine million public employees are classified as educational (including teachers, administrators, and workers in supportive roles), and there are approximately one million law enforcement personnel and firefighters in the USA.

Not only do public DB plans attract a diverse group; they also promote retention efforts by rewarding length of service. This is because DB plan formulas usually base the retirement benefit on a worker's salary during his final years of service and on his length of service. Since salaries tend to rise over time, DB plans typically calculate pension benefits based on the worker's final three or five years (final average salary or FAS). As the workforce changes, all employers will be challenged to compensate workers who possess required knowledge, skills, and institutional memory (see Chapter 7). DB plans may be key to retaining quality employees.

DB plans also encourage orderly turnover of personnel by allowing employees to depart from the workforce with a clear knowledge of their pension benefits and with the assurance that the benefit payment will continue for life. By contrast, the DC plan provides no assurance that an employee will be financially prepared for retirement at any specific age or level of experience. Unfortunately this uncertainty (or, in some cases, certainty of the inadequacy of one's benefits) causes employees to remain on the job even when their ability to perform job duties is in decline. Clearly this may also complicate the employer's role, forcing decisions with unpleasant consequences for everyone.

In recent years, public DB plans have grown more flexible in their ability to meet a range of new employer (and employee) objectives. Developments include shorter vesting periods; a majority of public employees now participate in plans with a vesting period of five years or fewer, down from ten years a decade ago. In addition, many large statewide public retirement plans now allow participants to purchase service earned at another retirement system or in the military. Also many plans now permit terminating participants to take all or part of the employer contributions, and some allow retired participants to return to active employment while continuing to receive their pension benefits. The number of public sector hybrid plans, having both DB and DC plan characteristics, has risen, as has the number of plans permitting retiring participants to take a portion of their benefit as a lump sum at retirement. Some plans also now permit participants to share in investment earnings during the accumulation period.

Another feature of DB plans particularly valuable to public employers is their ability to help public employers temporarily adjust the criteria used to determine retirement eligibility (typically, age and years of service requirements). Such incentives target employees who qualify already for retirement or who are close to qualifying, many of whom may be older and have more experience and salary than other employees. Once the worker retires, his position can be held vacant temporarily or permanently, or he may be replaced with lower-paid employee. Structured and managed properly, early retirement incentive plans have been deemed useful to public employers, especially in the short-term.

Public DB plans as Financial Engines

A not-yet-discussed beneficial aspect of public DB plans is that their assets promote economic growth and vitality. Through their size, broad diversification, and focus on long-term investment returns, public pension funds stabilize and add liquidity to US and foreign financial markets. The Board of Governors (2004) reported that the $2.3 trillion held by public retirement systems equaled over 20 percent of the nation's entire gross domestic product and approximately 20 percent of the nation's total retirement market. Public pension assets are well-diversified: approximately $1.3 trillion of public pension assets are held as corporate equities; $800 billion is in US treasury notes and bonds and corporate debt; and another $90 billion is in real estate and mortgages (Board of Governors 2004). Most of these assets are invested on a long-term basis, while public pension cash and short-term holdings add essential liquidity to financial markets.

The cost of public pension funds to taxpayers, which is generally reported as employer contributions was $38.8 billion (in FY 2002). Public pensions paid over $110 billion in benefits in FY 2002, and a substantial majority of these funds derived from sources other than employer (taxpayer) contributions—mainly investment gains and employee contributions. Over the two-decade period from 1983 to 2002, public pensions had total receipts of $2.7 trillion: investment earnings represented $1.65 trillion of all system receipts, dwarfing employer (government) and employee contributions (US Census Bureau 2003). Through professional asset management and benefiting from favorable investment markets, public funds leveraged contributions from employers and employees into sizable investment earnings during the 1980's and 1990's. The sources of public pension revenue are summarized in Figure 12-1.

It is worth noting that these revenue sources shifted dramatically between 1983 and 2002, with investment earnings ring from 42 percent in 1983 to 62 percent in 2002. Meanwhile, the employer (taxpayer) share of cumulative public pension revenue declined from 42 percent to 26 percent. Unlike DB plans in private industry, most public DB plan participants contribute to their plans: 13 percent of public pension contributions came from employees during this period, and investment earnings made up the remainder. The time-series change in the distribution of revenue sources is depicted graphically in Figure 12-2.

By sponsoring DB plans with professional investment functions, instead of DC plans with assets managed by individual plan participants, public employers increased the value of retirement plan assets by an amount greater than the entire cost of their contributions during this same period.

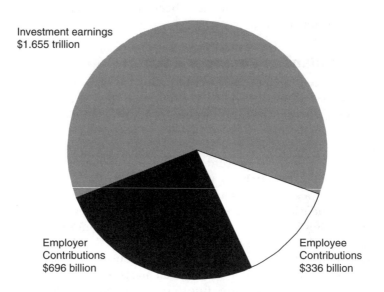

Figure 12-1. Sources of public pension revenue.
Source: US Census Bureau (2002).

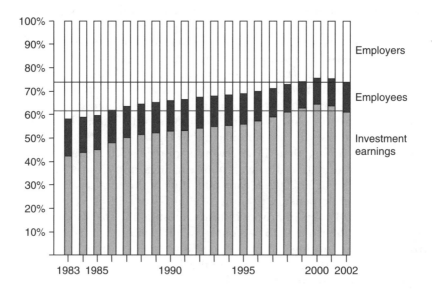

Figure 12-2. Changes over time in public pension fund revenue by source, 1983–2002.
Source: US Census Bureau (2002).

Venture capital provides financing for new and rapidly growing companies; the innovations and efficiencies generated by start-up companies are considered critical to long-term economic growth. In the last decade, many public retirement systems have established target allocations to venture capital projects within their own state (PSRS/NTRS 2002). These investments seek to provide a return to the pension fund commensurate with the investment's level of risk, and also to promote economic growth and development in the state. Venture capital typically requires at least ten years to fully mature, making it a natural match for DB assets (McDonald 2002). This is because of DB funds' focus on long-term investment results and because these funds pool assets for large numbers of participants, accumulating portfolios large enough to commit to venture capital projects. In addition, DB plans also invest in other asset classes with the same long-term focus they demonstrate with venture capital.

As consumers, retired pension participants spend their benefits on a range of goods and services. These expenditures increase economic demand and promote employment, generating additional economic activity, which begets additional demand and employment. This is known as the multiplier effect: the effect of a single dollar has an economic impact greater than one dollar as it ripples through the economy. In an analysis described in more detail in the Appendix, we estimate the impact of the higher earnings from DB plans versus those available from DC plans which take into account lower investment earnings. We evaluate the impact of these higher investment gains on the gross product of the five states with the largest public pension distributions in fiscal year 2002 (California, New York, Texas, Ohio, and Illinois). In particular, we assume a marginal propensity to consume (MPC) of 0.67, which implies an economic multiplier effect of 3.0. Benefit payments from these five states comprised approximately 44 percent of the $110 billion in public pension benefit payments in FY 2002. The difference between the actual benefits distributed by DB plans, and the estimated value of available DC benefits in these states of $25.78 billion. represents the marginal value added by public DB plans as a result of their investment returns over the inferred value of available DC benefits (see Table 12-1).

Next we compute for each of the five states the value added to the gross state product (GSP) by the higher payments from DB plans attributed to superior investment returns. The value added, shown on Table 12-1, is determined by multiplying the marginal value-added by public DB plans' higher investment returns by the economic multiplier of 3.0. The table also shows the percentage value added to each state's gross state product, which in these five states totaled a weighted average of 2 percent to states' GSP. If we were to extrapolate these computations to the entire economy, a national 2.0 percent impact would yield a value added from public DB plans of $203 billion: *$10.137 trillion (GDP)* × *2.0% = $203 billion*. This contribution

TABLE 12-1   Estimated Benefits from DB and DC Plans, Assuming Lower Returns
to DC Investments, 2002 (in $ billions)

State	Actual benefit payments made by public DB plans	Assumed payments from DC plans	Value added by higher DB plan returns	2001 Gross state product	$ Value Added to Gross state product by higher returns	% Value Added to Gross state product by higher returns
California	14.88	6.20	8.68	1,359.27	26.05	1.9
New York	12.48	5.20	7.28	826.49	21.85	2.6
Texas	5.87	2.45	3.42	763.87	10.28	1.3
Ohio	5.62	2.34	3.28	373.71	9.85	2.6
Illinois	5.36	2.24	3.13	475.54	9.39	2.0
Total	44.21	18.43	25.78	3,798.88	77.42	2.0

Note: Columns may not add due to rounding.

Source: United States Dept of Commerce (2003).

to the nation's economy dwarfs the employer contributions of $39 billion to public retirement systems in FY 2002. Indeed, setting aside all the other benefits to employers and employees of DB plans, contributions to public pension plans may be among the best investments a state or local government can make.

Conclusions

The economic boost of public pension benefits is likely to grow as public employees of the baby boomer cohort begin to retire, and public retirement systems begin to pay out increasingly larger benefit amounts. In our view, public pension plans are in a strong position to handle the coming influx of retirees, since, unlike Social Security (mainly a pay-as-you-go program); public pensions are rather well-funded (approximately 95 percent in 2003). Investing the $2.3 trillion in public pension assets and the flow of benefit payments to annuitants promises a continuous, predictable, and growing source of economic stimulus. Moreover, through efficient asset management and pooling of resources, public DB pension plans have a significant, positive effect on financial markets and the economy.

In general, public employers recognize that DC plans have many positive attributes, but to make them work well, many factors must fall into place: participants must consistently make sound investment decisions over their working and retired lives; they must remain in the workforce steadily, avoiding lengthy time-off for having children, raising a family, completing an education, or for illness; they must have a sufficient amount withheld from their pay; they must avoid borrowing against and spending their retirement assets; and they must make appropriate decisions regarding withdrawal rates during retirement. Even then, employees might exhaust their assets after retirement. Hence having a DB plan as the primary retirement benefit protects public sector employees against many of these problems.

Public DB pension plans have also enabled public employers to achieve important objectives related to the recruitment and retention of quality workers. These plans provide financial security in retirement and reduce retiree reliance on public assistance programs. The fact that these plans have evolved relatively independently of the federal regulatory structure governing private pensions has allowed the public plans to engage in an ongoing process of creating and modifying plan designs and governance structures to meet the unique needs of public sector employers. The independence, flexibility, and profitable prudence of these plans will continue to support public employers in their ongoing mission to serve taxpayers, while providing financial security to retired public employees and significant economic benefits to their communities. Public plans are, indeed, a useful component of the new retirement paradigm of the future.

Technical Appendix

The multiplier effect described in the text is based on the MPC which refers to the proportion of each additional dollar of household income used for consumption. As Keynes (1936) noted, people tend to consume more if their income rises, but this consumption gain tends to be less than the rise in their income. The MPC states that a worker who receives an increase in salary of $100 per month will spend some, but not all, of the entire $100; savings and taxes will make up the difference. It can be expressed as a formula: $MPC = \Delta I - MPS - t$, which simply means that the marginal propensity to consume equals the change in income minus savings minus taxes. The multiplier effect can be derived from the MPC as $1/(1 - MPC)$.

To compare actual benefits paid by public DB pensions and the benefits that might have been payable by DC plans earning lower assumed investment returns, we reduced by ten percent the amount paid by public DB pensions to reflect migration of retired participants from the five states. This reduces the DB payments figure to $44.2 billion. For the 20-year period ended in 2002, public DB plans experienced annualized investment returns of 10.03 percent. As a base of comparison, using the Nebraska benefits adequacy study and the Investment Company Institute report on the asset allocation of 403(b) and 457 plan participants as a guide, we assume a net annualized investment return for DC plans during the same period of 6.5 percent. Based on these rates, the DC plan portfolio would have returned 41.7 percent of the investment gains accrued by the DB plan. Applying this proportion—41.7 percent—of the investment earnings DC plans would have generated, to the benefits actually distributed by public DB plans in the five states, yields $18.4 billion. This amount is referred to here as the *inferred value of available DC benefits,* and represents a level of assumed DC plan benefits that can be compared with the amount actually distributed by DB plans.

While this exercise illustrates how public DB plans can have a positive effect due to their superior investment returns, relative to DC plans, there are other factors that must also be mentioned. For instance, we assumed that DC plans would pay benefits in the same proportion to their invest- ment earnings as DB plans, but in fact we cannot know at what rate DC plan assets will actually be spent. Also we assumed that DC and DB contribution rates would have been the same. In view of the fact that some DB contri- butions over this period were actually intended to reduce underfunding, it is possible that contributions to DC plans would have been lower than these. In any event, our central finding—that DB contributions yield posi- tive long-term economic results—suggests that higher contribution rates literally have been a good investment, not only for taxpayers, but also for public employers and employees. Additionally, this analysis assumed a consistent contribution rate relative to investment gains and benefit pay- ments, though actual contribution rates varied across states. Also we did not attempt to determine additional tax revenues generated by higher DB payments; rather we assumed that the DC and DB plans produced similar rates of leakage, though most public DB plans do not permit loans. Finally, we assumed that the administrative cost of the plan types is identical, though public DB plans typically have administrative expenses consider- ably lower than those of DC plans. Factoring this in would likely strengthen the case for the economic value of DB versus DC plans.

Endnote

The authors wish to acknowledge the significant contributions made to this paper by Cathie Eitelberg, Gary Johnson, Jeannine Markoe Raymond, Bill Wallace, and Paul Zorn.

1. For the 25 percent of state and local government employees who do not partici- pate in Social Security, pension benefits are generally higher to compensate for the absence of Social Security benefits.

References

Board of Governors of the Federal Reserve System (Board of Governors) (2004). 'Flow of Funds Accounts of the United States First Quarter 2004'. Federal Reserve System: New York.

Brainard, Keith (2003). *Myths and Misperceptions of Defined Benefit and Defined Contri- bution Plans.* Denver: National Association of State Retirement Administrators.

—— (2004). *Public Fund Survey.* Denver: National Association of State Retirement Administrators and National Council on Teacher Retirement.

Buck Consultants (2000). *Benefit Review Study of the Nebraska Retirement Systems.* Denver: Buck Consultants.

Clark, Robert L., Lee A. Craig, and Jack W. Wilson (2003). *A History of Public Sector Pensions in the United States.* Philadelphia: University of Pennsylvania Press.

Congressional Budget Office (CBO) (2003). *Baby Boomers' Retirement Prospects: An Overview.* Washington, GPO.

Eitelberg, Cathie G. (1997). *An Elected Official's Guide to Public Retirement Plans.* Chicago, IL: Government Finance Officers Association.

Findlay, Gary (1997). 'In Defense of the Defined Benefit Plan', *Government Finance Review,* Chicago: December.

Government Finance Officers Association (GFOA) (1992). 'Federal Regulation of Public Employee Retirement Systems', *Public Policy Statements.* Adopted June 23. *www.gfoa.org*

Investment Company Institute (ICI) (2004). *Fundamentals,* 13(2), June.

Keynes, John Maynard (1936). *The General Theory of Employment, Interest, and Money.* Cambridge: Macmillan/Cambridge University Press.

McDonald, Ian (2002). 'Fundholder's Lament: All Bear, No Bull', *Wall Street Journal,* April 25, 2002.

Metz, Joseph G. (1998). *The Taxation of Public Employee Retirement Systems.* Chicago, IL: Government Finance Officers Association.

Mitchell, Olivia S. and Edwin C. Hustead (eds.) (2001). *Pensions in the Public Sector.* Philadelphia: University of Pennsylvania Press.

Public School Retirement System/Non-Teacher Retirement System of Missouri (PSRS/NTRS). (2002). '2002 Summary of Findings'. Study by Missouri Venture Capital Research Initiative, Jefferson City, MO. August, *www.publicfundsurvey.org*

Rajnes, David (2002). 'An Evolving Pension System: Trends in Defined Benefit and Defined Contribution Plans'. Washington, DC: Employee Benefits Research Institute, September.

United States Bureau of Labor Statistics (USBLS) (2003). '2003 National Compensation Survey: Employee Benefits in Private Industry in the United States'. Washington, DC: USBLS.

—— (2002). '2002 National Occupational Employment and Wage Estimates—Protective Service Occupations', Washington, DC: USBLS.

United States Census Bureau (US Census) (2002). 'Federal, State, and Local Governments—State and Local Government Employee-Retirement Systems'. Washington, DC: USBLS.

United States Department of Commerce (US Dept of Commerce), Bureau of Economic Analysis (2003). 'Regional Economic Accounts, 2001 Gross State Product', Washington, DC: USGPO.

Part IV

**In Search of a New Pension Paradigm:
The Global Outlook**

Chapter 13

The Future of Pensions in Canada

Silvana Pozzebon

The Canadian public pension system has been characterized as one of the best in the world. Over time, it has succeeded in decreasing poverty among the elderly by the institution of a series of targeted, flat-rate benefits which redistribute income to pensioners. Reforms in 1997 are widely held to have increased the financial sustainability of the first pillar pay-as-you-go earnings-related element in the public retirement income scheme. To bolster it against the pressures of an aging population, measures have been implemented to partially fund the plan. As a consequence, there appears to be a general sense of increased confidence, at least among the Canadian population, in the future of public pensions. The second pillar of the Canadian retirement income system consists of voluntarily provided occupational pensions, also known as private pension plans. Until recent media attention raised questions about the financial viability of many of these plans, particularly those of the defined benefit (DB) variety, most plan members took their occupational pension promises for granted. Yet with 84 percent of registered, employer-sponsored pension plan membership in 2000 covered by plans of the DB type in Canada, there is increasing cause for concern (Statistics Canada 2003*a*).

This paper assesses the resilience of these two key components of the Canadian retirement income system. The public pension scheme is reviewed first, as it has been the subject of various studies in the last few years, including several of a comparative nature (e.g. Disney and Johnson 2001). Attention is then focused on occupational pensions. This second pillar of the retirement income system has been less studied, yet it is currently facing numerous challenges in Canada. The retirement system's third pillar consists of private savings. Only private retirement savings vehicles that receive tax treatment comparable to occupational pension plans will be discussed in this paper. We argue that future challenges to both the public and private pension pillars of the Canadian retirement system will require regulatory reform in the medium term.

The Public Pension System in Canada

The Components. Canada's state pension scheme consists of two main pillars.[1] The first, the *Old Age Security* (OAS) program, includes three subcomponents: *OAS pension, Guaranteed Income Supplement,* and *Spouse's Allowance.* The OAS pension is a flat benefit available to those aged 65 and over with at least 10 years of residency. To receive a full pension, which represents approximately 14 percent of average earnings, forty years of residency after the age of 18 are required; the OAS pension is reduced proportionally for each year of nonresidency. Originally a universal pension, the OAS pension became a targeted benefit with the introduction of a 15 percent benefit 'clawback' in 1989 for higher income individuals. The benefit reduction applied to those with net incomes above C\$56,968 in 2001; once net income reaches C\$92,435, no OAS benefit is received.[2] The OAS pension is taxable and indexed quarterly to the Consumer Price Index (CPI).

The other two subcomponents of the OAS program, the *Guaranteed Income Supplement* (GIS) and the *Spouse's Allowance* are means-tested flat-rate benefits. The GIS targets low-income OAS recipients while their spouses (or widow/ers) with a minimum of 10 years of residency are eligible for a Spouse's Allowance. Both are nontaxable, and like the OAS pension, indexed quarterly to the CPI and financed out of general revenues. Benefits for recipients who receive maximum benefits from these two income supplements represent 31 percent of average earnings for a single person and 50 percent for a couple (World Economic Forum Pension Readiness Initiative 2004b, henceforth WEFPRI)

The second major pillar of Canada's state pension is a compulsory, pay-as-you-go earnings-related scheme. Except for the residents of Quebec, who contribute to the provincially administered Quebec Pension Plan (QPP), employed residents of the rest of Canada are covered by the federally administered Canada Pension Plan (CPP). Contributions between plans are fully portable and the two plans offer similar benefits under its four major transfer programs—retirement benefits, survivor benefits, disability benefits and death benefits.[3]

CPP retirement benefits are set at approximately 25 percent of average pensionable earnings over the contributory period, adjusted for the mean increase in maximum pensionable earnings during the five years before retirement.[4] A person's contributory period spans the years between his eighteenth and sixtyfifth birthday (or the retirement date if retirement occurs between age 60 and 64). Some periods of low or no income can be dropped from the contributory period including up to 15 percent of the months when earnings were lowest. The normal retirement age under the CPP is 65, though benefits can be obtained as early as age 60 or as late at 70; a 6 percent annual reduction (increase) in benefits applies for those who opt to receive a pension before (after) age 65. Retirement benefits accounted for 70.5 percent of total benefits paid out in July 2003 by the CPP and QPP combined (author's calculations using Table 13–1, Chawla and Wannell 2004). The lion's share of the remaining payouts was attributed to survivor benefits (15 percent) and disability benefits (11 percent).

As the pay-as-you-go pillar of the public scheme matured since its inception in 1966, the C/QPP share of total transfer payments to seniors increased relative to that of the OAS program. In 2001, C/QPP benefits accounted for 48 percent of total government transfers to families receiving C/QPP whose major income recipient was 65 and over, while the OAS share was 43 percent the comparable figures for 1981 were 62 percent for OAS and 30 percent for C/QPP (Chawla and Wannell 2004).

The CPP plan is financed essentially by contributions split evenly between employees and employers. Combined premiums increased slowly at a rate of 0.2 percent annually from 1986 to 1996 when they reached 5.6 percent of maximum contributory earnings. As a result of demographic changes and benefit improvements, CPP transfer payments exceeded contributions by the early 1900s. To respond to the crisis, a reform in 1997 implemented a rapid increase in contributions to the 2003 level of 9.9 percent where they are projected to remain for some years.[5] Premiums have been set high enough to permit the accumulation of surpluses until 2021 (MacNaughton 2004).

Under the 1997 reform, the management of CPP surpluses was relegated to the CPP Investment Board. Created in December of 1977, the CPP Investment Board is an independently governed and managed Crown corporation. It was set up to oversee the investment of CPP reserve assets 'to maximize return without undue risk' in a diversified portfolio of securities including stocks, real estate, bonds, and private equities (MacNaughton 2004). For some five years now, the CPP Investment Board has been actively investing funds that are segregated from general government revenue. Professional investment managers have been employed to assist the CPP Investment Board in managing the private equity components of the reserve fund. Though independent, the CPP Investment Board is held to high standards of accountability; it is subject to external audits and has a wide-reaching disclosure policy. In September 2003, CPP reserve assets totaled C$64.4 billion (about 2.9 years of benefits)[6] and they are projected to reach some C$160 billion over the next ten years (MacNaughton 2004).

How Resilient is Canada's Public Pension System? As is true for many developed countries, Canada's population is aging rapidly. Those 65 and over accounted for eight percent of the population in 1971, 13 percent in 2001, with the percentage projected to rise to 15 in 2011, 19 in 2021, and 21 by 2026 (Duchesne 2004). While Canada's situation may not currently be as 'critical' as that of some European Union countries, such as Italy or Spain whose population age structures already exhibit an inverted pyramidal form, declining fertility rates (from 3.7 in 1950 to 1.6 in 2000), rising life expectancies, and the looming retirement of the baby boom generation is expected to produce a labor shortage over the 2020s in Canada (WEFPRI 2004a, b).

Dependency ratios, defined as the ratio of the inactive population over 55 years of age to the labor force 15 years and older, are projected to almost double between 2000 and 2030 in Canada from 0.31 to 0.60 respectively (WEFPRI 2004b). These figures suggest an important rise in public pension plan expenditures in the future.

The evidence indicates that Canada's public retirement scheme has successfully reduced poverty among the elderly and income inequality among pensioners to date (cf. Hoffman and Dahlby 2001). These results are in part attributed to the highly progressive nature of the public pension system, as it favors low income earners. Some would advocate an even more progressive system (as the 1996 debate over the rejected Seniors Benefit Program suggests; see Battle 2003), while others, such as the Association of Canadian Pension Management (ACPM) (2000), characterize Canada's retirement income system as already unfair for higher income workers. The ACPM goes further, stating that poverty-level measures used to assess the adequacy of minimum government transfer payments for the elderly (OAS and less important supplemental assistant programs from the provinces) are too generous.

The Chief Actuary of Canada appears optimistic that changes made to partially fund the CPP will ensure its long-term viability, but there is room for pessimism here as well. For example, higher contribution rates may be required if the CPP Investment Fund does not attain its projected rate of return or if other actuarial assumptions, which underlie the long-term maintenance of the 9.9 percent premium, are not met. Additionally, the management of public pension reserves has typically been fraught with problems related to governance, investment policy, reporting, and disclosure, among others (Pension Research Council 2003). In fairness, it should be noted that the creation of the CPP Investment Board has been welcomed by leading experts as a positive experiment in how reserves from partially funded pay-as-you-go systems can be insulated from political interference[7] (Pension Research Council 2003; MacNaughton 2004).

In view of Canada's already high tax rates and sizable public debt, there is also some cause for concern that future generations will bear a disproportionate tax burden to support rising public pension expenditures (financed both from general tax revenue and payroll taxes on earnings). Yet high tax rates can act as a disincentive for employees, reducing labor productivity that can, in turn, slow economic growth (WEFPRI 2004a). Moreover, the effects of higher pension costs must be considered in the context of rising expenditures required to support Canada's already ailing public health care system.

To sustain economic growth needed to maintain living standards as the population ages, two broad levers are available: increasing productivity growth and increasing labor supply (WEFPRI 2004a). Like most developed countries, Canada has experienced labor productivity growth since World War II, though its pattern of growth during the last three decades appears to have been more consistent than that of other Organization for Economic Cooperation and Development (OECD) nations (WEFPRI 2004a). The increasing service orientation of the economies of developed countries like Canada makes significant future growth in labor productivity unlikely, however.

A second, more publicized, solution to alleviate the economic consequences of aging populations in rich countries is to increase labor supply. Three possibilities exist: induce greater labor force participation among seniors, do the same for other demographic groups (e.g. women or young people) with low workforce active rates; and increase immigration. It is believed that targeting efforts to increase labor force activity of those age 55+ will have an important impact in Canada, because the gap in the labor force participation rate for this age group is largest when compared with the average participation rates of the five OECD countries with the highest workforce activity (WEFPRI 2004b). In fact, the median retirement age in Canada was sixty-five in 1975, which then fell slowly until 1986 and then more sharply to 60.6 in 2002 (Duchesne 2004; Statistics Canada 2003b). Data also show that 43 percent of retirees were under sixty years of age during the five-year period from 1997 to 2001. Factors contributing to the early retirement trend were the lowering of the minimum age requirements from sixty-five to sixty for Q/CPP eligibility, other early retirement incentives introduced in corporate pension plans as a response to downsizing, and restructuring efforts during the last two decades.

Expanding labor force attachment among the elderly poses several challenges, among which are the need to make structural adjustments to pension programs (delaying early retirement eligibility is one obvious option); and tax laws which often act to decrease pension wealth for those who delay retirement in Canada. Though gradual withdrawal from the labor force may offer an interesting alternative for seniors who would like both more income and time to pursue leisure activities, the current system penalizes those who opt for phased retirement (Smolkin 2003). The quest for labor market flexibility in the new economy has begun to generate an unprecedented number of atypical employment opportunities (part-time, contractual, on call, seasonal, etc.) that may prove increasingly attractive to seniors in the future. This is particularly likely as the elderly now face longer lifespans in better health than in the past. Encouragingly perhaps, the labor force participation of Canadians age 65+ rose faster than the overall growth of the same age group in the population recently (20 percent vs 11 percent from 1996–2001), and the average senior still on the job is aging (Duchesne 2004).

Employers also have a role to play by offering agreeable work environments to attract and retain older employees. Yet the high stress levels and increasingly heavy work loads that characterize the Canadian health and educational sectors are often said to have driven many of these workers, typically covered by good pension plans, to early retirement. Of course, if employers respond to high labor costs in developed countries such as Canada by outsourcing jobs to less developed nations, the projected labor shortage may never develop. An optimistic scenario would anticipate that the capital invested by Canada's funded private occupational pensions and partially funded public system (for example, the CPP Investment Board) would sustain aggregate consumption and output levels.

When all is said and done, one can conclude that Canada's public pension system currently meets income adequacy standards for lower income individuals and poor seniors. The move towards partial funding of the public pension scheme has likely increased the financial sustainability of its earnings-related component, the CPP, for the medium term. But the impact of future challenges and the ability of the system to adapt remain uncertain. The example of the QPP, whose population base is aging faster than that of the rest of Canada, is perhaps indicative. A recently released Working Paper by the Régie des Rentes du Québec (2003*b*) which administers the plan, includes a proposal to modify the calculation of the QPP benefit so that, in the future, eligible individuals who have worked fewer than forty years between age 18 and retirement (e.g. many of those who retire early) will receive lower benefits than under the current system. In fairness, the QPP Working Paper also proposes other provisions to encourage later retirement, such as allowing those who work after age 65 to accumulate benefits up to the age 70 at a rate of 0.7 percent per month of work, rather than at the current 0.5 percent.

Private Pensions in Canada

The Components. The second major pillar of the Canadian retirement income system consists of occupational pensions that are voluntarily provided by employers and some unions. Canada belongs to a group of developed nations where such private plans play a relatively important role in providing income for the elderly (Disney and Johnson 2001). Thus private pension payments to elderly Canadians amounted to 29 percent of their total income (in 1999; Statistics Canada 2003*a*). Evidence also suggests that pensioners age 60–64 receive a higher percentage of their income from private plans than do older pensioners (Hoffman and Dahlby 2001).

Under Canadian law, *registered pension plans* (RPP) are the most common type of employer-sponsored plans. These are subject to minimum standards prescribed by federal and provincial pension legislation. Contributions for both employers and employees are tax-exempt and subject to annual limits.[8] In 2000, the percentage of paid workers covered by RPPs was 40.6 (Statistics Canada 2003*a*).[9] Of the 5.4 million RPP participants in that same year, 54.3 percent worked in the public sector. The vast majority of Canadian RPP members have historically belonged to DB plans, with virtually all others in defined contribution (DC) plans of the money-purchase type. DB plans accounted for 84 percent of RPP membership in 2000; the proportion of overall RPP participants in final earnings plans was sixty; 73 percent of RPP members are in contributory plans. While virtually all public sector employees belong to contributory plans, only half (51 percent) of private sector workers do. Contribution rates are set at five or more percent of earnings for 72 percent of workers in such plans. Most Canadian jurisdictions now set vesting provisions at two years of membership or service.

Despite the historical bias toward DB plans, an increasingly popular form of occupational pensions in Canada is *group registered retirement savings plans* (group RRSPs). These are similar to registered DC plans mentioned above, in that contributions made by workers and investment returns receive tax-deferred treatment. By contrast, group RRSPs typically offer a wider range of investment choices, and employer contributions to these plans are treated as nondeductible employee earnings. Group RRSPs are essentially 'pooled' individual registered retirement savings plans (RRSPs) (see below) to which employers typically 'facilitate' access by underwriting administrative charges and deducting employee contributions directly from payroll. Group RRSPs are not subject to pension legislation, so that, unlike RPPs, employers are not required to contribute to them and lump sum withdrawals are permitted unless the plan specifies otherwise.

Briefly, individual RRSPs are voluntary retirement savings vehicles available to those with work income. Canada's income tax law since 1991 accords tax advantages to employee RRSPs contributions similar to those granted RPPs. As a consequence, workers not covered by RPPs (or the self-employed who are ineligible for RPP participation) can save up to 18 percent of earnings in a tax-sheltered individual RRSP to the maximum allowable (C$14,500 in 2003). Additionally, employees for whom the pension adjustment (a calculated value of annual pension credits accumulated in their RPP) is lower than the tax-exempt limit set for RRSPs, may elect to contribute to an RRSP, or a group RRSP if one is offered, up to the allowable limit. Investment returns on funds accumulated in RRSPs are also not taxable. RRSP savings can be withdrawn at any time[10] but, unless used to buy a home or to finance full-time education, taxes are withheld when funds are removed.

Unfortunately, no official statistics are collected for group RRSPs. Using annual data reported by *Benefits Canada*, probably the best-known publication for employee benefit professionals in Canada, it is estimated that assets held in group RRSPs have grown 178 percent during the last decade, from C$9.4 billion in 1993 to C$26.1 billion in 2003 (Benefits Canada 1993; Sharratt 2003). As a relative measure of the importance of group RRSPs, consider that in 2003 they accounted for 47 percent of all administered assets for the DC plan market, which includes both plans covered and not covered by pension legislation (Sharratt 2003).

A number of changes have affected the configuration of the Canadian private pension system, at least since the early 1990s. Official statistics are suggestive and anecdotal evidence from professional publications and the wider media provide strong hints that at least two trends are discernable. The first is a decline in the relative importance of pension plans covered by pension legislation (i.e. RPPs) in favor of savings vehicles, such as group RRSPs, which are not covered by these laws. A second trend, which complements the first, is a shift from DB plans, which have traditionally been the focus of most pension legislation, to those of the DC type. Growth in the latter segment is probably most pronounced outside the pension regulatory framework.

Pension plan coverage data is perhaps most revealing of the decreasing role of RPPs. Coverage of paid workers by a RPP fell slowly from 1991 when it was 45.4 percent to 40.6 percent in 1998, where it stabilized to 2000 (Statistics Canada 2003*a*). Several reasons may explain this decrease: structural shifts in employment patterns from sectors such as manufacturing to services and the related decline in unionization; shrinking public sector employment during most of the 1990s; important job growth during this same decade among the self-employed who are ineligible for RPP membership; and high pension administrative and financial costs in a context of increasing global competition (see Pozzebon 2002 for an overview).

While official statistics are suggestive, other evidence supporting the move from DB to DC plans is more anecdotal. Statistics Canada data does show that the proportion of total RPP plan membership in DB plans fell 9 percent between 1984 to 2000 (from 93 to 84) while that of DC plans rose by almost the equivalent amount (8.6 percent) (Pozzebon 2002; Statistics Canada 2003*a*). No official statistics support the allegation, and as the discussion above on group RRSPs indicates, growth in DC plans has not been confined to those covered by pension laws. A quick scan of the contents of professional journals in the benefits area over the last decade, such as *Benefits Canada*, further suggests that change is afoot. Unfortunately, it is difficult to discern from the information currently available how much, if any, of the DB to DC shift involves conversions to plans covered by pension legislation or can be attributed to the creation of new plans both within and outside the regulatory framework.

The loss of popularity of DB plans may have been fuelled by many of the same reasons noted above for RPPs (Pozzebon 2002). These include a fall in employment among more highly unionized industries like manufacturing and the public sector where DB plans have been prevalent. The market boom of the 1990s, coupled with easier access to financial information and opportunities to self-direct one's investments through the Internet, also contributed to making DC plans more attractive. And, younger workers who no longer expect long-term employment relationships probably appreciate the greater portability of DC plans relative to their less flexible DB counterparts. Employers too may be drawn to DC plans which are less complex to administer and have more predictable costs that DB pension plans.

How Resilient is Canada's Private Pension System? Many have argued that the slow decline in RPP coverage should be a matter of concern to those interested in retirement security. If the purpose of pension legislation is to protect plan beneficiaries and the soundness of pension funds, then one might surmise that workers would be better off with plans operating in a regulatory framework. Plans outside this protective umbrella, like group RRSPs, may result in lower levels of retirement savings if, for example, employers fail to contribute to them; or they make only sporadic, low, or stock-option-only contributions; or if employees are permitted to withdraw funds and make their own investment decisions.

Though group RRSPs are induced to some extent by tax incentives, there are also many other types of pension agreements outside the regulatory framework that offer an even less certain promise. The case of higher income earners is illustrative here. Due to Canada's much criticized low limits for tax-advantaged RPP contributions, it has become more difficult over time for higher-income earners (earning approximately twice the average wage) to set aside retirement savings sufficient to maintain living standards in old age. The maximum amount of pension entitlement per year of service that could be earned under RPPs remained frozen at C\$1722.22 from 1977 to 2003; the amount rises to C\$2000 in 2005, after which it will be indexed to increases in the average Canadian wage. As a consequence of these limits, some employers have provided a supplementary employee retirement plan or stock option plan. The extent to which such plans are pre-funded is unknown, and in the wake of the Enron scandal, it is legitimate to question the security of pension arrangements built on company stock. These factors must further be considered in the context of Canada's progressive public pension system which emphasizes the role of private pension income for higher earners.

The DB to DC shift may be worrisome, in that DB plans are viewed by many as synonymous with retirement security. They offer fixed pension benefits payable on a regular basis and employees assume no responsibility for investment or saving decisions. But recent events have increasingly threatened the notion of security traditionally associated with private DB plans in Canada, as elsewhere. For instance, various high profile cases have demonstrated the fragility of DB pension plans in situations of corporate insolvencies (or near-insolvencies), which incidentally have been linked to large unfunded pension liabilities. The Air Canada and Stelco cases are two examples from a long list of established firms that have been adversely affected by competitive pressures over the last decade. Moreover, Ontario is the only Canadian jurisdiction that has established a pension insurance fund that secures partial benefits (to a maximum of C$1000 per month) in the case of a DB plan insolvency. Set up in 1980 and funded by employer contributions, the Ontario Pension Benefits Guarantee Fund is currently under scrutiny. With only some C$230 million in reserves, questions about its sustainability are being raised should it be called upon to help bail out Stelco's C$1.25 billion pension shortfall (Livingston 2004; Reguly 2004).

Another related consideration is that the market downturn that followed the boom of the 1990s produced substantial DB plan unfunded liabilities. No Canada-wide estimates appear to be available, but a study of the nation's 104 companies on the SandP/TSX index with DB plan assets over C$10 million indicates that 78 percent of these firms had pension shortfalls in 2002 (Church 2003a). Another report by the Dominion Bond Rating Service found 84 percent of the 263 Canadian DB plans studied had deficits at the end of 2002, with close to one-quarter of the plans being less that 70 percent funded (McFarland 2003). Using a larger sample of 1040 Canadian DB pension plans, a joint study by three consultancy companies—Mercer, Towers Perrin and Watson Wyatt—concluded that funding levels were generally about 85 percent (Church 2003b). These figures approximate those of the Régie des rentes du Québec (2003a) which supervises that province's private pension plans. It estimates that, as of December 31, 2002, some 70 percent of DB plans under its jurisdiction were underfunded, but assets covered more than 80 percent of obligations in the majority of cases. Finally, a recent estimate places the collective balance sheet deterioration of Canadian DB plans at 30 percent for the three-year period ending in 2002 (Ambachtsheer 2004).

Sizable pension asset shortfalls have brought to light 'fuzzy' embedded risks in DB plans, and they have also focused attention on problematic pension accounting, investment practices, and governance issues (Ambachtsheer 2003, 2004). For instance, a generally accepted accounting and actuarial practice, smoothing techniques for the calculation of pension assets and liabilities, has served to 'camouflage' the unfunded status of many private Canadian pension plans. Accounting standards bodies all over the world have recently undertaken initiatives to review these practices (see Chapter 10). Though the market upturn in 2003 may draw attention away from the issue, the events of the last few years have highlighted the need for more transparency and communication so employees better understand the risks associated with DB plans and investors in general (many of whom are investing pension assets) can better evaluate the financial health of firms.

The booming markets of the 1990s resulted in more risky behavior among pension fund managers, many of whom increased equity exposure. As a consequence, several pension funds accumulated surpluses that were used to justify contribution holidays, and sometimes, to improve benefits. But the subsequent financial instability of many funds raises questions about pension fund governance practices. The response of the Canadian pension community was exemplified in a 2003 release of draft pension governance guidelines and a draft self-assessment questionnaire by the recently created *Canadian Association of Pension Supervisory Authorities* (CAPSA 2003). It may be anticipated that the promotion of better governance practices would help address issues arising from the inherent conflict between the increasingly short-term financial horizon of many firms, and the longer view required for the effective management of pension plans. How successful this effort will be remains an open question, particularly since the application of these principles appears to be voluntary.

What about the DC promise? While many workers embraced DC plans during the 1990s when financial markets were doing well, the negative returns from the 2000 period have brought home a harsher reality. There is growing awareness of the vulnerability of employees with DC pension plans; they may simply not accumulate enough retirement saving, especially if plans allow them control over participation, contribution, and investment decisions. By now, few would argue that the average employee has the savvy to construct an adequate investment portfolio focused on long term goals. The fact that many DC retirement savings vehicles are not covered by pension legislation and supervision in Canada adds to concerns.

Some have sought to address the problems raised by allowing employees to select investment options in retirement savings arrangements. For instance, the *Joint Forum of Financial Market Regulators*, a Canadian industry taskforce, has recently proposed guidelines for capital accumulation plans (defined as DC plans and other investment vehicles where employees are entitled to make investment decisions; JFFMR 2001). The stated purpose of the guidelines is to harmonize protection of the many different types of investment products across varying regulatory regimes (securities, insurance or pensions) so that members of capital accumulation plans have the information and assistance needed to make investment decisions. While these efforts are well-intentioned, they must be considered in light of the Canadian context where the nature of the pension sponsor's fiduciary duty remains unclear. Even if the Joint Forum's efforts are successful, they could prove more useful in bolstering protection for employers than employees.

Sponsors who adopt guidelines may be better armed against legal actions that could be brought against them by retiring employees unhappy with pension plan returns (Smolkin and Satov 2004).

Whether the provision of financial education will be effective in helping employees with capital accumulation plans make better investment decisions is far from clear. One of the least 'radical' solutions might be a return to something resembling the more cautious, early DC pension market approach, of offering a very limited number of investment bundles with different risk levels. Such an approach would be doubly interesting if it served to reduce the management fees for DC plans offering investment options. Estimates indicate that the median fee on mutual fund products targeted to individual investors was 2.4 percent in Canada (in 2000), some 1.4 percent higher than the median fee for pooled funds[11] offering institutional products to corporate investors (Ripsman 2000).

Looking ahead, the question arises as to whether the decline in RRPs and DB plans will persist. What many employers perceive as burdensome pension legislation which targets DB plans especially may discourage some from continuing to offer these plans. This is particularly true for firms that operate in different provinces, and hence, must obey separate regional pension regulations; firms with employees in more than one province sponsor some 23 percent of Canada's pension plans (Rubin 2004). In an effort to promote greater statutory uniformity across Canada, the CAPSA has circulated proposed regulatory principles for a model pension law (CAPSA 2004). This model law is derived from current 'best practices' intended to serve as examples when jurisdictions amend their pension statutes.

This first consultative step toward greater harmony and simplification of pension legislation is intended to conserve RPPs. Yet some of the proposals inspired by Quebec's pension law—immediate vesting and the establishment of a pension committee[12] to act as administrator of the plan—may be interpreted by some sponsors as an added burden. Exempting small plans from the pension committee provision may, on the other hand, generate a more favorable response from other employers.

Even if greater legislative harmony is achieved, the administrative and financial burdens of DB plans make it unlikely that many employers will establish new DB plans, given the highly competitive global economy. The need for flexibility in employment relations will grow in the future in the context of the projected labor shortage. Turnover reduction efforts will probably be focused on a core group of employees whose services employers expect to retain at most for a handful of years. And it is hard to imagine that small and medium sized employers, particularly those that increasingly serve as lower-cost subcontractors for large firms, will be able to offer expensive and administratively cumbersome DB plans.

The shaky financial situation of Canadian DB plans may provide further motivation for some firms to terminate them altogether, though other employers may opt to switch to a DC plan which will retain pension assets under the purview of pension regulation. Tax incentives for employers may also mean that not all new retirement savings arrangements will be made outside the pension regulatory framework. Moreover, DB plans are likely to persist for employees of Canada's large public sector where they are strongly entrenched.

Evidently, the private pension industry in Canada is at a crossroads. This far, change has been relatively gradual, as employers have adapted to environmental pressures by repositioning themselves in or around the old pension paradigm. These adjustments have tended to increase retirement income insecurity for employees, generally speaking, whether they had DB or DC pensions, but especially so when employees were permitted to make investment decisions. Responses so far have been piecemeal. Pension law harmonization efforts and recommendations to improve pension plan governance may prove effective, or they may just be wishful thinking. Of course given the poor performance of many investment professionals over the last few years, it seems doubtful that providing better investment education to employees will increase their economic security in retirement.

Conclusion

A multi-pillar approach with both funded and unfunded components is believed to provide a solid foundation for retirement income, due to the opportunities that such a system offers to balance long-term risks (Holzmann 1999). In Canada, the public pension scheme has both an unfunded component and a funded element, the CPP Investment Fund. The latter was adopted as a measure to improve public pension retirement security. The public system also embodies a balance between poverty reduction (the OAS program) and retirement income support (Q/CPP). The private pension system is generally considered the funded component of Canada's retirement system. It has proved successful in providing income replacement, particularly for those with higher incomes, who receive lower replacement rates from the OAS program due to the progressive nature of the public pension system.

Some might conclude from this overview that Canada's retirement system stands on reasonably solid ground at present. Nonetheless, it faces many challenges in the future. In particular, the private sector component appears to have weakened substantially during the last decade. The gradual shift from DB to DC, with a parallel move away from retirement saving arrangements covered by pension regulation, portend increasing insecurity for tomorrow's retirees.

To the extent that this shifting paradigm raises future retirees' dependence on the public component of the system, it may destabilize a system already susceptible to demographic transition. As a result, more determined efforts to improve Canada's voluntary occupational pension system are needed, along with reforms to the Q/CPP. For instance, methods to encourage delayed or phased retirement could be a good starting point, along with a systematic overhaul of tax policy toward retirement saving. Additional review of pension governance rules and the plan sponsor liability environment would also be in order. In sum, strengthening the multi-pillar foundation of Canadian retirement income will require concerted and wide-ranging efforts.

Endnotes

1. The description of the public pension system draws especially on Hoffman and Dahlby (2001); WEFPRI (2004*b*) and Chawla and Wannell (2004).
2. The exchange rate in March 2004 was C$1.32 = US$1.00.
3. To simplify the presentation, the discussion below focuses only on the CPP and retirement benefits.
4. Before 1998, a three-year average was used. The move to a four-year average that year and a five-year one in 1999 was part of the benefit reductions implemented by the 1997 reform described below. See Table 3.4 in Hoffman and Dahlby (2001) for a summary of other changes.
5. In 2003, contributory earnings equaled C$36,400.
6. Author's estimate. Chawla and Wannell (2004) report that benefits paid under the CPP in July 2003 were C$1.86 billion. Multiplying the monthly figure by twelve yields estimated annual benefits of C$22.32 billion. C$64.4 billion in the CPP divided by C$22.32 equals 2.9.
7. The CPP Investment Fund was modeled on the Caisse de dépot et placement du Québec which manages QPP funds in addition to those of other public and private sector depositors. But results for 2002 show that the Caisse experienced a 9.6 percent decrease in net assets (C$8.6 billion) which represents its largest loss since its creation in 1966 (Sanford 2003). Much media attention has been focused on the Caisse's poor performance which is in part attributed to questionable investment decisions and lavish spending excesses for new corporate headquarters. Better market conditions and a major 'restructuring' of the fund has seen substantial improvement in the Caisse's performance in 2003 when it posted weighted average returns of 15.2 percent on overall funds held (Sharratt 2004).
8. The limits on employee contributions in 2003 were C$15,500 for DC plans and the maximum annual pension accrual for DB plans was C$1722.22.
9. Statistics throughout the paragraph are from this same source and for 2000.
10. Withdrawals are not permitted for locked-in RRSPs to which employees transfer their accrued RPP pension savings upon termination of RPP membership.
11. The median pooled fund fee of 1 percent assumes a 0.5 percent recordkeeping fee in addition to a 0.49 percent investment management fee.
12. At least two members of the committee must be designated by plan members, one to represent active participants and the other nonactive members.

References

Ambachtsheer, Keith (2003). 'The Real Pension Crisis', *Financial Post Editorial*. July 16: FP15.

—— (2004). 'Cleaning Up The Pensions Mess: Why It Will Take More Than Money', C. D. Howe Institute *Backgrounder*, No. 78 (February). Consulted online March 30, 2004: *http://www.cdhowe.org/pdf/backgrounder_78.pdf*

Association of Canadian Pension Management (ACPM) (2000). *A Retirement Income Strategy for Canada. Dependence or Self-reliance: Which Way for Canada's Retirement Income System*, 23 pages. Consulted online March 1, 2004: *http://www.acpm-acarr. com/acpm/Attachments/DependenceOrSelfRelianceENG.pdf*

Battle, Ken (2003). 'Sustaining Public Pensions in Canada: A Tale of Two Reforms', in Noriyuki Takayama (ed.), *Taste of Pie: Searching for Better Pension Provisions in Developed Countries*. Tokyo: Maruzen Co., Ltd, pp. 37–91.

Benefits Canada (1993). 'A Walk Down Easy Street: Canadian Employers Are Trading In the Pension Promise In Exchange For a Low-hassle Group RRSP', *Benefits Canada*, 17(11): 31.

Canadian Association of Pension Supervisory Authorities (CAPSA) (2003). *Pension Plan Governance Guidelines and Self-Assessment Questionnaire*. (January). Consulted online March 1, 2004: *http://www.capsa-acor.org*

—— (2004). *Proposed Regulatory Principles For a Model Pension Law*. A report by the Canadian Association of Pension Supervisory Authorities. (January). Consulted online March 1, 2004: *http://www.capsa-acor.org*

Chawla, Raj K. and Ted Wannell (2004). 'A C/QPP Overview'. *Perspectives on Labour and Income* (Statistics Canada Catalogue no. 75-001-XIE), 5, 1: 19–27, January 2004 online edition.

Church, Elizabeth (2003*a*). 'Pension Shortfalls Threaten To Explode'. *The Globe and Mail*. Consulted online March 30, 2004: *http://www.globeandmail.com/servlet/story/ RTGAM.20030512.wxrpensx/BNStory/Business/*

—— (2003*b*). 'Pension Plans Face $225-billion Shortfall'. *The Globe and Mail*. Consulted online March 30, 2004: *http://www.globeinvestor.com/servlet/ArticleNews/story/ RTGAM/20030523/upens0524*

Disney, Richard and Paul Johnson (2001). 'An Overview', in Richard Disney and Paul Johnson (eds.), *Pension Systems and Retirement Incomes Across OECD Counties*. Northampton, MA: Edward Elgar, pp. 1–47.

Duchesne, Doreen (2004). 'More Seniors At Work'. *Perspectives on Labour and Income* (Statistics Canada Catalogue no. 75-001-XIE), 5, 2: 5–17, February 2004 online edition.

Hoffman, Michael and Bev Dahlby (2001). 'Pension Provision in Canada', in Richard Disney and Paul Johnson (eds.), *Pension Systems and Retirement Incomes Across OECD Counties*. Northampton, MA: Edward Elgar, pp. 92–130.

Holzmann, Robert (1999). 'The World Bank Approach to Pension Reform', Social Protection Discussion Paper Series, no. 9807. Consulted online March 1, 2004: *http://wbln0018.worldbank.org/HDNet/hddocs.nsf/View+to+Link+WebPages/ A9F42F871DE2FA9985256794005E9816?OpenDocument*

Joint Forum of Financial Market Regulators (JFFMR) (2001). *Proposed Regulatory Principles For Capital Accumulation Plans*. A Report by the Joint Forum of Financial Market Regulators' Working Committee on Investment Disclosure in Capital

Accumulation Plans (April 27). Consulted online March 30, 2004: *http://www.osc.
gov.on.ca/en/About/Publications/JF_010427.pdf*

Livingston, Gillian (2004). 'Ontario Not Concerned About Teachers' Pension Plan
Shortfall, Watching Stelco'. Consulted online March 30, 2004: *http://money.
canoe.ca/News/Other/2004/02/22/357388-cp.html*

MacNaughton, John. A (2004). 'The Challenge of Investing CPP Assets'. Presentation made to the Calgary Chamber of Commerce, January 20. Consulted online
March 1, 2004: *http://www.cppib.ca/info/speeches/Calgary_Jan_04.pdf*

McFarland, Janet (2003). 'Our Pension Mess Could Be Worst'. *The Globe and Mail.*
Consulted online March 30, 2004: *http://www.globeandmail.com/servlet/ArticleNews/
TPStory/LAC/20030731/RJANE/TPBusiness/TopStories*

Pension Research Council (2003). *Risk Management for Global Aging: Perspectives on the
Challenges Facing Industrialized Countries.* The Wharton School of the University of
Pennsylvania WP 2003–1.

Pozzebon, Silvana (2002). 'Have Employer-Sponsored Pension Plans Outlived
Their Usefulness?', in Selected Papers from the 38th Annual Canadian Industrial
Relations Association Conference, Gregor Murray et al. (eds.), *Rethinking Institu-
tions for Work and Employment.* Les Presses de l'Université Laval, pp. 137–53.

Régie des Rentes du Québec (2003*a*). 'La situation financière des régimes de
retraite à prestations determinées: Une invitation à la responsabilisation et à la
prudence', *La Lettre Express.* (May 2003). Consulted online March 30, 2004: *http://
www.rrq.gouv.qc.ca/fr/services/Publications/let05-2003fr.pdf*

Régie des Rentes du Québec (2003*b*). *Adapter le Régime de rentes aux nouvelles réalités
du Québec.* Consulted online March 30, 2004: *http://www.rrq.gouv.qc.ca/fr/services/
Publications/ConsPub2003.pdf*

Reguly, Eric (2004). 'Stelco Plan May Hit Taxpayers Hard'. News from the *Globe and
Mail.* March 11. Consulted online March 30, 2004: *http://money.canoe.ca/News/
Other/2004/02/22/357388-cp.html*

Ripsman, Colin (2000). 'Focus On Fees', *Benefits Canada,* September edn. Consulted online March 30, 2004: *http://www.benefitscanada.com/content/legacy/
Content/2000/09-00/focusonfees.html*

Rubin, Sandra (2004). 'Ottawa Gears Up For Pension Overhaul: "Ridiculous" To
Have 10 Provincial Regimes For Plan', *National Post,* March 17. Consulted online
March 30, 2004: *http://www.zsa.ca/En/Articles/article.php?aid=832*

Sanford, Jeff (2003). 'Caisse Reports Biggest Investment Loss In 37-Year History',
Benefits Canada, April. Consulted online March 1, 2004: *http://www.benefitscanada.
com/content/legacy/Content/2003/04-03/industry.pdf*

Sharratt, Anna (2004). 'Caisse Releases Financial, Corporate Governance Results'.
Benefits Canada News Headlines, February 18, 2004. Consulted online March 1, 2004:
http://www.benefitscanada.com/news/article.jsp?content=20040218_141502_1180

Sharratt, Anna (2003). '2003 Defined Contribution Plan Report', *Benefits Canada*
(December) Consulted online on March 1, 2004: *http://www.benefitscanada. com*

Smolkin, Sheryl (2003). 'Tax, Pension Rules Make Phased Retirement Difficult',
Canadian HR Reporter, 16(19): 7.

Smolkin, Sheryl and Lori Satov (2004). 'Year of the CAP'. *Benefits Canada* (January)
Consulted online on March 1, 2004: *http://www.benefitscanada.com*

Statistics Canada, Income Statistics Division, Pensions and Wealth Program (2003*a*). *Canada's Retirement Income Programs: A Statistical Overview (1990–2000)*. Catalogue no. 74-507-XIE. Ottawa, Canada: Ministry of Industry.

Statistics Canada (2003*b*). 'Fact-sheet On Retirement', *Perspectives on Labour and Income* (Statistics Canada Catalogue no. 75-001-XIE), 4, 9: 1–7, September 2003 online edition.

World Economic Forum Pension Readiness Initiative (WEFPRI) (2004*a*). 'Living Happily Ever After: The Economic Implications of Aging Societies', Executive Summary of a Report to the World Economic Forum Pension Readiness Initiative developed in partnership with Watson Wyatt Worldwide. Consulted online March 1, 2004: *http://www.weforum.org/pdf/Initiatives/pension_report_2004.pdf*

——. (2004*b*). 'Canada—Country Profile'. Consulted online March 1, 2004: *http://www.weforum.org/pdf/Initiatives/pension_canada.pdf*

Chapter 14

The Future of Retirement in Sweden

Annika Sundén

In 1998, the Swedish Parliament passed pension legislation that transformed Sweden's public pension scheme from a pay-as-you-go defined benefit (DB) plan to a Notional defined contribution (NDC) plan. In addition, that reform introduced a second-tier defined contribution (DC) individual accounts plan. The new pension system went into effect in 1999 and benefits were first paid in 2001. This reform fundamentally changed the provision of public pension benefits and redefined the benefit promise. Under the new system, government-provided benefits are closely linked to contributions and lifetime earnings determine benefits. The reform also recognized how increased life expectancy influences the system's financial stability, and so it built in an automatic benefit adjustment process that responds to changes in longevity. The new system also boosted individual responsibility due to the introduction of a funded individual-account component. The reform also had implications for the Swedish occupational (industry-based) employer schemes, and three of the four occupational plans changed their formats as a result.

In this chapter we discuss the transformation of the Swedish retirement income system and comment on how it may change the future of retirement. First we outline the reform, and compare it to the system in place before the reform. Next we explore the reform process, and then discuss future challenges. A final section offers some lessons for other countries.

The Pre-reform Retirement System in Sweden

The retirement income system in Sweden has long involved two pillars: a public national pension that covered all individuals; and an occupational pension system that built on collective bargaining agreements between labor market players (akin to employer pensions in the USA). The pre-reform public pension system provided a flat benefit (FP), introduced in 1913, intended to protect old-age income security, and a supplementary benefit (ATP) introduced in 1960 to provide earnings-related benefits.[1] The ATP benefit was based on a worker's fifteen years of highest earnings; it also required thirty years of covered earnings for a full benefit; and it replaced 60 percent of earnings up to a ceiling. The ceiling was approximately 1½ times the average wage. People with no or very low ATP benefits received an additional benefit, the pension supplement. Together with the FP benefit, the pension supplement provided a minimum benefit level worth approximately 30 percent of the average wage. Earned pension rights, retiree benefits, and the income ceiling were all indexed to consumer prices. Benefits were taxed as regular income, although low-benefit retirees received an extra deduction. The normal retirement age was 65, but the benefit could be taken at age 60 with an actuarial adjustment or postponed until age 70. A partial retirement benefit allowed older workers to reduce the number of hours worked and receive a benefit that partially replaced lost earnings.

The FP and ATP benefits were financed primarily through payroll taxes levied on employers. Payroll taxes for the FP and ATP systems were 5.86 percent and 13 percent respectively in 1997, and the financing of the FP benefit was supplemented by general tax revenues. Although pension rights were earned only up to a ceiling, the payroll tax was levied on all earnings. The system was pay-as-you-go with partial funding. When the system was first introduced in 1960, the contribution rate was set so that the system would build up a surplus to act as a buffer against cyclical contribution changes and offset an expected decrease in private saving following the introduction of a universal earnings-related scheme. The surplus was invested in several so-called 'buffer' funds (AP funds). At the time of the 1998 reform, assets in the buffer funds equaled approximately five years' worth of benefit payments. The majority of these reserves (85 percent) were invested in low-risk assets, mainly Swedish government and housing bonds.

Occupational plans in Sweden included four types of plans for national government workers; local government workers; white-collar workers, and blue-collar workers. All told, these covered most workers (90 percent) and pay benefits worth, on average, 10–15 percent of income. With the exception of the blue-collar worker plan, Swedish occupational pensions also replaced a portion of earnings above the public plan benefit ceiling. At the time of the public pension reform, all four occupational plans were of the DB variety, and as a rule, benefits were determined by earnings during the ten-year period before retirement.

The Reform Process

In the early 1990s, projections showed that the system's buffer funds would be exhausted within 20–25 years, and contribution rates would have to be increased dramatically to continue to pay promised benefits. This was because under the old pay-as-you-go Swedish system, a generous benefit formula combined with slowing productivity growth produced large projected system deficits. Pension benefits as well as earned pension rights were indexed to prices rather than wages; the lack of a link between benefits and real wage growth meant that earned pension rights and benefits rose faster than wages and contributions in times of low or negative productivity growth. Indeed, the fact that the system targeted benefits to capped income, and the earnings cap tracked consumer prices, meant that over time, successively larger fractions of the population earned wages above the ceiling as real wages grew.

The system also exhibited other problems, including unsystematic and inequitable relationships between contributions and benefits. One reason was that contributions were paid on all earnings from age 16 until retirement, whereas benefits were based only on the highest fifteen years of earnings. This formula thus redistributed income from people with long working lives and a flat life cycle income (typically low-income workers), to those with shorter work histories and rising earnings profiles (typically high-income workers). Finally, there was little incentive to delay retirement as a result of the benefit formula and the fact that contributions were levied on all earnings (Sundén 2000).

Reform Process. The reform process began in 1991 when Parliament appointed a committee to review the system and propose reform. The goal was a financially and politically sustainable system for the long run. Compared to financial problems predicted for the USA, the problem in Sweden was even more severe. Projections showed that, with a future real wage growth of 1.5 percent and unchanged contribution rates, the buffer funds would be exhausted sometime between 2010 and 2015. To maintain financial stability, contribution rates would have to rise from 18.86 percent to about 24 percent by 2015, and continue to rise thereafter. Indeed, the system was thought to be sustainable only with a real wage growth of 2 percent (Ministry of Health and Social Affairs 1994).

Broad political consensus was important and the policymakers faced strong pressures to find a compromise. A first government commission, in 1990, could not agree on a reform proposal but proposed keeping the system's framework unchanged while indexing system parameters to economic growth; it also recommended increasing the normal retirement age and the number of years required for a full pension. Shortly thereafter, Sweden entered a deep recession and pension reform became a top priority leading to the appointment of a parliamentary group representative of all seven parties then in the Parliament.[2] The gradual changes suggested by the previous pension commission were rejected by this new group, which instead recommended a complete overhaul of the system.

The group ultimately agreed that the several key principles would govern the new pension system: benefits would be determined by contributions from lifetime earnings, indexation would be based on the growth of the contribution base; and benefits at retirement would incorporate changes in life expectancy (Palmer 2002). Overall, the outcome was a compromise, in that it included both pay-as-you-go and DC elements. A DC plan was favored because it established a close link between contributions and benefits, and implied a contribution rate that would remain unchanged in the future. Since payroll taxes were high in Sweden, it was widely believed that future financial imbalances could not be resolved by additional increases in contribution rates.

The new system also included a small component of funded individual DC accounts. Though the Social Democrats initially opposed these, the DC accounts were eventually adopted in exchange for keeping the scale of the public program unchanged. The conservatives had argued for a decreased role of the public scheme but they agreed on a contribution rate of 18.5 percent, if individual accounts were added to the system. Parliament finally passed the legislation in June 1998: the outcome was a NDC plan which is a plan financed on a pay-as-you-go basis, and the Premium Pension plan which is a funded individual account component.[3]

How Does the New Swedish Pension System Work?

In the new system, the total mandatory contribution rate is 18.5 percent of earnings. This is divided into two portions, with 16 percentage points credited to the notional account, and 2.5 to the Premium Pension. Contributions are split equally between employees and employers; employee contributions are limited by a ceiling, while the employer's share is levied on all earnings.[4] Participants earn pension rights from labor income, benefits from unemployment insurance, and other social insurance programs, as well as from years spent at home taking care of children, time in military service, and in education.[5] The system also provides a guaranteed basic benefit, to ensure a minimum standard of living in retirement. This guaranteed benefit is means-tested and offset by the income from the NDC component; it is financed by general tax revenues; and it is conceptually separated from the earnings-related scheme.[6] The guarantee is payable from age 65 and the benefit is worth approximately 35 percent of the average wage of a blue-collar worker. Currently, around 30 percent of retirees collect at least some pension income from the guarantee benefit. The benefit amount is indexed to prices, so real wage growth will over time reduce the import of this guarantee in total retirement income.

The NDC Component. The key concept in the new Swedish pension system is the NDC. Under this framework, contributions are recorded in each worker's individual record, and the resulting account values represent that individual's claims to future pension benefits. But contrary to a conventional funded DC scheme, annual contributions in the NDC plan are used to finance current pension benefit obligations as in any pay-as-you-go system. Hence, the individual accounts are 'notional'.

This individual account balance grows over time, by annual contributions and due to a rate of return credited to the account each year. To link earned pension rights to workers' earnings, the rate of return is set equal to national per capita real wage growth. It is interesting that formulating the rate of return on the individual accounts was a sticking point in the reform discussions. Initially, policymakers considered using the change in the total wage bill as the measure of the rate of return, to ensure the system's financial stability. However a competing reform goal was to ensure that earned pension rights and benefits followed the average wage growth among the working population, so that relative income growth would boost pension income irrespective of when people earned their pay during their lifetimes. It was felt that these goals were best achieved by using per capita wage growth. Accordingly, to ensure financial stability, policymakers added an 'automatic stabilizer' mechanism that abandons wage indexation if the stability of the system is threatened.

Under the NDC, retirement ages are flexible: that is, benefits may be drawn as of age 61. At retirement, annual benefits are calculated by dividing the notional account balance by an annuity divisor. The divisor is determined by the cohort's age 65 life expectancy at retirement, and an imputed real rate of return of 1.6 percent (the expected long-term real growth rate of the economy assumed by the reformers). Since the annual pension benefit is equal to the net present value of benefits using a real interest rate of 1.6, the initial benefit at retirement is higher than if benefits were adjusted fully for economic growth each year (as long as growth rates exceed 1.6 percent). The rationale was to provide a relatively high initial benefit, rather than having an increasing benefit profile after retirement. The divisor is the same for men and women, which implies that a unisex mortality table is used. It is fixed at age 65 and no adjustments are made for cohort changes in life expectancy after age 65. Benefits are also adjusted each year for inflation. Since the initial benefit calculation already includes an implicit rate of return (1.6 percent), the post-retirement indexation takes this into account. For example, if real wage growth were 2 percent and consumer prices changed by 1 percent, benefits would be adjusted by 1.4 percent. On the other hand, if real wage growth fell below the norm, benefits would be adjusted by less than inflation. Over a worker's lifetime, this type of indexation produces the same result as regular wage indexation (Palmer 2002).[7]

Financial Stability. A key goal of the pension reform was to ensure that the system would be financially stable, even if the system faced adverse demographic and economic developments. On the other hand, the system is still a pay-as-you-go program; pension payments are financed by annual contributions. Increasing the contribution rate is not a viable option in the NDC framework, since higher payments automatically boost benefit promises. Therefore, the buffer funds and the introduction of an automatic balancing mechanism are crucial for the system's financial stability.

Buffer Funds. The buffer funds play an important role in the implementation of the new pension system. In the short term, these funds alleviate pressures on the general budget due to the reform. Several programs previously were financed through payroll taxes (the guarantee pension, disability pension, and survivor pension) are now financed through general tax revenues. In order to offset this change, revenue was transferred to the general budget from the buffer funds in 1999, 2000, and 2001. The amount was equal to a one-time transfer of about one-third of the balance in the funds.[8] The remaining buffer funds are needed to cover projected deficits in benefit financing in the future, when the baby boom generation starts to retire. Thus, although the pension reform created a pension system that is financially stable in the long run, the reform did not pay for all of the costs of baby boomer retirement.

Since these buffer funds are so important to the system's financial stability, the rules regarding their governance and investment have recently been reevaluated. Currently, fund management practices are similar to those in Canada (Pozzebon Chapter 13). In the past, the Swedish buffer funds have been criticized for sacrificing returns in order to achieve political goals, and in particular, subsidizing housing. Accordingly, the new investment rules require that investments be made using risk and return considerations; economically-targeted investments are disallowed. The guidelines also allow a larger share to be invested in equities than in the past (up to 70 percent of the portfolio) and international assets (up to 40 percent of the portfolio may be exposed to currency risk). Members of the investment boards are appointed by the government and selected on the basis of financial competence.

Automatic Balancing. Because the system is still a pay-as-you-go system it remains sensitive to demographic change. In particular, two features in the design of the system could introduce financial instability: the indexation of benefits to average wage growth rather than to the growth in the total wage bill, and the use of fixed divisors in annuity calculations. In particular, pension rights and retiree benefits grow with per capita earnings, while contributions are linked to the total wage bill. This makes the system sensitive to shocks: for instance, a decline in the workforce would mean that average wages would grow faster than the total wage bill, so, in turn, benefit payments would grow faster than the contributions financing them.

Another reason why financial imbalances might occur has to do with how the annuity divisor in the NDC is calculated. Annuities are based on a cohort's longevity when it reaches age 65, rather than a projection of that cohort's life expectancy. Further, the divisors are fixed after that point, and not adjusted to take into account changes in *ex post* longevity. If a cohort's actual longevity is longer than anticipated, benefit payments to that cohort will exceed their total contributions.

An automatic balancing mechanism was designed to deal with these two sources of financial instability without raising taxes. Thus if shortfalls are projected, per capita wage indexation will be reduced, to bring the system back in balance. The idea is that this mechanism will work automatically, so it does not require an explicit action by politicians. The hope was that protecting the pension system from discretionary changes would minimize the risk of manipulation for political gain.

Of course, this automatic balancing mechanism still requires that system financial stability measures can be calculated. Before the reform, the National Social Insurance Board (NSIB) traditionally undertook system projections to set contribution rates. The new pension system also specifies the financial information that must be reported, including a system income statement and balance sheet. A balance ratio relating the pension system's assets to its liabilities and summarizes its financial status must also be calculated annually. The balance ratio is defined as follows:

$$Balance\ ratio = (Capitalized\ Value\ of\ Contributions$$
$$+ Buffer\ Funds)/Pension\ Liability$$

System 'assets' consist of the capitalized value of contributions and the current value of the buffer funds. The capitalized value of contributions is equal to the pension benefits that the annual contributions could finance in the long run. It is derived by multiplying annual contributions by the turnover duration, which is the expected average time between when a contribution is made to the system and when the benefit payment based on that contribution is made.[9] The current turnover duration is approximately thirty-two years (NSIB 2004). The pension liability is thus the system's current vested liability.[10] A balance ratio of one means that the NDC system is in financial balance (i.e. assets and liabilities are equal). When the balance ratio is below one, the system is in imbalance and liabilities exceed assets. If the balance ratio exceeds one, the system has an accumulated surplus. Table 14-1 shows the financial balance of the NDC for the period 2001–3.

The automatic balance mechanism is intended to be activated as soon as the balance ratio falls below one; at that point, indexation of earned pension rights and current benefits will be lowered from average wage growth.[11] The indexation will be reduced by multiplying the change in

TABLE 14-1 Assets and Liabilities NDC 2001 and 2002 (Billions of
Swedish Crowns)

	2001	2002	2003
Contribution asset	5,085	5,293	5,465
Buffer funds	56	488	577
Total assets	5,650	5,780	6,042
Pension liability	5,423	5,729	5,984
Assets/liabilities	218	52	58
Balance ratio	1.0419	1.0090	1.0097

Note: 1 US$ = 7 Swedish Crowns.

Source: National Social Insurance Board (2004).

average wage growth by the balance ratio. The reduced indexation will
continue as long as the balance ratio is less than one. Currently, the
automatic balance mechanism is intended to be applied only in the event
of a system deficit. However, under certain economic and demographic
conditions, the system might build up a permanent and substantial surplus.
In that event, if the surplus becomes too large, the excess would be
distributed to participants; not yet resolved is what might be too large.[12]

Transition. The transition to the new system is to take place over sixteen
years.[13] The first cohort to participate in the system is the 1938 cohort; it is
to receive one-fifth of its benefit from the new system, and four-fifths from
the old system. Each succeeding cohort will then increase its participation
in the new system by 1/20, so that those born in 1944 will receive half of
their benefit from the new and half from the old system.[14] Workers born in
1954 or later will participate only in the new system, but not until 2040 will
benefits be paid fully by the new system. In other words, soon after the baby
boom generation has begun to retire in 2015, a large share of benefits will
still be paid by the old system, even though new retirees will get most of
their benefits under the new system.

The Individual Account—the Premium Pension. The new plan also
requires that workers pay 2.5 percent of earnings to a mandatory funded
individual account. These accounts are self-directed and participants may
invest in domestic and international mutual funds. A new government
agency, the Premium Pension Agency (PPM), has been established to
administer the funded pillar and acts as a clearing-house. The clearing-
house model was chosen to keep administrative costs down by drawing on
economies of scale in administration.

Contributions are withheld by employers and submitted to the National
Tax Authority. Swedish employers make monthly tax and contribution

payments, but they report information on individual earnings on an annual basis. For this reason, individual pension rights cannot be established until each worker has filed his income taxes; these reports must then be consolidated with employer reports, and the process takes an average of eighteen months. Until pension rights have been established, pension contributions are placed on an interim basis in a government bond fund at the National Debt Office; after individual rights are determined, participants decide how to invest their funds. Contributions are invested by the PPM in lump sums; fund companies only know the total investment of pension contributions, not the identity of each individual investor. The PPM keeps all individual account and fund share value records. Individuals are allowed to change funds on a daily basis, and all transactions are aggregated by the PPM which then transmits them as a net purchase or redemption to each fund.

The Funds. Policymakers decided to offer investors broad choice in the Premium Pension, so any fund company licensed to do business in Sweden is allowed to participate in the system. Fund companies seeking to participate must sign a contract with PPM that governs reporting requirements and fees. The fee schedule is two-part, involving a money management fee and a fixed administrative fee charged by the PPM. Fund managers charge the same fee for participants in the pension system as they do in the private saving market. Because the account administration is handled by the PPM, costs for fund managers would be anticipated to be lower; managers must rebate to the PPM a share of the fees, which PPM then passes on to participants. The rebate is set by a formula and determined by the level of the gross fees and the size of the fund; popular funds and high-fee funds have to pay a larger rebate.

In order to keep the number of funds manageable, each fund manager is allowed to register a maximum of fifteen funds. At the time of the first investment elections in 2000, approximately 460 funds were registered with the PPM (see Table 14-2). Currently, more than 650 funds participate in the system. About two-thirds are equity funds, and 6 percent are life cycle funds (i.e. funds in which the asset allocation automatically changes as participants approach retirement). About a quarter of the funds invest mainly in Sweden. Almost 60 percent of the funds were established for the Premium Pension system. The average gross fund fees (before rebate) vary from 1.16 percent for the equity funds to 0.47 percent for the funds that invest only in interest-earning assets. After the rebate, fund fee average 0.43 percent of assets. The fixed administrative fee charged by the PPM is 0.3 percent of assets, resulting in a total cost of 0.73 percent of assets for an average participant. These administrative costs are relatively high compared to, for example, the US Thrift Savings Plan (the individual account plan for federal employees): that has expense ratios of 0.1 percent of assets.

TABLE 14-2 Distribution of Funds in the Individual Account
System

Type of fund	Share(%)	Average fund fee (%)
Equity	68	1.16
Balanced equity and interest-earning	10	0.86
Life cycle	6	0.61
Interest-earning	16	0.47

Source: Säve-Söderbergh (2003).

On the other hand, fund costs in Sweden are considerably lower than those observed in Latin American countries with individual accounts (Mitchell 1998). For example, net fees in Chile were 1.36 percent of assets in 1999 (James et al. 2001).

The government also established two additional funds one being a default fund for participants who did not choose a fund, and a second for participants who wanted to make an active choice but also wanted the government involved in the asset management. In initial discussions, reformers suggested that the default would be a low-risk fund mostly invested in interest-earning assets. But policymakers then worried that such a strategy would have a negative effect on the distribution of benefits, if low-income workers were more likely to take the default. Consequently, the default fund's investment strategy was reformulated to mirror the asset allocation of an average investor in the system.

Currently the default fund seeks to achieve a high long-run rate of return at an overall low risk level.[15] That fund follows a fixed allocation of stocks and bonds, where equity holdings cannot exceed 90 percent of the total value and may not fall below 80 percent; of which a maximum of 75 percent may be invested in foreign stock. Other funds may invest 100 percent in equities, but the default must hold a minimum in interest-earning assets. Currently, the default fund holds 65 percent of its assets in international equities and 17 percent in Swedish equities; 60 percent of all assets are managed passively. The money management fee for the default fund is quite low: in 2003, the gross fee was 0.5 percent, and only 0.16 percent after the PPM rebate.

The government-managed fund is also required to incorporate environmental and ethical concerns in its investment decisions. Consequently, the government-managed fund may invest only in companies that follow international conventions (to which Sweden has agreed) on human rights, child labor, environment, and corruption. That fund invests in between 2,000 and 2,500 companies worldwide; when in 2001 the firms were screened the

250   Annika Sundén

review indicated that thirty companies violated the screen, which were then excluded from the portfolio.[16] It should be noted that the policy only excludes companies that have violated international conventions, broken laws, or have admitted wrongdoing. No exclusions are to be made on basis of the goods that the company produces; for example, tobacco companies are allowed. Government fund managers do not have voting rights for their holdings.

Investment Behavior. Participants in the Premium Pension plan may choose up to five funds. A participant who makes an active investment choice may not invest any share of the portfolio in the default fund or shift the portfolio to the default at a later date.[17] The first investment election for the Premium Pension occurred in 2000, and the objective was to induce as many participants as possible to make an active choice.[18] Accordingly, the agency launched a large advertisement campaign and actively encouraged participants to select their own portfolios. Private fund managers also offered ad campaigns to attract investors. At that time, some two-thirds of participants made an active investment choice, selecting 3.4 funds on average (see Table 14-3). The bulk of the contributions were invested in equities: 74 percent of the portfolios for men and 69 percent of the portfolios for women were placed in equity funds. Of course, since life cycle and balanced funds also include equities, the total share in equities is higher (Säve-Söderbergh 2003). Participants also exhibited 'home bias'—almost half of the portfolios were invested in Swedish stocks.

Women were somewhat more likely than men to make a choice, and as expected, high-income participants were more likely to take an active role than low-income participants. We caution that one cannot draw firm conclusions about the share of participants that actively thought about the investment decision from these results. This is because no action was

TABLE 14-3 Investment Allocation, Men and Women, 2000

	Men	Women
Average amount invested (Swedish crowns)	19,800	15,500
Number of funds elected	3.4	3.4
Average share of portfolio in:		
Equity funds	0.74	0.69
Balanced funds	0.07	0.09
Life cycle funds	0.17	0.19
Interest-earning funds	0.02	0.03

Source: Säve-Söderbergh (2003).

Note: 1 US$ = 7 Swedish Crowns.

needed to select the default fund, so one cannot separately identify those that actively decided that they wanted to invest in the default fund, from those who defaulted into it through lack of taking action.

One surprise has been that the share of participants actively selecting their portfolio allocations has fallen considerably, among new system entrants. For instance, in 2004, only 9 percent of enrollees selected their own portfolios. One explanation might be that new entrants are mostly young workers entering the labor market and far from retirement. Nevertheless, in the first investment period during 2000, close to 60 percent of participants in the same age group selected a portfolio instead of defaulting (Cronqvist and Thaler 2003). One explanation might be that the Premium Pension received much less attention in more recent enrollment periods: advertising fell dramatically, as did private fund manager publicity efforts as compared to the initial election period. Another explanation is that the default fund performed better than the average portfolio. The initial investment selections in 2000 coincided with the peak of the run-up in the stock market, and following that, the stock market tumbled. Since the fall of 2000, the default fund returned −29.9 percent, while the average investor who actively chose funds lost 39.6 percent of his assets (Cronqvist and Thaler 2003).

Annuities. Benefits in the individual account component can be withdrawn from age 61 and annuitization is mandatory. The PPM is the sole provider of funded-system annuities, and participants can select between a fixed or variable annuity. The level of the annuity is based on standard insurance practices, and the PPM uses unisex life tables of persons in the age cohort from the year the calculation is made. The survivor benefit in the funded component is voluntary. If a survivor benefit is elected and the individual dies before retirement (during the accumulation phase), the survivor benefit pays a fixed amount for five years. If the individual dies after retirement, the survivor benefit will be paid as a lifelong annuity to the surviving spouse.

Following the pension reform, three of the four occupational schemes also introduced individual accounts to their workers. Contribution rates in these schemes vary between 2.5 and 4 percent, which means that most workers in Sweden now contribute between 5 and 6.5 percent of their earnings to individual accounts.

Information and Education

Since the reform completely changed the pension scheme, it was crucial to provide information to participants during the implementation period. The new system puts more of the risk and responsibility on individuals to plan for retirement, so in 1998 a broad information campaign was launched to educate participants about the new system. This campaign sent to participants a detailed brochure describing the new system, fielded numerous public service announcements on radio and television, and included discussions in newspapers and a website on the reforms. During the campaign, participants also received their first annual account statement for the pension scheme, the 'orange envelope'. This orange envelope is sent out annually and includes account information as well as a projection of benefits for the NDC as well as the premium pension.

Following the initial campaign, the annual mailing remains the primary source of information to participants about the pension scheme. It not only provides information about expected benefits, but it also summarizes how the new pension system works and promotes the main message that lifetime earnings determine benefits. For the individual account component, the PPM also sends out annual information on fund choices, investment risk, and fees, and the agency has its own website where participants can review and manage their accounts.

To evaluate the success of information efforts and participant knowledge about the new pension system, the National Social Insurance Board has fielded an annual survey since 1999 (National Social Insurance Board 2003). The most recent survey showed that almost everyone—93 percent of respondents—knew the public pension had been reformed. Furthermore, about two-thirds of participants say they read at least part of the orange envelope. Yet when respondents were asked to rate how they perceived their knowledge about the system, fewer than 40 percent indicated that they had a good understanding of the new system (Figure 14-1). About half reported that they had some understanding of the new system but they viewed their knowledge as poor. The share of participants who said that they did not understand the new system at all fell from about 30 percent in 1998 to 13 percent in 2003. Not surprisingly, older individuals were more likely than younger individuals to report that they had good knowledge of the system. Men viewed themselves as more knowledgeable than women, and formal education was positively correlated with system knowledge.

Challenges for the Future

One of the most important objectives of the Swedish pension reform was to design a pension system that would be financially stable over time, even when faced with adverse demographic and economic developments. The new system also seeks to provide increased work incentives and give participants a possibility to control some of their pension funds. Next we investigate whether the reform will achieve its goals, and assess the challenges for the future.

Financial stability. While the Swedish reform introduced several features to ensure financial stability, the system is still mainly pay-as-you-go, since

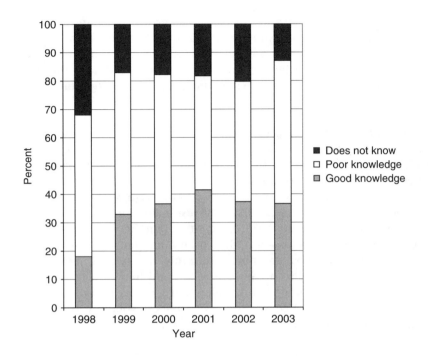

Figure 14-1. Self-reported knowledge about the Swedish pension system.
Source: National Social Insurance Board (2003).

pension payments are financed by annual contributions. Because the contribution rate in an NDC scheme is fixed by definition, the system's financial stability then relies on adjusting benefits. This means that the system shifts the risk of financing benefits from future to current generations (Palmer 2002).

The automatic balancing mechanism adjusts benefits immediately, as soon as the system slips into financial imbalance. It is interesting that the mechanism does not distinguish between financial imbalances caused by temporary downturns, from more serious economic and demographic developments. Thus it is possible that the automatic balancing might be triggered unnecessarily; the benefit impact of such an event would be small, but it could have an impact on the system's political stability. In fact, when the automatic balancing mechanism was introduced, it was described as an 'emergency brake' that would only be used rarely and only in situations when the system was in crisis. The result is that when automatic balancing occurs, it may be taken as a signal that the system is in crisis and that people's benefits are threatened. A better strategy might have been to characterize the automatic balancing mechanism as a regular component of the indexation of earned pension rights and benefits. In general, benefits will grow with average earnings but the return can vary the same way the rate of return on capital varies. Because automatic balancing is very likely to occur (the current balance ratio is 1.01), for the system's survival it will be important to change the image of the automatic balancing mechanism.

Benefits. In general, replacement rates will be lower in the new versus the old pension system. The shift from a DB to a NDC plan makes it difficult to estimate expected benefits. In fact, only 38 percent of participants in 2003 knew that lifetime contributions determined benefits (National Insurance Board 2003). Participants also had poor knowledge regarding the benefit components, and they tended to overestimate the importance of the Premium Pension for the level of benefits. Benefits will also depend on the investment decisions in the premium pension and currently participants' portfolios are almost entirely invested in equities. The average investor today is forty-two years old and hence relatively far from retirement. On the other hand, unless participants reduce their equity holdings as they approach retirement, market volatility could have a negative effect on retirement benefits.[19]

Fairness and Redistribution. The new system creates a close link between contributions and benefits for many employees, but for those in the lower half of the wage distribution, this link is broken by the guarantee pension which is offset by the NDC benefit. For low-wage individuals, additional work does not necessarily increase pension benefits one-for-one. The choice of retirement age is also less flexible for retirees dependent on the guarantee pension, since that benefit is only payable from age 65. But a high guarantee pension was important to ensure income security for individuals with no or low earnings. The system also redistributes income from high earners by putting a ceiling on earnings used in determining benefits, while levying the employer payroll tax on full earnings.

The choice to index the system to the change in average wages supplemented by an automatic balancing mechanism has implications for the distribution of benefits between cohorts. The activation of the automatic balancing mechanism reduces the indexation of earned pension rights and current benefits by the same amount. Participants in the beginning of their careers have longer horizons to recoup the loss in benefits compared to retirees who have started to collect their benefits. The expected size of this type of redistribution has not yet been fully examined, but some cohorts are likely to bear a larger share of the burden and may demand to be compensated.

Incentives to Work. The retirement age under the new pension is flexible and the increase in benefits from an additional year's work is actuarially fair, which was a design aimed at encouraging incentives to work. Evidence from the USA supports this view, since they suggest that a DC plan is likely to increase work among older individuals (see Chapter 5). Furthermore, the Swedish system does not have an age limit for covered earnings: that is, participants earn pension credits as long as they work. For example, a worker could start collecting benefits, and then return to work and continue earning pension credits. In practice, however, labor market legislation makes it difficult for workers to continue working past age 67; further employers are often unwilling to continue employing workers after age 65. In response to the pension reform, the age limit in labor legislation was increased to 67, but workers are still not covered by sickness and unemployment insurance after age 65.

Currently, most workers in Sweden exit the labor market much earlier than age 67—the average retirement age is approximately 62 (National Social Insurance Board (NSIB) 2000). Several of the occupational schemes provide early retirement incentives, and disability insurance has been used in the past as a path to retirement (Palme and Svensson 1999). As health improves and life expectancies continues to rise, the relationship between the ages stipulated by the pension system and labor legislation may have to be revisited.

Investments Under the Premium Pension System. The individual account component of the Swedish reform was constructed to provide wide investment choice. While at first active involvement was encouraged, more recently the PPM has taken a more passive role and limited its communication to provide information about fund risks and fees. Its objective has been to improve public financial knowledge so that workers can make good investment decisions. The question is whether this strategy will be successful; the USA experience has shown that investment decisions are complicated and participants are prone to make mistakes (Munnell and Sundén 2004). Furthermore, participants are not necessarily better off by choosing their own portfolio from a wide selection of funds (Benartzi and Thaler 2002). Finally, participants who are dependent on the guarantee pension have incentives to follow risky investment strategies in order to try to maximize their Premium Pension benefit because the level of the guarantee pension is determined by a participant's earnings-related benefit if the full contribution went to the NDC.

Members of Parliament and representatives from the PPM and the default fund have begun discussing the possibility of reducing the number of fund choices offered. It may be difficult to limit the number of funds given that the system had started out with broad choice. Another issue is whether maintaining such broad choice is cost-efficient. The fixed administrative fee for the PPM is relatively high, at 0.3 percent of assets (compared to 0.05 percent of assets for the notional accounts), and the money management fee for the default fund is considerably lower than the majority of funds.

The experience with the Swedish Premium Pension makes clear the importance of the default fund. Currently, the fund's investment strategy requires that most of the portfolio is invested in equities. Representatives from the fund have expressed that this strategy needs to be modified and that life cycle funds should be part of the default's portfolio. The rule that once participants have made an active choice, they cannot return to the default, also needs to be reviewed.

Information and Education. The new system is complicated and surveys of participants show that knowledge is limited about how the system function. A majority of participants is unaware of how benefits are determined, and the notion that the individual account component, Premium Pension, is more important for retirement income than the NDC benefit seems to be widespread. At the same time, participants also report that they need more information. But given the amount of information currently available, more information is probably not the solution. A challenge for the NSIB is to consider alternative ways of communicating with participants.

Conclusions

The Swedish experience with pension reform provides some important lessons for other countries considering reforming their retirement income systems. One of the most interesting insights was that Swedish policymakers recognized pension systems are dynamic institutions and hence must adjust to changing demographic and economic circumstances. They also recognized that it may be politically difficult to make needed adjustments, or that governments may try to manipulate the pension system for political gain. They therefore sought to 'tie politicians' hands', by introducing automatic adjustments that would help insulate the system from political risk and contribute to maintain its stability. Of course, the NDC approach implies that all such adjustments involve changes in benefits. Increasing contributions is not a viable option, because it also increases the benefit promise. If the system comes under financial pressure, this design feature could lead to substantial benefit cuts which in turn could threaten retirement income security. Furthermore, the adjustments of benefits in response to increasing life expectancy implies that individuals will have to work longer to reach a given replacement rate. It is always going to be difficult for some groups, such as those with physically demanding jobs, to extend their worklife so these groups may end up with lower replacement rates than in a system that adjusted benefits as well as taxes. The Swedish system provides a minimum guaranteed benefit that is well above the poverty level why adjusting only benefits may be less of a problem than in countries with lower minimum benefits. For such countries, pension schemes in which adjustment take place both on the benefit and the contribution side may be preferable.

The introduction of funded individual accounts was one area of much disagreement in the reform process. In the end, a small funded pillar with very broad investment choice was introduced. Participants were encouraged to choose their own portfolios—in fact, participants were given the impression that they gave up their opportunity to affect their pension benefits by investing in the default fund. However, the investment experiences during the first three years underscore the importance of a well-designed default fund. The sharp decrease after the initial elections in the share of workers making an active choice implies that the Swedish system may have too broad a choice. Another topic of keen interest to countries considering the introduction of individual accounts is whether the clearing-house model will be cost-effective in the long run. Plan administration requires a well-developed infrastructure, and plan implementation has been more costly and complicated than anticipated. Finally, it is important to note that funds are not accessible before age 61, to ensure that they are not used for other purposes than retirement; further, annuitization is mandatory when the money is withdrawn.

Overall, the new pension system puts more responsibility on individuals to plan and prepare for retirement. The system is not perfect: it is complicated and the focus on contributions makes it difficult to predict benefits. Information and education are important components of the reform but the Swedish system could be made easier for participants. Finally, although the pension system is constructed to be financially stable, it does not solve the financial pressures associated with the retirement of the large baby boom generation. The transition to the new system was facilitated by the fact that Sweden had accumulated large reserves in the old system in order to meet this obligation.

Endnotes

1. The introduction of the public earnings-related scheme primarily affected blue-collar workers in the private sector, because white-collar workers and employees in the public sector were already covered by earnings-related benefits through their occupational schemes. The public earnings-related system was the 'jewel in the crown' for the Social-Democratic party and its introduction was only won after one of the toughest political fights in modern Swedish history.
2. The Working Group on Pensions was organized along rather unconventional lines for a Swedish commission. It was headed by the Minister for Health and

Social Insurance and included high-ranking members of the parties represented in Parliament. However, membership was confined to the parliamentary political parties; no representatives of labor market organizations or retired peoples' associations were included. Although the labor market parties were not included in the group, a 'reference group' consisting of the unions was continuously briefed on the progress of the group.

3. Following the Swedish reform, several other countries have introduced NDC schemes including Italy, Poland and Latvia (Palmer 2002).

4. The ceiling is approximately 1½ times the average wage.

5. Credits for child rearing are earned until a child is four years old.

6. After the reform, the system for earnings-related benefits became a separate system—schemes such as disability insurance that had previously been a part of the pension system were transferred outside. The calculations of disability benefits were changed and linked closer to the scheme for sickness benefits.

7. Survivor benefits are provided for outside of the pension system and are temporary.

8. Currently the buffer funds amounts to about three times' the annual benefit payments.

9. The inverse of the turnover duration is the discount rate of the flow of contributions.

10. The calculation of the balance ratio involves only current values and no projections are made for assets and liabilities. Traditional projections of the financial status of the pension system are presented in an appendix to the annual report.

11. To smooth out the effects of temporary downturns, a three-year moving average is used in the calculation of the balance ratio.

12. During 2004, a government inquiry analyzed the issue. Their task was to examine the level of the balance ratio at which a distribution can be made without threatening the system's financial stability. Of course, it is not likely that a surplus distribution would occur any time soon; however the reason that the issue is being decided now is the goal of an autonomous system—future governments should not be tempted to use the buffer funds for other purposes than to pay pension benefits.

13. The transition period was originally twenty years but it was shortened because the reform was delayed.

14. Although individuals born in the late 1940s and early 1950s will get 50 percent or more of their pension benefits from the new system, many of their decisions about labor supply (these cohorts have had already been in the workforce for twenty years or more) and savings were made under the old system. In part for this reason, the pension rights for the transition cohorts earned in the old system until 1994 are guaranteed in the event their benefits in the new system is lower.

15. The five-year return should be in the top quartile of the returns for all funds.

16. The effect on returns was very small. Simulations done by the fund indicates that the portfolio excluding the thirty companies had a rate of return that was fifteen basis points lower than the full portfolio.

17. The reason for this rule was that the center-right parties wanted to limit the government's involvement in money management.
18. According to the original time table for the reform, the elections should have taken place in 1999 but were delayed due to implementation problems of the computer systems handling the administration.
19. The experience from 401(k) plans in the USA show that participants exhibit inertia and are not likely to rebalance their portfolios on their own as they age (Munnell and Sundén 2004).

References

Benartzi, Schlomo and Richard H. Thaler (2002). 'How Much Is Investor Autonomy Worth?', *Journal of Finance* 57 (4): 1593–1616.

Cronqvist, Henrik and Richard H. Thaler (2003). 'Design Choices in Privatized Social Security Systems: Learning from the Swedish Experience', Paper presented at the American Economic Association annual meeting in San Diego January 2004.

James, Estelle, James Smalhout, and Dimitri Vittas (2001). 'Administrative Costs and the Organization of Individual Account Systems: A Comparative Perspective', in Robert Holzman and Joseph Stiglitz (eds.), *New Ideas about Social Security*. Washington, DC: The World Bank.

Ministry of Health and Social Affairs (1994). *Reformerat Pensionssystem* (A New Pension System). Stockholm: Allmänna Förlaget.

Mitchell, Olivia S. (1998). 'Administrative Costs of Public and Private Pension Plans', in M. Feldstein (ed.), *Privatizing Social Security*. NBER. Chicago: University of Chicago Press, 1998, pp. 403–56.

Munnell, Alicia H. and Annika Sundén (2004). *Coming Up Short: The Challenge of 401(k) Plans*. Washington, DC: Brookings Institution Press.

National Social Insurance Board (2000). *Social Insurance in Sweden 2000*. Stockholm: National Social Insurance Board.

—— (2003). *Survey of the Orange Envelope 1999–2003*. Stockholm: National Social Insurance Board.

—— (2004). *The Swedish Pension System Annual Report 2003*. Stockholm: National Social Insurance Board.

Palme, Mårten and Ingemar Svensson (1999). 'Social Security, Occupational Pensions and Retirement in Sweden', in Jonathan Gruber and David Wise (eds.), *Social Security and Retirement Around the World*. Chicago: University of Chicago Press, pp. 355–402.

Palmer, Edward (2002). 'Swedish Pension Reform: Its Past and Its Future', in Martin Feldstein and Horst Siebert (eds.), *Social Security Pension Reform in Europe*. Chicago: University of Chicago Press, pp. 171–210.

Sundén, Annika (2000). 'How Will Sweden's New Pension System Work?', *Issue in Brief*, No. 3. Boston: Center for Retirement Research at Boston College, March.

Säve-Söderbergh, Jenny (2003). 'Pension Wealth: Gender, Risk and Portfolio Choices', *Essays on Gender Differences in Economic Decisions-Making*. Ph.D. Dissertation. Institute for Social Research, Stockholm University.

Chapter 15

Risk Management and Pension Plan Choice in Japan

Masaharu Usuki

Pension plan sponsors and managers of defined benefit (DB) plans in Japan faced many hardships over the last fourteen years. Above all, the depressed stock market and declining interest rates have contributed to the rapid spread of DB plan underfunding. In addition, new accounting standards introduced in fiscal 2000 made unfunded pension liabilities a greater concern for plan sponsors. Further, plan sponsors have been disappointed with the ineffectiveness of measures taken in the field of asset management, because of the narrowing risk premium in capital markets since 2000. Increasingly they are turning their eyes to the field of liability management and benefit design, seeking to control the financial risks of the pension plans offered. Measures taken include plan termination, benefit reduction, put-back of the contracted-out portion, and adoption of cash balance or defined contribution (DC) plans.

In this chapter, we evaluate whether and to what extent these changes in benefit design were influenced by sponsors' desire to control financial risk. We select several plan financial characteristics that affect risk tolerance and asset allocation decisions, such as the funding ratio, and examine whether these variables influence decisions regarding plan termination and put-back of the contracted-out portion of Employee Pension Funds (EPFs). In particular, we examine the hypothesis that plan sponsors have altered the plan type they offer, as a way to control risks in pension management. We find that the pension plan's funding ratio, volatility of the plan sponsor's return on equity, and the size of the pension plan relative to the plan sponsor's total assets do exert an influence on decisions to change pension plan types.

This research is of general interest for at least two reasons. First, pension plans in other countries today face similar challenges that their Japanese counterparts have experienced in the last decade. These challenges consist of a depressed stock market, declining interest rates, increasing longevity risk, and unfavorable regulatory changes (especially in the accounting arena). Japanese plan sponsor reactions, in terms of changing their benefit design, may offer valuable insights for others in similar circumstances.

Second, how financial risk influences pension plan offerings is an important area of pension research that has yet to be thoroughly explored. We seek to shed light on these issues by analyzing what drives pension plan design in Japan.

Defined Benefit Plan Sponsor Risk Sensitivity

The Tokyo stock market began to plummet in 1990, and since then, Japanese investors have grown increasingly concerned about financial risks. DB pension plan sponsors were no exception. A key problem was that it became difficult for pension funds to earn higher returns by taking investment risks. The Nikkei stock average fell 80 percent, from the 1989 year-end peak of 38,916 yen the April 2003 level of 7,831 yen. Assuming the average stock market risk premium of 5.44 percent from 1953 to 2002 is maintained, and adding this to the nominal risk free rate of 1.95 percent (from 1990 to 2002), the *ex ante* probability of the historical rate of return on the Tokyo Stock Exchange Index (TOPIX) is below one percent (Usuki 2003).[1] Such disappointing rates of return on pension fund investments were naturally of grave concern, since domestic stocks constitute 30 percent of DB plan assets in Japan.

Over the last forty years, Japanese DB plans have been of two main types, namely the EPFs and the Tax Qualified Pension Plans (TQPPs; see Clark and Mitchell 2002). The EPFs have a contracted-out portion that is managed by the plan sponsor as a partial substitute for a component of the public retirement benefit. As a consequence, the EPFs have some quasi-public characteristics not found in TQPPs, and accordingly, data on EPFs are more easily obtained than for TQPPs. Published data indicate that the average return on assets managed by EPFs was two percent in nominal terms and −0.4 percent in real terms in the 1989–2003 period (Pension Fund Association 2003).

Especially from 2000, the premium per unit of risk or volatility declined, as compared to the preceding period. Yen-based premiums over the risk-free rate fell in asset classes such as domestic and foreign stocks, and also in domestic bonds although to a lesser degree. At the same time, volatility, as gauged by the standard deviation of return, increased notably in foreign bonds and stocks. As a result, the 60-month Sharpe Ratio decreased uniformly for all asset classes. This clearly hurt DB plans, since in addition to holding domestic as well as foreign bonds and stocks, DB plans also tend to invest around fifteen of total assets in fixed-yield contracts sold by life insurers. But the guaranteed yield of these contracts was lowered from 2.5 percent to 1.5 percent in 1999.

A typical Japanese DB plan allocates, respectively, 25, 30, 10, 15, 15, and 5 percent of assets to yen-bonds, yen-stocks, foreign bonds, foreign stocks, insurance contracts and money market products, the Sharpe Ratio declined drastically after 2000 (see Figure 15-1). In other words, while investment risks increased, investment returns were associated with a declining risk premium.

Pension plan sponsors also had to take into account the impact of interest rate changes on the liability side of the DB balance sheet. The twenty-year Japanese government bond yield which stood at 5.7 percent at the end of 1989, then fell to 2.2 percent in 1999, and 1.3 percent in 2002. These government bond rates are used to discount DB pension liabilities, so this decline augmented the economic value of pension liabilities and increased plan sponsor burdens.

The stagnant rate of return on assets, combined with growing liabilities caused by the lower discount rate, have contributed to the increasing pension funding shortfall or decreasing surplus, which is a major downside risk for Japanese pension plan sponsors. Figure 15-2 shows that the share of underfunded EPF plans has continued to rise over time, and it has exceeded 90 percent in 2001. Plan sponsors have voiced the concern that these funding shortages will worsen corporative financial ratios under the

Note: Asset allocation in model portfolio and return indexes of each asset class are as follows:

Asset class	Allocation (%)	Index
Yen bonds	25	Nomura-BPI
Yen stocks	30	TOPIX Total Return
Foreign bonds	10	Citigroup World ex Japan Government Total Return
Foreign stocks	15	MSCI World ex Japan Total Return
Insurance contracts	15	Nippon Life Insurance General Account Contract
Cash (Risk-free asset)	5	Treasury Bills

Figure 15-1. Monthly Sharpe Ratio of model portfolio returns.
Source: Author's calculations using data provided by Ibbotson Associates Japan, except for insurance contracts.

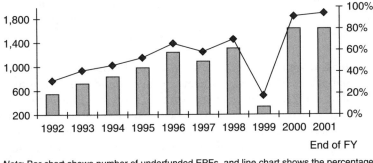

Note: Bar chart shows number of underfunded EPFs, and line chart shows the percentage to total number of EPFs.

Figure 15-2. Number of underfunded EPFs.
Source: Ministry of Health, Labor and Welfare (2003).

new accounting standard explained below, and that they could damage firm market valuation.

Impact of New Accounting Standards. Another factor causing Japanese pension plan sponsors to become more vividly aware of DB plan financial risks was the new accounting standard adopted in 2000. Before that, DB plans recorded only what was contributed to a plan as an expense on the income statement, without recognizing any liabilities on the balance sheet. As a consequence, it was unusual for top executives to devote any attention to DB fund management, unless a large increase in the contribution was requested.

In 2001, however, an accounting standard became effective, similar to Financial Accounting Standard 87 in the USA and International Accounting Standard 19 (see Chapter 10). This new standard stipulated that the difference between the market-based value of pension assets and liabilities (the Projected Benefit Obligation (PBO)) had to be recognized and disclosed as an item called 'accrued pension benefits' on the liability side of the plan sponsor's balance sheet.

When the new accounting standard was first applied, the average reported ratio of DB plan assets to liabilities was 54 percent for companies listed on the First Section of the Tokyo Stock Exchange (year-end fiscal 2000).[2] However, this ratio fell to 46 percent at year-end fiscal 2001 and 42 percent at 2002, because of the above-mentioned poor return and ballooning value of liabilities. Plan sponsors were then forced to recognize these deteriorating funding conditions every six months when financial statements were published. According to Benartzi and Thaler (1995), the more often people watch the result of their financial activities, the more risk-averse they become. If this hypothesis holds true for plan sponsors, disclosure of bad results under the new accounting standard would be predicted to make them more sensitive to risks in pension fund management and think about adopting measures to control risks in pension finance.

Shift of Focus from Assets to Liabilities. From the plan sponsor viewpoint, DB plan management is similar to that of other financial institutions (Davis 1995; Peskin 1997). That is, plan sponsors owe a long-term debt to employees (the promised pension) which is backed by invested funds. In these circumstances, changes in investment strategy and benefit design can both be effective in financial risk management. As a primary measure to control risk, however, the traditional and universal response in developed countries has been for DB plan sponsors to change investment strategies and tactics, especially their asset allocation policies.

As a result, many pension plans in Japan have reduced their allocation to riskier asset classes since 2000, especially with regard to domestic and foreign stocks. Some have boosted the share of fixed-yield insurance products, while others moved to long-term domestic and foreign bonds seeking to bring the duration of assets closer to that of liabilities. Yet such measures on the asset management side have not served as a panacea. That is, even if a DB plan successfully engaged in duration-matching or immunization by investing in fixed income products such as bonds and insurance products, this would mean that the plan would forego the potential for higher returns. In the Japanese case, expected rates of return would fall far below the discount rate used in actuarial calculations. Consequently, no matter how hard pension funds have tried to reduce risks on the asset side, they have not succeeded in keeping unfunded liabilities from growing.[3]

Changes in Pension Plan Types and Benefit Design

Finding it difficult to contain DB plan risk using asset management measures, Japanese plan sponsors have begun to alter the way they design the pension plan itself. If we consider benefit obligations to be akin to financial institution debt, there are two ways to control risks on the corporation's balance sheet. One is to eliminate or reduce the debt (or at least stop its growth), and the other is to reduce the interest rate risk due on debt by shortening the debt duration. Next we identify five tools that can serve that the purpose. The first, introducing a cash-balance plan, has the effect of shortening duration, while the other four (plan termination, benefit reduction, put-back of contracted-out portion, and introducing a DC plan) help reduce, contain, or eliminate pension liabilities and the shortfall of assets relative to liabilities.

Plan Termination. The two major types of DB plans, EPFs and TQPPs, declined in number by 12 percent and 28 percent respectively from their

TABLE 15-1 Number of EPFs and TQPPs

Fiscal year	EPFs Termination (dissolution)	EPFs Put-back of contracted-out portion	EPFs Existing fiscal year end	TQPPs Existing fiscal year end
1991	0	N.A.	1,593	90,434
1992	0	N.A.	1,735	92,082
1993	0	N.A.	1,804	92,467
1994	1	N.A.	1,842	92,355
1995	1	N.A.	1,878	91,465
1996	7	N.A.	1,883	90,239
1997	14	N.A.	1,874	88,312
1998	18	N.A.	1,858	85,047
1999	16	N.A.	1,835	81,605
2000	29	N.A.	1,814	77,555
2001	59	N.A.	1,737	73,582
2002	73	481	1,656	66,741

Source: Pension Fund Association (2003).

peaks (see Table 15-1). Termination eliminates the risk of growth in pension liabilities due to falling discount rates. As a rule, when a Japanese pension plan is terminated, accumulated assets must be distributed first to beneficiaries in the form of annuities, and then to active members either in the form of on-the-spot lump-sum payments or annuities after retirement. Also employers can establish DC plans and use the accumulated assets that otherwise would be distributed in cash to contribute to employees' accounts in DC plans.

Benefit Reduction. Another way to manage pension risk is to reduce DB plan benefits. The reduction of benefits accrued from past service was legalized in 1997, provided that certain conditions are met, including agreement between labor and management, and the existence of business difficulties. From fiscal 1997 through 2001, the number of EPFs whose benefits have been reduced each year was 7, 16, 52, 177, and 114 respectively. The most common pattern has been where pension plans reduced the annuity amount, by lowering the assumed rate of interest for the conversion of original lump-sum value into annuities.[4] Of late, this reduction has not been limited to monthly annuity amounts, but rather it has also affected the value of the lump-sum amount. Another notable development has occurred in a few cases where pensioners' benefits have been pared down.[5]

Put-back of Contracted-out Portion. Another way to adjust DB pension risks applies only to EPFs. This involves the put-back or return of the assets and liabilities of the contracted-out portion to the public retirement system. This has become attractive because the decline in interest rates and increase in longevity have boosted the liability due to the contracted-out portion. Until recently, however, the rebate rate offered by the government was too low to compensate for that increase. As a result, plan sponsors faced the risk of a growing funding shortage in the contracted-out portion of the benefit.

Very recently, in 2002, the new Defined Benefit Corporate Pension Plan Law has permitted the return of the contracted-out portion by EPFs on more attractive terms. This put-back not only relieves DB plan sponsors of the risks associated with a potential increase in benefit obligations and shortfalls, but it also enables a plan sponsor to record one-time profits on its income statement. This is because the value of obligations recognized on the balance sheet is larger than the value of assets the sponsor must pay back to the government.[6] Plan sponsors have devoted much attention to this new rule, and by year-end 2003, the government had approved put-backs by 702 EPFs out of a total of 1,700 plans, including those of blue chip firms such as Toyota, Hitachi, and NEC.

Cash Balance Plans. Another approach to pension risk management involves the introduction of cash balance plans. In this new format, each participant's account balance increases periodically by the sum of service credits and interest credits, the latter of which equals the account balance at the end of the previous year multiplied by the base interest rate. Plan participants receive the balance of that cash value at the time of job termination or as an annuity at retirement.

An appeal of this scheme is that falling interest rates boost benefit liabilities via a declining discount rate, but this increase is offset by smaller interest rate credits. A lower interest rate, therefore, increases liabilities in a cash balance plan by much less than in a traditional DB plan. For this reason, benefit obligations in cash balance plans have a much shorter duration and their sensitivity to interest rate movements is smaller, than in traditional DB plans. Hence cash balance plans help plan sponsors to shift a portion of interest rate risks to plan participants.

This adjustment mechanism can be applied even to the post-retirement period when annuities are paid. Pension plans can adjust the interest rate by which the value of the lump-sum payment is converted into annuities, in synchrony with changes in market interest rates. This adjustment mechanism applied to annuitants is similar to the one for variable annuity products of life insurance companies.

Defined Contribution Plans. A final way to adapt benefit design for risk management purposes is to introduce a DC plan. In 2001, the law permitted a modest level of employer contributions to this type of pension under tax-exempt status, and by September 2003, some 538 employers with 529,000 employees had adopted this plan type.[7] Some firms established their new plans from scratch, while others did so as a complete or partial substitute for existing DB pensions or book-reserve severance-pay schemes. Plans established as a full or partial replacement for DB plans have the effect of shifting investment risks from employers to employees.

Managing Pension Portfolios of Liabilities. While the portfolio risk management process of financial institutions always integrates assets and liabilities, DB pension management has traditionally focused only on the asset side. One reason may be that pension benefits have typically been construed as an exogenous factor to fund managers. Yet the reality now is that pension plan liabilities have become a more or less controllable variable in Japan. Pension plan sponsors are seeking ways to control risks by redesigning benefits, selecting appropriate plan types, reducing the amount of pension liabilities, and adjusting their duration.

As the concept of 'portfolio' management extends beyond investment vehicles, plan sponsors are beginning to realize that they must also manage their plan's liability portfolio. They then begin to question what the trade-off might be for lower risk in liabilities: that is, should they accept a lower expected return in exchange for lowering risk, as in the case of an investment portfolio? To answer this question, we use the analogy of financial institutions trying to change the composition of liabilities where the composition of assets is constant. Here the DB plan may be conceptualized as a financial operation which borrows money from plan participants and invests the funds thus gained. Plan termination or put-back of the contracted-out portion has the effect of suspending this operation completely or partially. The cost of this suspension is the lost opportunity of earning a higher rate of return than the interest rate on borrowed money and enjoying resulting profits. Changing a DB into a DC plan has the same effect. Adopting a cash-balance plan has the effect of converting long-term fixed interest rate liabilities into floating rate notes. The opportunity costs are profits potentially achieved by the rise in discount rate when the duration of liabilities is longer than that of assets.

Whether this perspective is generally applicable in the Japanese context can be evaluated by examining whether plan sponsors' financial characteristics are related in sensible ways to the pension plans they offer. In the next section, we therefore examine what factors actually affected plan sponsor decisions regarding the termination of DB plans and the put-back of the contracted-out portion to the government.

Empirical Analysis

We hypothesize that plan sponsors in Japan have sought to reduce risk by terminating their DB plans or returning the contracted-out portion to the government, instead of by reducing investment in riskier assets. In our empirical analysis we build on related studies from other countries, which relate plan sponsor financial characteristics to the decision to change pension plan type. In the USA, for instance, Friedman (1983), Bodie et al. (1985) and Petersen (1996) relate asset allocation decisions in DB plans to the risk tolerance of the pension plan sponsors. They find that the plan sponsor's profitability tend to increase risk tolerance; this may be represented by return on total assets (Petersen 1996) or return on net assets. Another important factor is the plan sponsor's financial stability, for which proxies include the standard deviation of profits (Friedman 1983; Petersen 1996) or the firm's bond rating (Bodie et al. 1985). In general, they find that financial instability narrows risk tolerance as well as flexibility to invest in riskier assets.

In the case of pensions, another important factor affecting risk tolerance is the plan's funding status, represented by the ratio of pension assets to liabilities. A higher funding ratio leads to a higher risk tolerance and allocation to riskier assets. Other controls include the maturity of the plan, usually represented by the ratio of beneficiaries to active participants (or active to total participants; Friedman 1983), and benefit payments divided by assets and the year the plan started (Petersen 1996). A more mature pension plan would be said to have less flexibility to invest in riskier assets.

Hypotheses. Drawing on these prior studies, we therefore hypothesize that plan sponsors with lower risk tolerance would be more likely to terminate their DB plans and return the contracted-out portion to the government. Specifically:

- Hypothesis 1. *Regarding Termination*: Financial characteristics of plan sponsors and pension plans that reduce risk tolerance expedite the termination of EPFs;
- Hypothesis 2. *Regarding Put-Back*: Financial characteristics of plan sponsors and pension plans that reduce risk tolerance expedite the put-back of the contracted-out portion of EPFs.

To evaluate these we use Probit multivariate regression models to explore the empirical relationships, controlling on several explanatory variables.[8]

Determinants of Termination. To Hypothesis 1, the dependent variable takes a value of 1 for EPFs terminated from April 2001 through June 2003, and 0 for those which did not terminate in this period. This variable y_t is estimated by the following probability function used in the Probit regression model:

$$y_t^* = \alpha_t + \mathbf{b_t x_r} + \mathbf{h_t x_h} + \varepsilon_t, \quad \text{where} \quad \begin{cases} y_t = 1, \ if \, y_t^* > 0 \\ y_t = 0, \ if \, y_t^* \leq 0. \end{cases}$$

The vector $\mathbf{x_r}$ consists of factors that may cause plan termination due to risk tolerance, while $\mathbf{x_h}$ is a vector consisting of control factors that may affect the decision to terminate. More specifically, we select four variables to include in vector $\mathbf{x_r}$: the 5-year average return on shareholders' equity (ROE), the volatility of ROE (VROE), the funding ratio (FNDGRAT), in the DB pension plan (pension assets divided by pension liabilities) and the ratio of pension liabilities or pension assets to the plan sponsor's total assets on the balance sheet (PAVSAST or PLVSAST). We hypothesize that risk tolerance would be reduced by lower profitability, higher volatility in profits, a lower funding ratio, and a larger ratio of pension plan assets or liabilities to business size of plan sponsor. Therefore, we expect the regression model to generate coefficients that are negative for ROE, positive for VROE, negative for FNDGRAT, and positive for PLVSAST and PAVSAST.

As control variables in vector $\mathbf{x_h}$, we include three elements: an industry dummy (INDUSTRY) indicating the plan sponsors' main line of business (where 0 means manufacturing and 1 means nonmanufacturing); the ratio of taxes paid in the last five years to shareholder equity (TOE); and a variable representing size which is the natural logarithm of plan assets (LNPA) or natural logarithm of the number of employees (LNEMP). The expected sign of the regression coefficient for INDUSTRY is positive, since it is said that manufacturing companies pay more attention to the maintenance of long-term employment which employers try to nurture by DB pension plans. Manufacturing companies are said to be more willing to take on the financial risks associated with DB pensions for the purpose of maintaining their employment practices. We expect a negative regression coefficient for TOE, since the termination of EPFs deprives plan sponsors having large taxable income of valuable tax deferrals. With regard to size (LNPA or LNEMP), we expect a negative regression coefficient, since there is a rule that requires a minimum number of plan participants.[9] (More precise variable definitions appear in Appendix Table 15-A1).

Determinants of Put-back. To test Hypothesis 2, we assign the value of 1 to EPFs that returned the contracted-out portion back to the government between April 2001 and June 2003, and 0 to the rest. The probability function used to estimate this variable y_p is as follows:

$$y_p^* = \alpha_p + \mathbf{b_p x_r} + \mathbf{h_p x_h} + \varepsilon_p, \quad \text{where} \quad \begin{cases} y_p = 1, \ if \, y_p^* > 0 \\ y_p = 0, \ if \, y_p^* \leq 0. \end{cases}$$

In this estimate, we exclude EPFs that terminated because it is impossible to return the contracted-out portion to the government once the EPF is terminated.

Vectors x_r and x_h consist of the same variables as above; we expect regression coefficients for each variable to have the same sign as indicated above, except for the size variables (LNPA or LNEMP). For those, we expect a positive regression coefficient, since we believe that from the perspective of cost-efficiency, there are scale economies in DB plan operation. Putting back the contracted-out portion may decrease the size of EPFs below critical volume and heighten the chances of scale diseconomies. This means that the larger the size of the EPF, the easier it is to return the contracted-out portion.

Data Sources. All accounting data and industry codes are taken from the Nikkei Needs electronic database (2004). Data on EPF decisions as to termination and put-back of the contracted-out portion were obtained from the Ministry of Health Labor and Welfare (2003).[10] Because of data constraints, samples are limited to EPFs in existence as of March 2001, when the new accounting standard was introduced. Further, we exclude multi-employer EPFs unless they were managed by companies that are consolidated for the purpose of financial reporting.

Results. Multivariate Probit regression estimates for termination models appear in Table 15-2 where we use PAVSAST and PLVSAST as alternative relative size controls, and LNPA and LNEMP as alternative absolute size controls.

Among variables reflective of risk tolerance, the funding ratio of pension plans (FNDGRAT) always generated coefficients with the expected signs and were significant at conventional levels in half the regressions. Among other variables, the coefficients for the ratio of pension plan assets or liabilities to sponsor's total assets (PAVSAST or PLVSAST), though significant only at 10 percent level, were consistently positive as expected. The coefficient for ROE was positive, contrary to expectations. Of the control variables, coefficients for TOE, the industry dummies (INDUSTRY), and logarithm of plan assets (LNPA) were insignificant. Notable are the coefficients for the logarithm of the number of employees (LNEMP), which were negative at statistically significant levels. This means that smaller EPFs are more likely to terminate, probably because of the legal requirement regarding minimum number of participants.

These results suggest that plan sponsors with less risk tolerance, which we attribute to larger volatility in return on equity, a lower funding ratio, and larger pension plans relative to plan sponsor total assets, were more likely to terminate their EPFs. In addition, the number of employees or participants seems to affect decisions to terminate EPFs.

TABLE 15-2 Probit Results For Plan Termination

	1	2	3	4
ROE	0.548	0.548	0.483	0.488
	(0.427)	(0.427)	(0.373)	(0.377)
VROE	1.586*	1.579*	1.446*	1.440*
	(1.942)	(1.932)	(1.726)	(1.719)
FNDGRAT	−1.543†	−1.126	−1.634†	−1.245*
	(−1.976)	(−1.509)	(−2.138)	(−1.722)
PAVSAST	1.849*		1.732	
	(1.656)		(1.559)	
PLVSAST		1.161*		1.084*
		(1.787)		(1.673)
TOE	0.200	0.264	0.643	0.690
	(0.057)	(0.075)	(0.183)	(0.197)
INDUSTRY	−0.066	−0.058	−0.031	−0.022
	(−0.302)	(−0.265)	(−0.141)	(−0.101)
LNPA	−0.092	−0.093		
	(−1.215)	(−1.227)		
LNEMP			−0.193†	−0.192*
			(−1.959)	(−1.948)

Source: Author's calculations from 416 observations.

*significant at 10% level; †significant at 5% level

To explore the second hypothesis, we evaluate similar models with a different dependent variable; results appear in Table 15-3. Coefficients on risk tolerance for PAVSAST and PLVSAST (the relative size of pension plan to sponsor total assets) were positive and highly significant. Coefficient estimates for ROE, VROE, and FNDGRAT were all insignificant. Among control variables, the LNEMP had a positive and statistically significant effect; this means that small plan sponsors found it difficult to return the contracted-out portion due to scale diseconomies after the put-back. We also found that coefficients for industry (INDUSTRY) were always positive, implying that plan sponsors in nonmanufacturing industries were more likely to return the contracted-out portion. This is possibly because of less risk in labor management as explained in more detail below. TOE was not significant.

From these findings, we conclude that plan sponsors with less risk tolerance, which we attribute to larger pension plans relative to plan sponsor total assets, were more likely to return the contracted-out portion. In addition, plan sponsors with larger EPFs and in nonmanufacturing sector were more active in returning the contracted-out portion.

TABLE 15-3 Probit Results for Put-Back

	5	6	7	8
ROE	0.334	0.352	0.333	0.353
	(0.252)	(0.266)	(0.253)	(0.268)
VROE	−0.497	−0.663	−0.490	−0.501
	(−0.542)	(−0.710)	(−0.537)	(−0.549)
FNDGRAT	0.005	0.602	0.044	0.693
	(0.009)	(1.067)	(0.080)	(1.299)
PAVSAST	3.201*		3.351*	
	(3.490)		(3.672)	
PLVSAST		1.823*		1.923*
		(3.287)		(3.484)
TOE	−2.659	−2.625	−3.329	−3.301
	(−0.930)	(−0.917)	(−1.154)	(−1.142)
INDUSTRY	0.273	0.250	0.278†	0.255
	(1.624)	(1.498)	(1.652)	(1.526)
LNPA	0.079	0.081		
	(1.544)	(1.574)		
LNEMP			0.185*	0.186*
			(2.660)	(2.679)

Source: Author's calculations from 379 observations.

*significant at 1%; **significant at 5%; †significant at 10%.

Risks in Labor Management

In addition to financial risks explored here, we also note two risks in the area of labor management that could influence employers' views of changing plan type and benefit design. One is the risk of demoralizing employees. Pension plan termination and/or the introduction of DC or cash balance plans appears to shift investment and longevity risks to employees. The put-back of the contracted-out portion often means a reduction in the amount of life annuity.[11] As a result, employees lose old age income that might be seen as more secure in a traditional DB plan. This is particularly important in an environment such as Japan, where the public old age pension is diminishing its role; that is, employees would be more likely to appreciate receiving a stable benefit from their company pensions. Indeed, unstable benefits might degrade employee morale, which in turn could lower productivity or increase employee turnover.[12] Employee demoralization could be a major deterrent to choosing a benefit design which lowered plan sponsor financial risks.

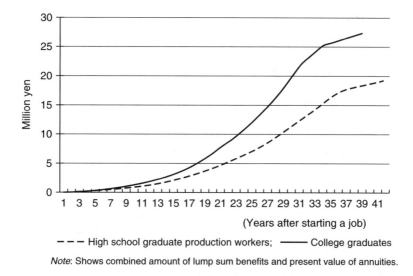

Note: Shows combined amount of lump sum benefits and present value of annuities.

Figure 15-3. Amount of retirement benefits by tenure.
Source: Author's calculations using the data from Staff of Central Labor Relations Commission (2002).

The other risk to note is the problems that arise if employee tenure cannot be well-controlled, and DB plan formulas have long been associated with control over employee tenure. Figure 15-3 depicts the present value of benefits on the vertical axis and employee age on the horizontal axis; it shows that this hypothetical plan sponsor wants employees to stay on the job at least fifteen to twenty years, but employee severance is preferred after thirty years of service or after age 50. In this way, the DB formula is an important tool to maintain long-term employment practices and to terminate them at some prearranged point. This use of a DB plan to effect labor management has been popular in automobile and other manufacturing industries where plan sponsors have sought to accumulate enterprise-specific employee expertise. If employers in these industries were to change DB into cash balance or DC plans, they might risk losing their ability to influence tenure.

Nevertheless, an increasing portion of plan sponsors in Japan is no longer focused on the maintenance of long-term employment practices. Instead, many firms have adopted merit-based compensation systems, even including retirement benefits. For example, several large companies have introduced cash balance plans because benefits there are based on average salary, and the benefit amount can easily reflect employees' performance over their careers.

Conclusions

This chapter suggests that that pension plan sponsors in Japan have sought to manage pension financial risks when choosing and changing pension plan types. This is a new development in Japan, especially regarding the termination of DB plans, though it confirms studies from other countries. Important determinants of DB plan termination include the VROE, the pension plan FNDGRAT, and the size of pension assets and liabilities relative to the size of the plan sponsor. In addition, we found that plan size also influenced decisions to terminate many Japanese EPFs. Regarding the decision to put-back the contracted-out portion of the EPF, we identified several significant factors. These include the size of pension assets and liabilities relative to plan sponsors businesses, and the total number of employees. In other words, plan-type choice is an important part of corporate risk management when the portfolio includes pension liabilities.

Data constraints preclude a direct analysis of firms' decisions to introduce DC or cash balance plans. Nevertheless, a research institute affiliated with the Ministry of Health, Labor and Welfare showed that plan sponsors most focused on pension financial risks (especially the volatility of liabilities caused by changes in the discount rate) had the strongest interest in adopting a cash balance plan (Research Institute for Policies on Aging 2003). Future research could extend our analysis to an examination of the introduction of DC plans and cash balance plans as well.

TABLE 15-A1 Variable Definitions

Explanatory variables

ROE	5-year average of net profits fiscal 1996–2000 divided by average of shareholders' equity in the same 5-year period.
VROE	Standard deviation of net profits from fiscal 1996–2000 divided by average of shareholders' equity in the same 5-year period.
FNDGRAT	Value of pension asset divided by projected benefit obligations disclosed in financial statements at March 2001.
PLVSAST	Value of projected benefit obligations divided by total assets of plan sponsors disclosed in financial statements at March 2001
PAVSAST	Value of pension assets divided by total assets of plan sponsors disclosed in financial statements at March 2001.
INDUSTRY	Nonmanufacturing = 1, manufacturing = 0.
TOE	5-year average of taxes paid from fiscal 1996–2000 divided by average of shareholders equity in the same 5-year period.
LNPA	Natural logarithm of pension assets.
LNEMP	Natural logarithm of number of employees.

Dependent variables

PUT back   EPFs putting back contracted-out portion since April 2001 through June 2003 = 1, no put-back = 0.

TERMINATE   EPFs terminated since April 2001 through June 2003 = 1, no termination = 0.

TABLE 15-A2 Descriptive Statistics

		Min.	Max.	Mean	Std. dev.
Test 1	ROE	−0.7271	0.5428	0.0057	0.0972
	VROE	0.0038	1.3282	0.0884	0.1306
	FNDGRAT	0.0608	0.9854	0.5954	0.1289
	PLVSAST	0.0071	0.7281	0.2392	0.1396
	PAVSAST	0.0014	0.4486	0.1412	0.0880
	TOE	0.0018	0.1988	0.0492	0.0311
	LNPA	4.3041	14.4228	10.0682	1.3476
	LNEMP	5.2204	11.4189	7.6916	1.0153
Test 2	ROE	−0.7271	0.1923	0.0075	0.0898
	VROE	0.0038	1.3282	0.0819	0.1179
	FNDGRAT	0.2000	0.9854	0.6001	0.1270
	PLVSAST	0.0071	0.7281	0.2353	0.1387
	PAVSAST	0.0000	0.4500	0.1401	0.0885
	TOE	0.0018	0.1930	0.0489	0.0290
	LNPA	4.3000	14.4200	10.0996	1.3645
	LNEMP	5.2204	11.4189	7.7286	1.0179

Our findings imply that financial risks will remain a main concern for pension plan sponsors in Japan. The future will likely witness an increase in plan terminations and put-backs of the contracted-out portion of EPFs, as well as additional conversions from traditional DB to cash balance and DC plans. Our analysis of Japan's experience in pension plan management also holds some implications for other developed countries. Since 2000, financial market conditions in Europe and North America have begun to resemble conditions experienced in Japan over the past decade. Stagnant rates of return due to the sluggish stock market, ballooning pension obligations, and changes in accounting standards, are forcing plan sponsors to pay far more attention to benefit design than ever before. Many of these factors are particularly familiar in the UK, where DB final salary based pension schemes have increasingly closed out new entrants and suspended benefit accruals (Veysey 2003). And in the USA, more than half of all corporate executives with DB plans are seriously considering changes in retirement programs (Feinberg 2004). Our analysis of the relationship between pension plan design and financial risk management is therefore relevant to and may be troubling for many DB stakeholders.

Endnotes

The author is grateful for comments and guidance by Robert Clark, Olivia Mitchell, and Stephen Utkus.

1. The probability is 0.88 percent in a log-normal distribution and 0.63 percent in a normal distribution.
2. These numbers are averages for 1,006 companies whose accounting data on pension assets/liabilities are available for three continuous accounting periods ending March 2003.
3. Those who advocate that pension fund management needs a paradigm shift (see Chapter 11) might suggest that plan sponsors could have improved funding by changing their asset allocation mix.
4. The original form of most of Japanese retirement benefits is a lump sum payment. After the establishment of DB plans, this lump sum value has increasingly been converted to an annuity using a specified interest rate.
5. This reduction is possible provided that two-thirds of pensioners agree, and that pension plans reimburse the present value of benefits in lump sum if any of pensioners so request.
6. In the case of a put-back, an asset amount equal to the liability for the contracted-out portion must be returned to the government, specifically to the Government Pension Investment Corporation, instead of to the Employee Pension Fund Association.
7. The maximum amount is 216,000 yen per annum if an employer has a DB plan, and 432,000 yen per annum if there is no other pension plan at the same employer. These ceilings will be raised by 60,000 yen and 120,000 yen respectively from 2005.
8. Unfortunately, data for DC plans, cash balance plans, and benefit reduction, and data for TQPPs are not publicly available, nor are variables to represent DB plan maturity in Japan.
9. The minimum number of participants is 500 for single-employer EPFs and 800 for multi-employer EPFs.
10. Descriptive statistics for variables appear in Appendix Table A2.
11. There is a rule that requires EPFs to pay at least 50 percent of their retirement benefits in life annuity combined with the contracted-out portion. This rule does not apply to EPFs after they return the contracted-out portion.
12. Although agreement with labor is required to alter the benefit design, it is difficult for the employees' side to refuse an employer's proposal, given loose labor market conditions in Japan at present.

References

Benartzi, Shlomo and Thaler, H. Richard (1995). 'Myopic Loss Aversion and Equity Premium Puzzle', *Quarterly Journal of Economics*, 110(1): 73–92.

Bodie, Zvi, Jay O. Light, Randall Morck, and Robert A. Taggart, Jr. (1985). 'Corporate Pension Policy : An Empirical Investigation', *Financial Analysts Journal* 41(5): 10–16.

Clark, Robert L. and Olivia S. Mitchell (2002). 'Strengthening Employment-Based Pensions in Japan', *Benefits Quarterly*, 2nd Q: 22–43. Reprinted in Toshiaki Tachibanaki (ed.), *The Economics of Social Security in Japan*. Surrey, UK: Edward Elgar. 2004.

Davis, Phillip E. (1995). *Pension Funds: Retirement Income Security and Capital Markets. An International Perspective*. Oxford: Clarendon Press.

Feinberg, Phyllis (2004). 'They Say "No" to DB plan', *Pension and Investments*, 3(2). Chicago, IL: Crain Communications, Inc.

Friedman, Benjamin (1983). 'Pension Funding, Pension Asset Allocation, and Corporate Finance: Evidence from Individual Company Data', in Zvi Bodie and John B. Shoven (eds), *Financial Aspects of the United States Pension System*. Chicago, IL: University of Chicago Press, pp. 107–76.

Ministry of Health, Labor and Welfare (2003). *Financial Conditions of Employee Pension Funds at the End of Fiscal 2003 (Kosei Nenkin Kikin no Zaisei Jokyo—Heisei 15 Nendo Zaisei Kensho no Kekka)*. Tokyo, Japan: Ministry of Health, Labor and Welfare.

Nikkei Needs Database (2004). *http://www.nikkeieu.com/needs/*

Pension Fund Association (2003). *Basic Data on Occupational Pension (Kigyo Nenkin ni Kansuru Kisoshiryo)*. Tokyo, Japan: Pension Fund Association.

Peskin, Michael (1997). 'Asset Allocation and Funding Policy for Corporate-Sponsored Defined Benefit Plans', *Journal of Portfolio Management*, 23(2) Winter: 66–73.

Petersen, Mitchell A. (1996). 'Allocating Assets and Discounting Cash Flows: Pension Plan Finance', *Working Paper*. Kellogg Graduate School of Management, Northwestern University.

Research Institute for Policies on Aging (2003). *Research Report on Retirement Benefits from the Perspective of Corporate Labor and Financial Management (Jinji Zaimu Ryoumen kara Mita Kigyounenkin nado Taishoku Kyuufu Plan no Arikata ni Kansuru Kenkyuu)*. Tokyo: Research Institute for Policies on Aging.

Staff of Central Labor Relations Commission (2002). *Survey of Retirement Benefits, Pension and Mandatory Retirement Age Conditions—Comprehensive Statistics on Wage and Other Conditions 2001 (Taishokukin, Nenkin oyobi Teinensei Jijo Chosa)*. Tokyo: Roui Kyokai.

Usuki, Masaharu (2003). 'Pension Funds and Retirement Benefits in the Depressed Economy and Market—Experience and Challenges in Japan'. Prepared for *11th Australian Colloquium of Superannuation Researchers*. Sydney, Australia: Centre for Pensions and Superannuation, University of New South Wales.

Veysey, Sarah (2003). 'An Unlimited Liability: U.K. Sponsors Continue Shift from Final Salary Schemes', *Pension and Investment*, September 29, 2003:39. Chicago, IL: Crain Communications, Inc.

Index